Refractions of the Third Reich in German and Austrian Fiction and Film

OXFORD STUDIES IN MODERN EUROPEAN CULTURE

GENERAL EDITORS

Elizabeth Fallaize, Robin Fiddian, and Katrin Kohl

The Oxford Studies in Modern European Culture series is conceived as a response to the changing modes of study of European literature and culture in many universities. Designed to combine focus with breadth, each title in the series presents a range of texts or films in dialogue with their historical and cultural contexts—not simply as a reflection of history but engaged in a mediation with history, conceived in broad terms as cultural, social, and political history. Flexible, interdisciplinary approaches are encouraged together with the use of texts outside the traditional canon alongside more familiar works. In order to make the volumes accessible not only to students of modern languages but also to those studying the history or politics of modern Europe, all quotations are offered in both the original language and in English.

REFRACTIONS OF THE THIRD REICH IN GERMAN AND AUSTRIAN FICTION AND FILM

Chloe Paver

OXFORD
UNIVERSITY PRESS

OXFORD

UNIVERSITY PRESS

Great Clarendon Street, Oxford OX2 6DP

Oxford University Press is a department of the University of Oxford.
It furthers the University's objective of excellence in research, scholarship,
and education by publishing worldwide in

Oxford New York

Auckland Cape Town Dar es Salaam Hong Kong Karachi
Kuala Lumpur Madrid Melbourne Mexico City Nairobi
New Delhi Shanghai Taipei Toronto

With offices in

Argentina Austria Brazil Chile Czech Republic France Greece
Guatemala Hungary Italy Japan Poland Portugal Singapore
South Korea Switzerland Thailand Turkey Ukraine Vietnam

Oxford is a registered trademark of Oxford University Press
in the UK and in certain other countries

Published in the United States
by Oxford University Press Inc., New York

© Chloe Paver 2007

The moral rights of the author have been asserted
Database right Oxford University Press (maker)

First published 2007

British Library Cataloguing in Publication Data
Data available

Library of Congress Cataloging in Publication Data
Data available

Typeset by Laserwords Private Limited, Chennai, India
Printed in Great Britain
on acid-free paper by
Biddles Ltd., King's Lynn, Norfolk

ISBN 978–0–19–926611–1

10 9 8 7 6 5 4 3 2 1

Acknowledgements

Many colleagues and friends contributed to the successful completion of this project. Arthur Williams, Elizabeth Boa, and Bill Niven advised on the original conception, supported me in grant applications, and commented on early drafts. Bill has been a particular source of support, both moral and practical. My Exeter colleagues have supported my work in all sorts of ways, but particular thanks are due to Helen Bridge and Gar Yates for reading and commenting on draft chapters. Mark Davie may feel that he hindered more than he helped, but he kept the admin at bay at important moments, for which I am very grateful. Helmut Schmitz has given me the benefit of his broad knowledge of the subject on a number of occasions, while, in discussions about his doctoral thesis, Markus Spitz helped me to clarify my ideas on *Morbus Kitahara*. Morven Creagh lent me valuable assistance in preparing the typescript and Tom Savage was kind enough to work on one of the image files for me. I very much appreciated Katrin Kohl's thoughtful, focused advice in the final stages. Last, but certainly not least, my OUP editors, most recently Tom Perridge, have been patient and helpful throughout the long writing process.

Work on the project was generously supported by the Arts and Humanities Research Board, which funded a semester's study leave, and by the British Academy, which financed several trips to German and Austrian archives. Other research trips were funded by the School of Modern Languages at the University of Exeter. I was able to carry out much useful work on film at the library of the Konrad Wolf Hochschule für Film und Fernsehen in Potsdam and at the Deutsche Kinemathek in Berlin. Staff at the Deutsches Literaturarchiv in Marbach have been unfailingly helpful during repeated visits. The Archiv der KZ-Gedenkstätte Mauthausen at the Ministry of the Interior in Vienna gave me generous access to its documents and photographs, as well as welcome help and advice: particular thanks are due to Christian Dürr and Stephan Matyus. Wolfgang Quatember at the Zeitgeschichte-Museum Ebensee pointed me in the direction of useful material about Ebensee's memorial sites.

For taking an interest in my strange and seemingly endless project, but mostly for distracting me from it, I am grateful to my Topsham friends, especially the Deasy family, Dave and Hazel McCabe, and the Sunday-night darts players in the Steam Packet. My parents, my brothers, and my sister deserve special thanks for lending their support even when work on the project made me elusive.

Images are reproduced by kind permission of the following: director Rolf Schübel (*Das Heimweh des Walerjan Wróbel*); Kinowelt GmbH, Leipzig (*Das schreckliche Mädchen*); Aichholzer Film (*Jenseits des Krieges*); Pro Babelsberg gemeinnützige Bildungsgesellschaft mbH (*Der Unhold*); Hamburger Edition (for a still from the CD of *Verbrechen der Wehrmacht. Dimensionen des Vernichtungskrieges 1941–1944* and for the 'Photo der jungen Frau', originally exhibited in *Vernichtungskrieg. Verbrechen der Wehrmacht 1941 bis 1944* and reproduced by Ruth Beckermann in the book of *Jenseits des Krieges*). I am grateful to the Archiv der KZ-Gedenkstätte Mauthausen and to the photographer Stephan. Matyus for permission to reproduce a photograph of the children's memorial at Mauthausen and for permission to reproduce the plan for an ossuary at Mauthausen. Every effort was made to obtain permission for other illustrative material.

Contents

List of Illustrations

Introduction   **Critical Approaches**

As an object of study, the response of German and Austrian writers and film-makers to the Nazi past is a moving target: each year, new novels and films about the Third Reich clamour for critical attention, and each of those works is a product of 'shifting memories'—ongoing social negotiations about the way in which the Third Reich and its crimes are to be remembered.[1] A periodic scholarly stocktaking is therefore inevitable, since neither the artists nor the cultural climate that nurtures them stand still. The end of the Cold War, which has changed for good the ways in which Germany and, to a lesser degree, Austria understand their relationship with their respective National Socialist pasts, has generated a flood of new creative reckonings with the Third Reich and a following wave of scholarly analysis.

Of course, to return to my shooting metaphor, it is not just the target that keeps moving, but also the marksman: scholarship no more stands still than do literature and cinema, so that, in principle at least, successive surveys of the field employ progressively more refined methods. Inasmuch as academics and artists are products of the same broad intellectual and cultural climate, one would expect this movement to happen in parallel, with potentially interesting divergences and disjunctions. The six decades' worth of German-language writing and film-making about the Nazi past have been the object of concerted scholarly enquiry for at least the last three of those decades, but while one of very few constants in this scholarship is the attempt to distinguish successive phases of 'coming to terms' in literature and cinema, it proves surprisingly difficult to distinguish an equally orderly sequence of phases in scholarly approach, perhaps in part because works of criticism number far fewer than primary works, leaving little scope for picking and choosing examples from which to fashion a neat narrative of academic development. It is nevertheless possible—and this is one of the tasks of this Introduction—to identify and evaluate key approaches and to discern some important methodological shifts.

---

[1] I have borrowed the term from Klaus Neumann, *Shifting Memories: The Nazi Past in the New Germany* (Ann Arbor: University of Michigan Press, 2000).

The 'refractions' of my title occur when the events of 1933–45 and their post-war legacies pass through a series of prisms: primarily, of course, the prism of the author's or film-maker's creativity, but also the prism of scholarly research and student analysis. The 'critical approaches' that concern me in this Introduction are therefore plural, in type as well as in number: (a) the approaches taken by novelists and film-makers towards the Third Reich and its aftermath, which are almost invariably critical, though in different ways and to differing degrees; (b) the approaches taken by scholars towards this artistic engagement with a murderous past; and (c) the approaches that students might take to these primary and secondary levels of criticism. Since academic writers are usually interested principally in elucidating (a) and students in understanding (a) through the medium of (b), in its simplest form this layered structure is fairly self-explanatory, but by the same token also unhelpfully self-reinforcing. Accordingly, the Introduction attempts to problematize the critical enterprise. It considers to what extent this particular object of study is constituted by the scholar's and/or student's critical approach rather than being a pre-existing, discrete entity that we simply take and place under the microscope (which is how, for the sake of simplicity, I presented it in my opening statement). I also examine the ways in which, explicitly or implicitly, academic writers assign degrees of value to works about the Third Reich. My findings point to unconscious processes of selection that define which works about the Nazi past are to be written about and how. I consider what this process of 'canonization' can tell us about the place of literary and cinematic representations of the Third Reich within the broader field of 'cultural memory' and also how one might integrate the study of literature and film with the study of other *lieux de mémoire* or 'sites of memory': Pierre Nora's term for any material or non-material 'space' in which collective memory takes form.[2]

These meta-critical considerations inform my examination, in the chapters that follow, of a range of works that engage with the Nazi past. This is therefore not so much a study (yet another study) of representations of the Third Reich as a book that asks what it is we think we are doing when we study representations of the Third Reich.

For reasons of space I restrict myself in the Introduction to discussing a series of full-length studies that, like this one, provide a survey of literary and cinematic responses to the Nazi past; it goes without saying, however, that much of what I say applies equally to shorter or multi-authored works

---

[2] Pierre Nora, *Les lieux de mémoire* (Paris: Gallimard, 1987; first publ. 1984); *Realms of Memory: The Construction of the French Past*, trans. Arthur Goldhammer (New York: Columbia University Press, 1996).

on the subject. The full-length studies in question are, like my own, primarily concerned with works produced by what Helmut Schmitz calls the 'perpetrator collective',[3] that is, they are not, or at least not principally, concerned with Holocaust experience as it is represented by the victims and by members of their successor communities.[4] Nearly all of the studies I address have been written by Germanists outside the German-speaking countries: the extensive and highly influential scholarship on Holocaust trauma and memory that has emerged from Germany and Austria has not been matched by a corresponding body of monographs on literature and film about the experience of the unpersecuted majority in the Third Reich. Whether this gap is the result of national differences in academic practice or of a more fundamental intellectual blind-spot is difficult to determine, but would be a matter for further enquiry.

Ethical Approaches

While it might seem odd to take up the story as late as 1983, Judith Ryan's study *The Uncompleted Past: Postwar German Novels and the Third Reich* makes a useful starting point precisely because it sees itself as belonging to a second generation of scholarship on literature and the Third Reich.[5] Studies written in the previous decade, argues Ryan, either debated the problems of writing after Auschwitz or read novels as a source of hypotheses about how the Nazi regime and its atrocities came about; Ryan's work, by contrast, aims to elucidate selected writers' views on personal responsibility and on the possibility of resistance to dictatorial rule, in order that 'the consciousness-building potential of these important texts [can] be released'.[6] Thus, the scholar becomes an exegete without whom the coded moral messages of the text—which constitute its main value—will remain obscure to the uninitiated. Ryan is open about the moral optimism that informs this approach:

> If keeping alive the memory of Auschwitz is to make any sense, it will surely be as a reminder of the problematic nature of human culpability. What responsibility do we bear as individuals and how much freedom do we have

---

[3] Helmut Schmitz, *On Their Own Terms: The Legacy of National Socialism in Post-1990 German Fiction* (Birmingham: Birmingham University Press, 2004), 8 and *passim*.

[4] See Further Reading and Viewing for studies of German-Jewish and Austrian-Jewish writing.

[5] Judith Ryan, *The Uncompleted Past: Postwar German Novels and the Third Reich* (Detroit: Wayne State University Press, 1983).

[6] Ibid. 18.

to exercise it? My judgments [. . .] are born out of the hope that the course of
history is something not entirely out of our own hands.[7]

Her Introduction ends in a celebration of her selected texts, which, she
says, 'have come to form the unspoken canon of literature on the Nazi
past':

> These novels are not just more complex; they are more significant than
> other German novels on the same theme, for they most tellingly lay bare
> the problematic nature of postwar Germany's incompletely resolved ideo-
> logical transition. [. . .] In a wider context, they also provide a model for
> literature whose aim is to initiate and develop responses to other political
> changes.[8]

Ryan nails her colours more firmly to the mast than most academics, but
if one looks beyond the explicit statement one can see that she has played
some role in constituting the subject matter in such a way that it lends
itself to her chosen analytical techniques. Her choice of overtly liberal
texts by writers such as Grass, Andersch, Böll, and Wolf makes possible
her enterprise of unlocking their 'consciousness-building potential'. This
is by no means an unreasonable approach, given that the Third Reich
has produced a clearer moral consensus than most historical periods
(or at least it had at the time when Ryan was writing, before the onset,
in the 1980s, of the Historians' Debate); nevertheless, as we shall see, it
would be possible not only to select for analysis more morally ambivalent
texts but also to take a more critical, less celebratory view even of those
indisputably moralizing texts that constitute the 'unspoken canon of
literature on the Nazi past'.

The main body of Ryan's study, though rather more critical than these
comments from her Introduction might imply, constructs an optimistic
literary-historical narrative in which, after some false starts, post-war
German fiction begins to stress the possibility of resistance to Nazism
and to call for an active moral conscience in the present. Fictional works
(mostly from the 1940s and 1950s) that fail to meet this standard are
criticized while those that achieve it (mostly from the 1960s and 1970s)
are celebrated; works that are open-ended, that activate the reader, are
valued over those whose form is closed.

As I intimated above, a neat succession of generations of scholarly
writing on this subject, such as Ryan evokes in her Introduction (in
what is perhaps no more than a conventional academic structuring
device), never really materializes, for various reasons. First, one clear

[7] Ryan, *Uncompleted Past*, 20.   [8] Ibid. 22.

constant in work on this subject is that academic writers elucidate the moral or political positions expressed in works about the Third Reich and, at the same time, adopt a morally informed intellectual position vis-à-vis those authorial positions. It seems to be in the nature of the subject that scholars who engage with it can neither show a postmodern disregard for authorial intention nor adopt a value-free attitude towards the material.

Secondly, Ryan's optimistically liberal approach continues to have its advocates. In her 2001 study *Family Secrets and the Contemporary German Novel*, Elizabeth Snyder Hook acknowledges explicitly her debt to Ryan; indeed, the fact that she picks up chronologically where Ryan leaves off (taking Ryan's last text, Wolf's *Kindheitsmuster*, as her first) evokes the passing of the scholarly baton from one to the other.[9] Snyder Hook offers what one reviewer has called 'affirmative readings' and, less charitably, 'a paraphrasing reading' of five novels, though, as the reviewer concedes, it is a very superior kind of paraphrase.[10] In practice this means that a chapter is complete once the psychology of the characters, in particular their psychological relationship to the past, has been made coherent and once the author's positive moral intentions and messages have been established; accordingly, chapters end within the frame of reference of the text, rather than at a meta-critical level (though, to be fair to Snyder Hook, writing the final sentence of a chapter from within the world of the novel or film, or from within the author's or director's world view, is the norm in this field, and is only really questionable if the writer does not reflect on his or her method elsewhere).

Finally, despite Ryan's view that a realist approach, one that looks to literary texts for information about the social reality of the Third Reich, is already passé, Donna Reed's *The Novel and the Nazi Past*, which was in preparation at about the same time, uses just such an approach,[11] and indeed her analysis, which also considers the way in which authors engage with the aesthetics and ideology of Nazism, is none the worse for its realist foundation. Her selection for analysis of three of the novels also examined by Ryan (Mann's *Doktor Faustus*, Grass's *Die Blechtrommel*, and Böll's *Billard um halbzehn*) confirms their canonical status at this time; like Ryan she sees in Grass's and Böll's texts a more sophisticated approach to the Third Reich than in Mann's exile novel, and she ends, not unlike Ryan, in

---

[9] Elizabeth Snyder Hook, *Family Secrets and the Contemporary German Novel: Literary Explorations in the Aftermath of the Third Reich* (Rochester, NY: Camden House, 2001).

[10] Andrea Capovilla, review of Snyder Hook, *Modern Language Review*, 98 (2003), 252–3.

[11] Donna K. Reed, *The Novel and the Nazi Past* (New York, Berne, and Frankfurt/Main: Lang, 1985).

6 **Critical Approaches**

praise of those newer works that 'leave open possibilities for change' and so 'hold out hope that we can become different from what they were'.[12]

The equivalents to Ryan's and Reed's work in the field of film studies are Robert and Carol Reimer's 1992 study *Nazi-Retro Film*, which judges films according to the degree to which they 'help Germans to locate responsibility for the past and help them come to terms with history',[13] and Anton Kaes's 1989 study *From Hitler to Heimat*, which identifies a shift in the New German Cinema of the 1970s, from a focus on 'questions of responsibility, guilt, and the legacy of history for the present' to a potentially more conservative 'quest for a German identity'.[14]

The Psychoanalytical Turn

If there is one clear shift in scholarship on this subject, it is the application of psychoanalytical theories of mourning to literary and cinematic representations of the Third Reich. All such work proceeds from Alexander and Margarete Mitscherlich's seminal *Die Unfähigkeit zu trauern* (*The Inability to Mourn*),[15] which argued that post-war Germans had not only failed to mourn the loss of Hitler and of associated nationalist ideals, with consequent psychological disturbances, but had failed even to reach the deficient state of melancholy that ought by rights to have resulted from their narcissistic emotional investment in Nazism. Although Reed cites the Mitscherlichs, her brief reference implies only that their theories can be used to confirm the insufficient process of mourning undergone by fictional characters (and therefore by the real Germans they represent);[16] by contrast, later critical works apply the Mitscherlichs' theories to the authors and their writing, not just to their characters, and break the mourning process down into its constituent phases and drives. Thus, post-war German and Austrian literature and film are read both as a symptom of a dysfunctional mourning process and as a space in which to dramatize that process.

[12] Reed, *Novel and Nazi Past*, 172.

[13] Robert C. Reimer and Carol J. Reimer, *Nazi-Retro Film: How German Narrative Cinema Remembers the Past* (New York: Twayne, 1992), p. xiii.

[14] Anton Kaes, *From Hitler to Heimat: The Return of History as Film* (Cambridge, MA, and London: Harvard University Press, 1989), 198.

[15] Alexander Mitscherlich and Margarete Mitscherlich, *Die Unfähigkeit zu trauern. Grundlagen kollektiven Verhaltens* (Munich: Piper, 1967).

[16] Reed, *Novel and Nazi Past*, 143–4.

The first major study in this vein, Eric Santner's *Stranded Objects: Mourning, Memory, and Film in Postwar Germany*, takes two steps at once: rather than simply apply the Mitscherlichs' theories, Santner engages critically with them, arguing that the German project of mourning described in *Die Unfähigkeit zu trauern* is part of a broader and longer historical process. For mourning is, according to deconstructionist thinking, the essential condition of postmodern humanity, which is (or ought to be) engaged in a 'perpetual leave-taking from fantasies of plenitude, purity, centrality, totality, unity, and mastery'.[17] Santner is aware of the risk of appearing to universalize the Holocaust, but argues that Nazism has not just *resulted* in an inability to mourn, but was itself an attempt to offer psychological compensations for the anxieties generated by mourning in the modern world.

For Santner, the main criterion for assigning value to a work is no longer how clearly it condemns the crimes of the Third Reich and post-war forgetfulness, nor how successfully it activates the moral energies of the viewer or reader, but how successfully it performs an act of mourning. Both of Santner's chosen film projects (Edgar Reitz's *Heimat* and Hans Jürgen Syberberg's *Hitler, ein Film aus Deutschland*) fail his test, on different grounds. The differences between Santner's approach and Ryan's are neatly illustrated by the fact that while Wolf's *Kindheitsmuster* fails Ryan's test of value because it is, in her view, insufficiently activating, it passes Santner's with flying colours because, so Santner reasons, Wolf succeeds in recuperating the suppressed feelings that generate trauma.

While Ernestine Schlant's *The Language of Silence: West German Literature and the Holocaust* works at a lesser level of abstraction than Santner's study, the notion of an 'inability to mourn' nevertheless underpins its analysis, and the *ability* to mourn is the yardstick by which the value of a work is measured.[18] That this will lead to more negative than affirmative readings is clear from the outset, when she speaks of post-war German literature's 'often groping and inept efforts to face up to the crimes of the Nazi regime'.[19] Her thesis is that most West German literature has avoided speaking of the Holocaust and failed to develop the empathetic understanding of the Jewish victims that would be necessary for mourning to commence. Schlant is able to take this critical stance partly by abandoning Ryan's 'unspoken canon'. Thus, she passes over Böll's canonical

[17] Eric L. Santner, *Stranded Objects: Mourning, Memory, and Film in Postwar Germany* (Ithaca, NY, and London: Cornell University Press, 1990), 7.

[18] Ernestine Schlant, *The Language of Silence: West German Literature and the Holocaust* (New York and London: Routledge, 1999).

[19] Ibid. 2.

Billard um halbzehn in favour of two of his lesser-known works; instead of celebrating Grass's *Die Blechtrommel* she looks askance at his *Tagebuch einer Schnecke*; and she examines authors such as Peter Härtling and Gert Hofmann who, while hardly minor writers, do not figure in other surveys of the field. This is not to imply that Schlant ignores works that she might have had to judge positively, since Jews and their sufferings barely figure in Ryan's 'unspoken canon'; rather, Schlant seeks out those works in which authors address the Holocaust most directly, but shows that in many cases talking about the Holocaust is a way of not mourning. Like Ryan, then, Schlant goes in search of the moral core of each text, but with a different scheme of values she arrives at different judgements. Though one could take issue with the detail of her argument, Schlant's reappraisal of the literary historical record, and in particular her willingness to criticize the great men, Böll and Grass, make this an important study.

Helmut Schmitz's *On Their Own Terms: The Legacy of National Socialism in Post-1990 German Fiction* also proceeds from the theories of the Mitscherlichs, though he contextualizes them by showing that they apply only to majority Germans, not to the victims, for whom a different model of mourning is necessary. He also homes in on one particular element of the Mitscherlichs' mourning model, the notion that the mourning process can only begin when members of the 'perpetrator collective' 're-empathize with their own libidinous Nazi selves, [through] a reinvestment of the past with emotion'.[20] This includes re-experiencing the negative emotions that accompanied bombing, expulsion, and defeat. Schmitz is therefore more willing than Schlant to take seriously those works that devote themselves to the majority experience, although he is careful to show that 're-empathizing' does not automatically lead to mourning, especially among younger writers for whom there was no original emotional investment. Like Schlant, he finds very few works that enact a positive mourning process, and, like Schlant, he ends with an analysis of W. G. Sebald, whom both see as the model for a more mature kind of mourning in literature. Thus, despite fundamental differences in method, Schlant, Schmitz, and even Santner (who ends with his positive appraisal of *Kindheitsmuster*) have in common with Ryan and Reed the construction of a positive progression in their corpus of texts.

To sum up, while the task of periodization plays a role in most studies on this subject, the terms in which change is understood themselves change over time: where, for Ryan, 'the German novel went through

---

[20] Schmitz, *Legacy*, 11.

several stages in its reflection on the ethical problems raised by the reckoning with nazism',[21] Santner, Schlant, and Schmitz see a psycho-historical narrative based on successive phases in a disturbed mourning process. My study proceeds from the assumption that at this time there is no very urgent need for another such literary-historical, film-historical, psycho-historical, and/or political-historical account of representations of the Third Reich, but that there is a need for a study that keeps the whole critical enterprise at arm's length.

Canon Formation and Cultural Memory

As we have already seen, in the two decades since Ryan's study, her 'canon of literature on the Nazi past' has both expanded and been called into question as a critical construction. This is a complex process because, as Jan Assmann has shown, canon formation is an important aspect of cultural memory.[22] If the novels and films analysed in this and similar studies are considered part of the wider field of 'cultural memory'—and there is still a tendency to restrict that term to public and political engagement with the past—then it is first and foremost because their plots recall the Third Reich, because they analyse processes by which the Third Reich is recalled, or because they are themselves symptomatic of those processes. But scholars also help to determine which of these works should be 'recalled' in future academic and public discourse. Conversely, while 'forgetting' is a key theme of many texts and films about the Third Reich, it is also, Jan Assmann argues, the inevitable fate of most written (and, by extension, filmic) material: writers and film-makers can remember the Nazi era as much as they like, but only memory that is kept in circulation will fulfil a memorial role. Though it is rarely explicitly acknowledged, studies such as this one play a part in the circulatory process.

At the same time, Aleida Assmann's work shows that, among theoreticians of cultural memory, interest is shifting from canon formation and other processes of selection for posterity to the nature of the 'rubbish' (*Abfall*) that is thereby discarded.[23] Of course, as soon as *Abfall* is made the object of intellectual attention it loses something of its quality as *Abfall*, so that one can arguably never completely step outside the

---

[21] Ryan, *Uncompleted Past*, 14.

[22] Jan Assmann, *Das kulturelle Gedächtnis. Schrift, Erinnerung und politische Identität in frühen Hochkulturen* (Munich: Beck, 1992), esp. ch. 2.

[23] Aleida Assmann, *Erinnerungsräume. Formen und Wandlungen des kulturellen Gedächtnisses* (Munich: Beck, 1999), esp. 383–407.

'archive' of preserved material. Besides, this shift in theoretical focus owes much to shifts in the professional practices of historians and archivists, who have broken down traditional boundaries between what is and what is not worth keeping. In his seminal study of French cultural memory, Pierre Nora judges these developments negatively, regretting 'la production indéfinie de l'archive' ('The indiscriminate [more precisely, 'endless', CP] filling of the archives') and the prevailing tendency to 'tout garder, tout conserver des signes indicatifs de mémoire, même si l'on ne sait pas exactement de quelle mémoire ils sont les indicateurs' ('to keep everything, to preserve every sign (even when we are not quite sure what it is we are remembering)').[24] In Danilo Kiš's dystopian story of a total archive, 'Enciklopedija mrtvih' ('The Encyclopaedia of the Dead'), which has been analysed by Aleida Assmann, Nora's fears about the new 'religion conservatrice' ('religion of preservation') are realized in fantastical form.[25]

In literary criticism and film studies, these developments in the way in which knowledge is passed down the generations (and in the role played by specialists in that process) have their equivalent in critiques of the ideological foundations of the canon and, amongst other things, of its privileging of 'high' over 'low' culture (in German *E-Kultur* and *U-Kultur*), with the result that works of literature and film that would once have ended up on the rubbish heap of cultural history are now considered worthy of scholarly attention. In the field that concerns us here, this has opened the way for an analysis of the more popular end of the market in fiction and film about the Third Reich. An example of this more inclusive approach is Louis Ferdinand Helbig's *Der ungeheure Verlust*, which examines literary representations of the flight and expulsion of German-speakers from Germany's former eastern territories, and sets major authors such as Wolf, Grass, Bienek, and Härtling alongside popular authors generally regarded—and therefore disregarded—as 'subliterarisch' (including Arno Surminski, Leonie Ossowski, and Hans Schellbach).[26] A second, more strictly germane example is the Reimers' *Nazi-Retro Film*, which gives as much space to the popular war film *08/15* as to Michael Verhoeven's Cold War satire *Das schreckliche Mädchen*, and has as much to say about the sentimental family drama *Die erste Polka* as it does about Katrin Seybold and Melanie Spitta's influential documentary *Es ging Tag und Nacht, liebes Kind*, about the murder of Sinti at Auschwitz. An advantage of the quantity-over-quality approach

[24] Nora, *Lieux de mémoire*, 32, 31; trans. pp. 10, 9.   [25] Ibid. 30; trans. p. 8.
[26] Louis Ferdinand Helbig, *Der ungeheure Verlust. Flucht und Vertreibung in der deutschsprachigen Belletristik der Nachkriegszeit*, 3rd rev. edn (Wiesbaden: Harrassowitz, 1996), 91.

is that it can identify common narrative formulae that offer psychological rewards to the reader or viewer (such as the conflict between the common soldier and the corrupt officer caste; or the scenario in which a non-Jewish German protects a Jewish neighbour). But by the same token, as the Reimers' study shows, it is difficult to avoid repetitiousness, since what can be said of one novel or film can be said of many.

Because of the way in which they are put together, drawing on the specialist expertise of a range of contributors, edited collections of essays are often a better source of analyses of lesser-known, non-canonical and/or popular writings and films than are monographs. Examples are listed in the section Further Reading and Viewing, but the volume *Gender, Patriarchy and Fascism in the Third Reich* deserves special mention for its role in extending the distinguished but nevertheless rather narrow circle of women writers habitually dealt with under the rubric 'gender and fascism'.[27]

So far I have equated the diminishing importance, in academic circles, of a 'canon' of literature and films about the Third Reich with a willingness to study a more diverse range of literary texts and films (though I maintain also that canon formation is not an entirely spent force, especially in literary studies, where four or five texts about the Nazi past that were published in the 1990s continue to receive a disproportionate amount of critical attention). But it is of course possible to pursue a different kind of inclusiveness, embracing those memorial objects and processes that have traditionally been the province of other disciplines. Interdisciplinarity is more in evidence in university teaching than in research, however (at least in the UK context that I know best), and monographs usually confine themselves either to literature and/or film or to other forms of cultural memory (as is the case in Bill Niven's nevertheless very wide-ranging *Facing the Nazi Past*).[28] This may be due in part to the fact that, as Astrid Erll has argued, the exact place of literature (and by extension also film) within the wider field of cultural memory has yet to be adequately theorized.[29] Thus, while Schlant's and Schmitz's recent work places literature in the context of public debates about remembrance, both nevertheless make a case for studying literature in isolation from film and from other material forms of memory. When Ryan and Reed

[27] Elaine Martin (ed.), *Gender, Patriarchy and Fascism in the Third Reich: The Response of Women Writers* (Detroit: Wayne State University Press, 1993).

[28] Bill Niven, *Facing the Nazi Past: United Germany and the Legacy of the Third Reich* (London and New York: Routledge, 2002).

[29] Astrid Erll, 'Literatur und kulturelles Gedächtnis: Zur Begriffs- und Forschungsgeschichte, zum Leistungsvermögen und zur literaturwissenschaftlichen Relevanz eines neuen Paradigmas der Kulturwissenschaft', *Literaturwissenschaftliches Jahrbuch*, 43 (2002), 249–76.

wrote their studies in the 1980s they felt no need to justify their exclusive focus on literature, which at that time represented standard disciplinary practice; Schlant no longer feels entitled to such unselfconsciousness: 'The use of purely literary works to analyze German attempts to come to terms with the crimes of the Nazi regime [. . .] needs, if not a justification, at least an explanation,'[30] which she bases on 'the privileged position of literature as the seismograph of a people's moral positions'.[31] Schmitz quotes this statement in support of his own exclusively literary focus and adduces a series of other reasons why literature has greater power than film and television to promote individual reflection and responsibility.[32] This stance recalls Ryan's contention that a certain brand of novel is the most 'telling' of Germany's struggle to come to terms with the sufferings inflicted by Nazism. As we have seen, however, Schlant and Schmitz have a more catholic definition than Ryan of the kind of fiction that can be made to 'tell', and the present study aims to be more catholic still, on the grounds that even if cinema, photography, memorial art, exhibitions, and sites of memory tell us something qualitatively different from fiction, they are still very telling indeed, as a large body of scholarship can attest. The particular role of literature as formulated by Schmitz, to which I am happy to assent, is no practical barrier to studying it alongside other forms of cultural memory, just as there is no practical barrier to studying post-Holocaust Austrian culture alongside post-Holocaust German culture, as I do here, even if nearly all full-length studies of the subject choose to focus on one or the other. Having said all that, this book is inevitably the product of my own disciplinary training, and literature and film play the major part in it.

While I am not concerned with establishing a canon of particularly 'telling' texts and films about the Third Reich, this book is, like all studies, necessarily selective. The first two chapters deal with works that have achieved a certain canonical status, but they question what this means for us as readers/viewers and as critics. Chapter 3 deals with lesser-known works—three pieces of documentary work by women—and identifies the critical challenges posed by their hybrid form. Chapter 4 sets a much-celebrated novel alongside a much-slated film version of a French novel and explores, amongst other things, the cross-cultural tensions evident in many works about the Third Reich. Chapter 5 considers issues surrounding memory and place, combining a model analysis of an Austrian memorial site with an exploration of the dystopian landscape of an Austrian novel. The deliberately eclectic selection of subjects is intended

---

[30] Schlant, *Language of Silence*, 3.   [31] Ibid.   [32] Schmitz, *Legacy*, 7–8.

to open up new perspectives in the study of texts and films about the Third Reich. In keeping with this aim I have discarded the conventional affirmative ending; in its place is a Conclusion that starts by calling to mind just how much of contemporary German and Austrian fiction is *not* concerned with the Nazi past (a fact that those involved in studying representations of the Third Reich can easily lose sight of) and ends by considering those contemporary 'pop' writers who cock a snook at the project of 'coming to terms'.

A few final remarks on method and organization. I have kept the text relatively footnote-free by using the section 'Further Reading and Viewing' to suggest other avenues worth exploring. All quotations appear in their original language, with English translations where necessary. Where I give details of a published translation at the first mention of a text, this is the source of the quoted translations; in such cases the page number of the translated text is given in brackets after the page number of the original. In all other cases translations are my own. Where a novel is not available in translation or where a film was not distributed in an English-language version I have provided as literal a translation of the title as the original title allows.

1 Beyond Celebration
Michael Verhoeven's *Das schreckliche Mädchen*

A close-knit community with skeletons in its cupboard, meddling young-sters who start asking awkward questions: these are staples of Western narrative, but also lived experience in post-1945 Germany and Austria. As screenwriter and director of *Das schreckliche Mädchen* (*The Nasty Girl*, 1989),[1] Michael Verhoeven is one of a number of writers and film-makers to exploit the narrative potential inherent in any unstable consensus of silence in order specifically to expose mechanisms of shame and shamelessness in post-Nazi communities. Produced shortly before the fall of the Berlin Wall, *Das schreckliche Mädchen* is one of the earliest works in this study, but as my approach is not primar-ily a film-historical or psycho-historical one (even if I rehearse some possible histories below) it earns its place in the first chapter for anoth-er reason, namely that of all the works studied here, it is probably the most straightforwardly moral, exposing the iniquities of the Nazi past and the silences that followed it with such a clearly educative agenda that it is difficult for the critic not to perform a straightfor-ward exegesis of its moral messages. The fact that Verhoeven questions the complacency of just such liberal attitudes to the Nazi past adds another layer to his moralizing without inviting a qualitatively dif-ferent critical method. I begin, therefore, by trying out what I am calling here a 'liberal' approach, before considering how one might step outside it.

Reading for the Message

In Verhoeven's film, Sonja is the model daughter and schoolgirl whose achievement in a national essay-writing competition is honoured by her home town of Pfilzing with a civic medal. By contrast, her research for a second competition, this time on the subject of her home town during the Third Reich, meets with obstruction from local officials and with increasingly open and violent harassment from other townspeople, for

---

[1] Michael Verhoeven, *Das schreckliche Mädchen* (FRG, 1989).

whom she becomes the 'awful girl' of the title,[2] fouling the prosperous nest of Pfilzing by exposing the Nazi allegiances of respected public figures. A series of court appearances, alternately as a plaintiff (fighting for access to files) and as a defendant (accused of defamation) attract growing media attention and, in its wake, a host of awards for civic courage. The town of Pfilzing eventually decides that it has more to gain from joining in this chorus of approval than it does from continuing to exclude Sonja and so honours her a second time, unveiling a bust of her at the Town Hall. The viewer's growing expectations of a happy ending are, however, disappointed when Sonja rounds on the assembled dignitaries, accusing them of using their tribute to silence her critical voice.

In film-historical terms *Das schreckliche Mädchen* is typical of works from the 1980s in subordinating the events of the Third Reich to the memory (and more particularly the forgetting) of those events: details of what happened in Pfilzing between 1933 and 1945 are relatively few and always framed by the act of remembering. The film also suggests that what Schlant argues for post-war literature, especially before 1990, is true also for film: that, however liberal in intent, it excludes the perspective of the Jewish victims. The only victim of Nazism who is embodied on screen, and given a character that invites sympathy, is a communist; by contrast, we know almost nothing of the Jewish man denounced by two priests.

On the other hand, viewed in psycho-historical terms, the film fulfils, if only fleetingly, one of the preconditions for mourning highlighted by Schmitz: that the perpetrator collective acknowledge the 'otherness' of Jewish culture rather than experience its loss narcissistically.[3] Sonja briefly appears in a stonemason's yard crouching to examine a stone fragment inscribed in Hebrew. She looks at it with evident curiosity, but clearly uncomprehendingly. In this way, Verhoeven acknowledges not just that Pfilzing has lost a part of its culture but also that that culture required, and still requires, an effort of empathy and interpretation by the non-Jewish majority. Interestingly, the cover of the DVD recording currently on sale reinforces this idea by showing Sonja actually fingering the Hebrew lettering rather like a blind person reading Braille (though she simultaneously studies it closely). The image has been faked—in the film she does not touch the stone and there is no overlap between her face and the lettering—but it suggests that by the beginning of the twenty-first century the idea that non-Jewish Germans

---

[2] The film was distributed in the UK and USA as *The Nasty Girl*. With its suggestion that the girl is inherently objectionable or even motivated by malice, 'nasty' is a poor translation of 'schrecklich' which implies rather the negative way in which she is judged by others.

[3] Schmitz, *Legacy*, 103.

must actively decipher the lost Jewish past was sufficiently mainstream to be understandable to consumers when symbolized in visual form, and sufficiently aspirational to encourage those consumers to part with their money.

In social-historical terms the film testifies to a wave of interest in the *Alltagsgeschichte* ('everyday history') of the Third Reich in 1980s Germany. In 1981, Sonja's real-life prototype, Anna Rosmus, entered the 'Schülerwettbewerb Deutsche Geschichte um den Preis des Bundespräsidenten' (German History Competition for Schoolchildren, Competing for the Federal President's Prize). The charity that has administered this biennial competition since its inception in 1974, the Körber-Stiftung, prides itself on the fact that its themed competitions encouraged young people to 'dig where you stand' some years before this became the motto of the grassroots *Geschichtswerkstatt* ('history workshop') movement in Germany. Verhoeven's 1989 viewers would have viewed Sonja's endeavours in the context of this trend, which was by then well established.

Like her cinematic counterpart, Anna Rosmus met with obstruction and evasion when she attempted to research the events of the Third Reich in her home town of Passau, and, like Sonja, her perseverance in the face of mounting abuse and physical attacks was rewarded with prizes and honours. Given its classic narrative topoi—a single-minded hero(ine) fighting a lonely battle for access to the truth, a conservative community that closes ranks against a perceived threat, and a sudden change of fortunes leading to unexpectedly generous rewards—and given, moreover, that the focus of this victory-against-the-odds narrative is the Nazi past, this is a story that could tell itself, a point to which I will return. One way in which Verhoeven keeps a certain distance from the ready-made story with which Rosmus supplied him is by stylizing and exaggerating it for satirical purposes. The cast, for example, consists of a limited array of types representing the local officials, dignitaries, and businessmen who together put the 'Filz' into 'Pfilzing'.[4] The tight knit of this network of power and influence is indicated by the reappearance of these and only these figures at each social occasion and by a stress on family connections (repeatedly, a character turns out to be somebody's father, daughter, husband, or sister). Verhoeven further emphasizes his characters' representative status by grouping them together in the credits as 'die Honoratioren' ('notabilities'), 'die Bürger' ('the locals'), 'die Stadtverwaltung' ('the local administration'), and so on, and by using

---

[4] 'Filz', literally 'felt', has the figurative sense of a corrupt network of local interests.

Brechtian social titles rather than names, for instance 'der General', 'die Diözesenrätin', and 'die Apothekerin' ('the general', 'the member of the diocesan council', 'the pharmacist'). Other defamiliarizing devices include the following: Sonja's commentary on the action from her standpoint in the present, which she often speaks directly to camera; still black-and-white images projected onto a studio backdrop, giving the impression of a crude stage-set; a mock-up of the family sitting room placed on the back of a lorry and filmed as it drives around Passau market; projections of Sonja's fears and fantasies; quick-fire sequences of very brief scenes; and a range of sound effects.

At its most general level the film attacks a community's complicity in Nazi policies and its desire to forget that complicity in the post-war era. Elizabeth Boa and Rachel Palfreyman identify three more specific targets: the moral bankruptcy of the town's institutions, all of which fail in various ways under Nazism and then cover for one another in the post-war era, in part by offering up one of their number, the former mayor Zumtobel, as a scapegoat; Allied denazification policies, which punish the powerless while protecting the powerful; and the right-wing violence that lurks beneath the peaceful surface of contemporary Germany.[5]

A few examples will illustrate Verhoeven's satirical technique. Having initially been refused access to the files concerning Mayor Zumtobel, Sonja has a lucky break: Zumtobel's grandson, Charly, who has just inherited the family confectionery business, agrees to lift the embargo. After delivering the news, Charly proudly demonstrates a machine that covers miniature weaponry in chocolate (Fig. 1), commenting: 'Das ist noch das alte Rezept von meinem Großpapa' ('We still make them to grandfather's old recipe'). Verhoeven makes no attempt to hide the artificiality of the sequence: the weapons are clearly plastic models, not made of sugar; there is a variety of weapons, not the single product that a real conveyor belt would carry; and they are lined up in military formation, as if on parade, not in the uniform lines required by mass production. The weaponry, I am reliably informed, includes a Kubel wagen, a Sturmgeschütz self-propelled gun, Flak-38 tracked anti-aircraft vehicles, Jagdtier tank destroyers, Krauss-Maffei half-tracks, and PAK105 artillery guns (all Second World War armoury); and Soviet Zil trucks carrying SA2 anti-aircraft missiles and a short-range nuclear weapon (products of the Cold War).[6] Of course, the average cinema-goer does not

---

[5] Elizabeth Boa and Rachel Palfreyman, *Heimat—A German Dream: Regional Loyalties and National Identity in German Culture 1890–1990* (Oxford: Oxford University Press, 2000).

[6] My thanks to Phil Weir for this information.

Fig. 1. Chocolate weaponry on parade in Michael Verhoeven's Cold War satire *Das schreckliche Mädchen*

know all this, but the close-ups are sufficiently close that the 1989 viewer would have recognized the mixture of pre-1945 and post-1945 armoury. Charly's comment about 'grandfather's old recipe' interprets the visual gag: post-war German industry supports Cold War military interests just as it supported Hitler's military interests; the arms race of the 1980s is thus a continuation of the alliance between business and militarist politics. The colour of the chocolate (the political colour of the National Socialists) also implies continuity. Moreover, by using chocolate, rather than some other industrial product, to make his point, by playing a fairground version of Offenbach's 'Can-Can' over the sequence, and by having Sonja show the chocolate toys to her toddler daughter, Verhoeven suggests that the saccharine, infantile pleasures of consumerism offer such gratification to his fellow West Germans that they fail to ask questions about where their prosperity comes from and what it hides.

The satire is only superficially contradicted by the approving tone with which Sonja's voice-over cites Charly. Elsewhere her naïve tone implies that her power as a muckraker comes from her youthful ignorance of the sensibilities she is treading on; here it creates an ironic gap between her gratitude towards Charly (with which the viewer identifies since his co-operation frees a narrative impasse) and Verhoeven's suspicion of him. 'Dem Charly war die Vergangenheit egal,' she says. 'Er sagt: "Hauptsache, das Geschäft blüht". Der Charly sagt, die Amerikaner haben seinem Großvater sogar angeboten, dass er in den USA eine Schokoladenfabrik aufmacht, darum glaubt er nicht, dass der alte Zumtobel ein Nazi-Verbrecher war' ('Charlie didn't care about the past. He says: "The important thing is that business is booming". Charlie says the Americans even invited his grandfather to open a chocolate factory in the USA, so he doesn't believe that old Zumtobel was a Nazi criminal'). Zumtobel junior here embodies an unencumbered 'third generation' that has nothing to hide, yet while Sonja profits from his lack of interest in history, it is not necessarily held up as a model; rather, it suggests that a cheerful insouciance about the Nazi past is a corollary of business success. At the same time, the audience is invited to question his confidence in his grandfather's innocence: that one capitalist country might see possibilities for commercial co-operation with another is not necessarily a guarantee of probity, Verhoeven hints.

The Cold War arms race and its capitalist foundations are evoked elsewhere. On two occasions the sound of military jets is heard overhead. The fact that the characters ignore the sound and continue their dialogue (though the sound effect must have been added post-production so that the actors are not literally ignoring it) suggests that the presence, in Germany, of increasingly sophisticated military firepower has become so accepted that it need not be remarked on. Sonja's Latin teacher has her pupils translate the phrase 'Auch die Armee kostet einen hohen Preis' ('The army costs a lot of money too') and Sonja demonstrates her conformism at this stage not only by rendering it correctly into Latin but also by identifying the grammatical structure as the *ablativus pretii* (ablative of price). The other sentence to be translated is 'Gründstücke sind teuer' ('Plots of land are expensive') and the teacher awards grades according to how much the girls' fathers have donated to the Church that year. These exchanges suggest that an acceptance of militarist and capitalist values is instilled in the young through education, not literally in Latin lessons but in correspondingly subliminal and unacknowledged ways.

Verhoeven points up the conflict between the Church's materialism and the spirit of the New Testament when, in a scene from the 1950s, he has Sonja's mother teach her school class about Jesus's ejection of the money-changers and stallholders from the Temple. With the aid of a blackboard drawing, the mother presents the children with a model of righteous anger—Jesus knocking over a money-changer's table—a model that her daughter will later emulate when she turns on the dignitaries of Pfilzing. Yet, despite his obvious sympathy for the figure of the mother, Verhoeven also criticizes her and, through her, Catholic education. By freezing the key elements of the chalk drawing behind the mother as she dismisses the class (letting her body mask the money-changers' table, but not the three human figures), Verhoeven gives us time to read the image. In its unthinking perpetuation of Nazi anti-Semitic iconography—the money-changers have exaggeratedly large hooked noses and oversized sacks of money—the drawing points to moral continuities between the Third Reich and the founding years of the Federal Republic. Moreover, Jesus is given a non-stereotypical physiognomy, which suppresses his cultural kinship with the money-changers and obscures Christianity's roots in Judaism. The frozen image of an angry Jesus (the momentum of his furious gesture rendered oddly static by the stylized figurative mode of the Catholic pictorial tradition) corresponds to other idealized, reified, and therefore ineffective images of heroic figures: the image of Sonja as a gilded statue, the tableau of Sonja as Joan of Arc at the stake, and the bust of Sonja destined for the Town Hall. Accordingly, the mother's lesson does not attempt to relate the gospel story to the lives of the girls, for whom it might serve as a model for modern-day *Zivilcourage*, but rather establishes a closed sign-system that refers only to itself: each girl has a copy of the blackboard drawing and her task is to colour it in. The bell that signals the end of the lesson precludes the possibility of discussion of Jesus's actions.

Of course, exposing the hypocrisy and complacency of the Catholic Church in prosperous conservative communities is about as difficult as knocking tin cans off a wall with a machine gun, and certainly no proof of satirical genius, but Verhoeven seems to know this, reserving his crudest shots for the easiest targets. Thus, the Latin teacher's reprimand to a schoolgirl who does not know her *ablativus pretii* and whose father's donations to the Church have suddenly dropped off is a crude pun: 'Von Ihnen hätte ich mehr erwartet' ('I expected more from you'). Even so, some of the details analysed above may seem to take us rather a long way from the Third Reich and its crimes, and might give the impression that Verhoeven is using forgetfulness about the Third Reich as a stick with which to beat his real *bêtes noires*: a society whose complacent materialism exasperates him and a government whose militarism he despises. However, the implication of the film as a whole is that one can only understand (and so overcome) the silence about the complicity of ordinary citizens in the crimes of the Third Reich if one understands the workings of the post-war social consensus. Equally, Verhoeven suggests that if Sonja must learn her *Zivilcourage* from her unconventional grandmother rather than from her social environment then this goes some way to explaining the fatal lack of *Zivilcourage* during the years of Nazi rule.

'Doing a Pfilzing'

In its contribution to Germany's and Austria's painful process of coming
to terms with the Nazi past, *Das schreckliche Mädchen* is unquestionably a good thing. So unquestionably, in fact, that it is one of a small
number of films whose study is supported, in the form of free teaching
materials, by Germany's government agency for democratic education,
the Bundeszentrale für politische Bildung. So unquestionably, too, that it
can be difficult to know what else to do with it but to extract its messages and celebrate its director's intelligence and right-mindedness. The
same could be said of many other works of German and Austrian fiction and film, but particularly of those that rescue previously neglected
aspects of the Nazi past from forgetfulness or dramatize such a rescue,
works such as Elisabeth Reichart's story *Februarschatten* (1984, about the
involvement of an Austrian community in hunting down and murdering
escaped Soviet prisoners), Ludwig Laher's documentary novel *Herzfleischentartung* (2001, about crimes committed in a little-known Austrian
concentration camp), Rolf Schübel's film *Das Heimweh des Walerjan
Wróbel* (1991, about the judicial murder of a young forced labourer), or
Margarethe von Trotta's film *Rosenstraße* (2003, about a group of women
who resisted the internment of their Jewish husbands).

Moral common sense tells one that these works deserve to be widely
known, but one needs to be at least a little suspicious of the psychological
rewards that studying them offers. In his comparative analysis of *Das
schreckliche Mädchen* and two films about the Weiße Rose resistance
group, David Levin questions the tendency to applaud works of art about
resistance to Nazism:

> For what do we celebrate in celebrating a cinema of resistance? Do we
> celebrate that which always renders resistance intolerable? Or are we too
> 'doing a Pfilzing', congratulating ourselves as we co-opt the resistance,
> making it speak the muted, and therefore reassuring, language that befits
> our admiration, and, in the process, joining in, rendering communal what was
> and remains an intensely solitary battle?[7]

Levin goes on to argue that *Das schreckliche Mädchen* frustrates such
attempts at assimilation, because Verhoeven uses Sonja's immediate
audience at the second civic reception as a double for the cinema
audience, with the result that our self-congratulatory identification with

---

[7] David Levin, 'Are We Victims Yet? Resistance and Community in *The White Rose, Five Last Days*,
and *The Nasty Girl*', *Germanic Review*, 73 (1998), 86–100 (92).

the 'schreckliches Mädchen' is externalized on screen. 'We have seen [Sonja] through her tribulations,' writes Levin, 'and now we can expect to share in her celebration', yet she excludes us with her foul-mouthed outburst, thereby exposing the falsity of our viewing position. By 'we', however, Levin appears to mean cinema-goers; in our role as critics we are still inclined to celebrate *Das schreckliche Mädchen*, as Levin himself does, precisely because it confronts viewers with their questionable desire for moral satisfaction in relation to the Nazi past. The circle of celebration is therefore difficult to break out of.

One possible criticism of Verhoeven's dramatization of the conflicts in West German society is that his portrayal of the neo-Nazi fringe is much too sketchy. At several points, the film cuts to a smoky beer hall where unidentified local people are carousing; some of the men in these shots appear in other scenes, including those in which Sonja is threatened or attacked. Verhoeven uses a visual shorthand for his extremists: displays of loutish and paramilitary behaviour, male–male interactions, and black clothes. Of course, the middle-classes are carica-tured too, but the two forms of stylization are not necessarily equivalent. The middle-class characters speak, they are defined by their institutional environments, and subtle differences between their actions and atti-tudes create a 'differentiated picture', a 'variegated mix' of behaviours that suggests a 'complex interplay of individual actions with local insti-tutional and wider national political factors'.[8] By contrast, the blackshirts are silent except when they sing or pray in chorus, and though their appearance and choice of locale suggest that they are working-class, the film gives us no way of understanding how their social environment acts to form their attitudes (beyond a hint that they, too, are deformed by Catholicism). Bernhard Schlink's *Der Vorleser*, discussed in Chapter 2, likewise conceptualizes middle-class attitudes to the Nazi past thor-oughly while the working class and its attitudes remain something of a blank.

On two occasions the film shows us pieces of left-wing graffiti, evid-ently genuine graffiti filmed on location in Passau. One piece reads: 'Wo wart ihr zwischen '39–'45? Wo seid ihr jetzt?' ('Where were you between '39–'45? Where are you now?'); the other: 'Braun sein heißt Mörder sein' ('To be brown is to be a murderer'). The unknown authors of these slogans are even more of a blank space than the blackshirts, but the very fact that the graffiti is written freehand lends it a reality that the celluloid neo-Nazis do not have, and its effect is to contribute to a more differentiated picture of Bavaria's political culture, suggesting as it does

---

[8] Boa and Palfreyman, *Heimat*, 167.

that Sonja's is not the only kind of protest against forgetting the Nazi past, that other, less mainstream and law-abiding dissenters exist.

Boa and Palfreyman demonstrate two complementary ways in which one might read *Das schreckliche Mädchen* aslant of its moral trajectory whilst nevertheless acknowledging its satirical intent. First, they place it in a cultural tradition that is tangential to the history of Nazism and its commemoration: the German *Heimat* tradition. In this connection, they suggest that Verhoeven does not, as one might expect of such an overtly critical writer, equate *Heimat* and Nazism, since the most sympathetic characters, those associated with resistance, are connected by their dialect and their simple country living with *Heimat* values. Secondly, they read the film in terms of gender. Again, they suggest that Verhoeven avoids a one-sided attack: while his satire pokes fun at the traditional role of women in the *Heimat* (for every shot of a woman preparing food, hanging out washing, chopping wood, or sewing, there is a shot of a man sitting behind a desk), the film nevertheless suggests that women draw strength from the more positive female traditions of *Heimat*.

A rather different way of gaining some critical purchase on the film is to consider it not as a film about remembering the Third Reich but as a biopic. Anna Rosmus, Sonja's real-life prototype, appears briefly as an extra in the film about her life, standing in the audience at Sonja's second investiture (wearing a red chiffon blouse), a playful gesture that puts her in the company of Maria von Trapp and Erin Brockovich, among others. This might sound like the stuff of film-trivia quizzes, but in Rosmus's case it is symptomatic of an unusually high identification with the narrativization of her life-story, or at least of that part of her life-story that has come to dominate it. Verhoeven's film can be seen as one stage in a much longer process by which Rosmus's story is told and retold. Even before the film was made, Rosmus's struggles had been recounted in newspaper articles, television reports, and documentaries.[9] Verhoeven's film only increased and broadened media coverage of her life, showing that the appetite for reports about the 'real-life' Sonja Wegmus had not been sated.[10] She was the subject of a Dutch documentary in 1991 and, in 1994, of one by German television station ARD,[11] while *60 Minutes*, the CBS current-affairs programme, profiled her twice (in 1994 and 2000). Rosmus herself

---

[9] Rosmus discusses the making of one such documentary, *Gegen den Strom* (FRG: ARD, 1987), in Anna Elisabeth Rosmus, *Out of Passau. Von einer, die auszog, die Heimat zu finden* (Freiburg im Breisgau: Herder, 1999), 146.

[10] e.g. Marc Fisher, 'The "Nasty Girl" and the Nazi Past', *Washington Post*, 7 Dec. 1990; Adrian Bridge, ' "Bad girl" of Passau Keeps the Holocaust Wounds Wide Open', *The Independent*, 15 Aug. 1993.

[11] Rosmus, *Out of Passau*, 152.

has told her story in various forms: in two full-length autobiographies;[12] in two essays;[13] and in an extended, annotated interview.[14] To this day, Rosmus makes her living partly through speaking engagements, mostly addressing university students at campuses across America, where she now lives, and where she is billed as the 'real-life heroine of *The Nasty Girl*'.[15] Often, Rosmus's talks accompany a showing of *Das schreckliche Mädchen*, allowing her to address the relationship between fact and fiction, and even when her subject is her current research project the narrative of her travails in Passau evidently provides a framework for her speech. The following report is typical: 'German historian and author Anna Rosmus spoke for two hours about her experiences uncovering the concealed Nazi past of Passau, Germany. [. . .] Rosmus described some of the difficulties and threats she encountered from many Passau residents, saying that *The Nasty Girl* accurately communicates the degree of her hardship and frustration, as well as some of the deep satisfactions her success had brought her.'[16]

No criticism of Rosmus is intended: her dedication, over more than twenty years, to uncovering forgotten details of Passau's past and her commitment to Passau's Holocaust survivors are remarkable by any measure. Nor am I trying to diagnose in Rosmus a compulsion to repeat her story: her speaking engagements, in particular, are a way of funding new research projects and of supporting her family. Nevertheless, the story of the fight to uncover the truth about the Nazi past appears to contain something so archetypal that it is both endlessly repeatable and such that one can build an identity around it ('identitätsstiftend'). The following billing of an event at which Rosmus was to share a platform with other speakers pinpoints the archetypal appeal of the narrative:

> You may not immediately recognize their names but once you hear their stories you'll never forget them. Shannon Lanier, Anna Rosmus and Patrick Douglas Crispin will recount how they each tenaciously searched for a truth that enabled them to succeed despite the obstacles. All three are scheduled to

---

[12] Anna Rosmus, *Was ich denke* (Munich: Goldmann, 1995), commissioned for the series 'Quer denken', and Rosmus, *Out of Passau*.

[13] Anna Rosmus, 'Leiden an Passau', in Marielouise Janssen-Jurreit (ed.), *Lieben Sie Deutschland?* (Munich: Piper, 1985), 98–106, and 'From Reality to Fiction: Anna Rosmus as "Nasty Girl"', *Religion and the Arts*, 4 (2001), 118–53.

[14] Hans-Dieter Schütt, *Anna Rosmus—die 'Hexe' von Passau* (Berlin: Dietz, 1994).

[15] The marketability of the 'real-life' prototype of a screen hero or heroine is illustrated also by Sally Perel, whose autobiography provided the basis for Agnieszka Holland's film *Hitlerjunge Salomon* (discussed in Ch. 4): originally published in French under the title *Europa, Europa*, the autobiography was subsequently rebranded for a German audience as *Ich war Hitlerjunge Salomon*.

[16] http://flathat.wm.edu/January242003/newsstory10.shtml. Accessed 22 Nov. 2006.

share their stories at the second general session of the American Association
of School Librarians' 11th National Conference and Exhibition.[17]

Verhoeven is just as much implicated in this process as he is an ironic
observer of it. In the film itself, Verhoeven displays a healthy suspicion of the ready recountability of the story, acknowledging from the
outset that this is a biography ripe for the telling, to a public eager
to listen. He has Sonja tell her story first as part of a slide show (and
therefore, by implication, to a local audience) and then to camera (to
a wider, perhaps national, audience). Other characters, too, are interviewed as if by a documentary team (in token of which the boom is
sometimes left amateurishly in the frame). At several points a media
scrum surrounds Sonja, though the idea of entrapment that this evokes
is counterbalanced by scenes in which Sonja uses the media to her
own ends. Verhoeven does not, therefore, simply recount the sensation-
al story of a woman who insisted on telling the truth about the Third
Reich; rather, he draws attention to his contemporaries' thirst for sen-
sational stories about people who insist on telling the truth about the
Third Reich.

Yet it is clearly not in Verhoeven's interests to undermine the story
value of the Rosmus material altogether: after all, he has chosen it
because the story of uncovering the Nazi past in the teeth of fierce local
opposition is far more satisfying and saleable than the story of uncovering the Nazi past in a relatively straightforward process of archival
research, with the odd bureaucratic hitch and the occasional uncomfortable encounter (that being the unsensational reality of most local-level
historical research in Germany and Austria). Moreover, Verhoeven himself exploited the demand, which existed before his film but was inflated
by it, for a 'doubling' of the story through a retelling of its prototype. In
his television documentary, *Das Mädchen und die Stadt*, extracts from
interviews with the 'original' characters from Passau are edited in such
a way as to recreate the linear narrative of the film, with its escalating
tensions requiring the ever greater fortitude of its protagonist.[18] The fact
that there is a measure of ironic distance here, too (though far less than
in the film), does not alter the fact that Verhoeven exploits the story's
inherent reproducibility. In one sequence, Rosmus's ex-husband claims
that his wife would have liked to play the lead role in *Das schreckliche Mädchen*; the film then cuts to Rosmus standing in front of a
poster for the film, telling us that while it is not entirely true to life she

---

[17] http://archive.ala.org/aasl/kc/news/second.html. Accessed 22 Nov. 2006.
[18] Michael Verhoeven, *Das Mädchen und die Stadt* (FRG: ZDF, 1990).

nevertheless recognizes herself in lead actress Lena Stolze: 'ich hoffe mit mir, ich zittere mit mir, ich triumphiere mit mir' ('I hope with myself, I tremble with myself, I triumph with myself'). By cutting this statement against the husband's somewhat bitter testimony, Verhoeven keeps his distance from Rosmus's identification with the dramatized narrative of her life. And yet Verhoeven's distance is precarious: when he publicized the English-language version of the film in the United States he took Rosmus with him and they appeared at press conferences together, where, interestingly, they took slightly different lines on the film, he stressing its fictional nature, she its authenticity.[19] It seems that Verhoeven needed Rosmus to validate his screenplay through the retelling of its story, even as he was suspicious of the repeated recycling of her story in the media.

The person of Lena Stolze can be submitted to a similar analysis. Both Boa/Palfreyman and Levin argue that Verhoeven's casting of Stolze establishes an implicit parallel between the bravery of Sonja and the bravery of Sophie Scholl, a member of the Weiße Rose resistance group whom Stolze had portrayed in two earlier films (one of them directed by Verhoeven); at the same time, because *Das schreckliche Mädchen* questions the public's need for heroic figures it is curiously at odds with the celebratory portraits of Scholl to which the person of Stolze alludes. A role from Stolze's later career complicates further this process of self-reference. The Hamburger Institut für Sozialforschung (Hamburg Institute for Social Research or HIS) employed Stolze to appear in a DVD that accompanied the second incarnation of the so-called 'Wehrmacht Exhibition'. Stolze's task was to give a virtual guided tour (Fig. 2). The blurb on the DVD jacket, also reproduced in advertising brochures, entices potential purchasers with the promise that: 'Lena Stolze, besonders bekannt geworden durch ihre Rolle der "Sophie Scholl" in dem Film *Die Weiße Rose* von Michael Verhoeven und der "Miriam Süßmann" im Film *Rosenstraße* von Margarethe von Trotta, führt Sie in verschiedenen Videoaufnahmen durch die Ausstellung' ('Lena Stolze, known especially for her roles as Sophie Scholl in the film *The White Rose* by Michael Verhoeven and as Miriam Süßmann in the film *The Women of Rosenstrasse* by Margarethe von Trotta, guides you through the exhibition in a series of video recordings'). While I hesitate to accord too much weight to a piece of advertising copy, there are various reasons why the choice of Stolze is not as self-explanatory as this statement would like to suggest. First, anyone trained in the rudiments of television presenting could have done the job of moving around the exhibition space while reading a factual text

---

[19] Schütt, *Anna Rosmus*, 124.

Fig. 2. The actress Lena Stolze gives a virtual tour of the exhibition *Verbrechen der Wehrmacht. Dimensionen des Vernichtungskrieges 1941–1944*

from an autocue (indeed, many would have read from the autocue more naturally); secondly, Stolze's earlier roles are not connected directly with the subject of the exhibition, which is the murder and maltreatment of Soviet prisoners of war, partisans, and non-combatants, including Jews, by Wehrmacht soldiers on and behind the Eastern Front; thirdly, her role in *Rosenstraße*, a film that was only moderately successful at the box office, was a minor speaking part easily eclipsed by five or six strong main parts, so that she cannot be said to be 'known' for it.[20] However, by stressing her link to two films about resistance to Nazism, and by spelling out that in one she played a Jewish victim, the HIS (or at least its publishing house Hamburger Edition) suggests that its consumers are buying into the correct way of dealing with the Nazi past. Possibly Hamburger Edition were also aiming the DVD at schoolteachers and calculated that Stolze, having portrayed sympathetic identificatory figures in films that are often shown in schools, would be acceptable to schoolchildren as a teacher-figure. Stolze has thus arguably become that embodiment of a publicly acceptable morality that her character in *Das schreckliche Mädchen* rejects. This might explain the omission of *Das schreckliche Mädchen*, Stolze's best and surely best-known performance, from the advertising copy.

[20] The Lumière database gives a figure of 600,605 for German ticket receipts to *Rosenstraße* in the year of its release; this compares well with, say, *Der Unhold* (163, 877), the Volker Schlöndorff film analysed in Ch. 4, but is small beer compared with major hits such as *Goodbye Lenin* (6,439,777).

Conclusion

A work like *Das schreckliche Mädchen* lends itself to an 'affirmative reading' of the kind that I discussed in the Introduction: a reading that values
a work for having something moral and/or new to say (whether inten-
tionally or symptomatically) about the Third Reich and its legacies. While
I see no reason to abandon such an assignment of value—what reason
could there be not to celebrate intelligent engagements with the Nazi
past?—there is a danger that the critical enterprise becomes circular and
self-affirming, with the coherence of the critic's analysis guaranteeing the
coherence (and therefore consequence) of the author's or film-maker's
messages, which in turn guarantee the value of the critic's analysis.
This chapter has suggested ways in which, faced with a self-evidently
enlightening work about the Nazi past, one might do more than simply
reconstruct its moral meanings: for instance, by acknowledging the processes of selection and exclusion that attend the construction of even
the most liberal of moralities; by recognizing the work's embeddedness
in contexts and traditions other than the Nazi past; or by analysing the
processes that keep stories about the Third Reich in circulation. The
example of Stolze's involvement with the 'Wehrmacht Exhibition' suggests that it is not just stories about the Third Reich that are subject to
commodification and circulation, but also liberal attitudes towards the
Third Reich.

2 Generation and Nation
Peter Schneider's *Vati* and
Bernhard Schlink's *Der Vorleser*

Though they fall either side of the watershed of 1989, Peter Schneider's story *Vati* (*Dad*, 1987) and Bernhard Schlink's novel *Der Vorleser* (*The Reader*, 1995) have such obvious points of contact that they have already been the object of comparative analysis.[1] Both record the emotional confusion of a central figure—respectively a lawyer and a legal historian—who discovers that a person he loves served in the concentration camps. As articulate professionals, the two men are able to formulate their emotional dilemmas very precisely, yet their self-knowledge is limited and both leave much unsaid. Taken together, the two texts lend themselves to a literary-historical approach that seeks to identify phases in German literature's approach to the Nazi past. In 1983 Schneider spoke approvingly of the recent spate of texts in which authors explored the involvement of their fathers (and, in a few cases, mothers) in National Socialism,[2] but when, only a few years later, he came to make his own contribution to this *Vaterliteratur*, the programmatically titled story *Vati*, he distanced himself from the earlier texts by questioning the way in which the student protesters (and by implication also the writers) of the late 1960s had dealt with their parents' involvement in National Socialism.[3] *Der Vorleser* continues this process of putting into historical perspective the student protest movement and the *Vaterliteratur* that it generated, and attempts, like *Vati*, to confront the unpalatable fact that the perpetrators of Nazi crimes were loved; at the same time it can also be seen to mark the point at which the overused formula of the father–son conflict is finally rejected.

---

[1] Peter Schneider, *Vati* (Darmstadt and Neuwied: Luchterhand, 1987); Bernhard Schlink, *Der Vorleser* (Zurich: Diogenes, 1995), *The Reader*, trans. Carol Brown Janeway (London: Phoenix, 1997). Page references to these editions appear in brackets in the text.

[2] 'Nous ne voulions rien avoir à faire avec la génération fasciste. Mais cette confrontation est devenue indispensable. Nous devons pouvoir dire que nous sommes les fils de nos pères' ('We wanted nothing to do with the fascist generation. But this confrontation has become indispensable. We should be able to say that we are the sons of our fathers'), 'Berlin, prison dorée', Peter Schneider in conversation with Philippe Boyer, *Nouvel Observateur*, 26 Aug. 1983.

[3] See Peter Morgan, 'The Sins of the Fathers: A Reappraisal of the Controversy about Peter Schneider's *Vati*', *German Life and Letters*, 47 (1994), 104–33 for a positive view of *Vati* in the context of *Vaterliteratur*.

My analysis is less concerned with placing *Vati* and *Der Vorleser* along a literary-historical timeline than with examining how the authors construct their moral and intellectual positions and how academic critics deal with texts in which such moral and intellectual positioning plays a major role.

Vati

Inspired by a series of magazine interviews with Rolf Mengele, son of Auschwitz doctor Josef Mengele, *Vati* caused a critical storm in a teacup, the story of which has been well rehearsed elsewhere.[4] If we pass over a spurious accusation of plagiarism, the substantive point of contention was whether it was defensible to present a Nazi criminal through the humanizing lens of his son, who narrates the story. In subsequent scholarly debate, widely divergent positions have been adopted: where, for Gordon Burgess, *Vati* turns good journalism about the Third Reich into bad literature, for Peter Morgan, on the contrary, it turns indifferent journalism into challenging literature; what for Adolf Höfer is proof that family-based narratives trivialize the Holocaust is for Karlheinz Fingerhut a cleverly managed disappointment of the reader's desire for moral satisfaction.[5]

For my present purposes an overview of the text's structure can take the place of a summary of the relatively uneventful plot. An unnamed lawyer recalls a visit, three years previously, to see his father, a Nazi doctor living in hiding in Brazil; the narrator's childhood, schooldays, and student years are recollected in flashback within this main narrative; rather more scattered references are made to events of the past year, since he announced news of his father's death to the media. During this most recent period a former schoolfriend makes contact, and it is to this anonymous 'Du' that the narrator addresses the narrative, which is, we learn, the latest in a series of attempts to explain his fraught relationship with his father. The earlier attempts had been characterized by a

---

[4] For a fuller account see Peter Schneider, *Vati*, ed. Colin Riordan (Manchester: Manchester University Press, 1993), 24–9.

[5] Gordon Burgess, '"Was da ist, das ist [nicht] mein": The Case of Peter Schneider', in Arthur Williams, Stuart Parkes, and Roland Smith (eds.), *Literature on the Threshold: The German Novel in the 1980s* (New York, Oxford and Munich: Berg, 1990), 107–22; Adolf Höfer, 'Vater-Sohn-Konflikte in moderner Dichtung. Symptome einer Verharmlosung des Faschismus am Beispiel von Peter Schneiders Erzählung *Vati*', *Literatur für Leser* (1994), 11–22; Karlheinz Fingerhut, 'Das Lebensziel: "Nicht so zu werden wie ihre Väter". Zu Peter Schneiders Erzählung *Vati*', *Diskussion Deutsch*, 21 (1990), 416–23.

compulsion to unburden himself (he indulges in 'nächtliche Monologe am Telefon', 'late-night monologues on the phone') coupled unhappily with an inability to express himself (his explanations are 'verhaspelt', that is, he trips over his words). What he hopes to gain by writing rather than speaking is 'Entfernung' ('distance'; p. 19).

The key point here is that the struggle to gain a rational perspective on events has not been fought and won before the narrator puts pen to paper. Rather, it is played out in the narrative, where it works as a second structuring principle. When writing about the most distant events the narrator confidently anatomizes his feelings and motives, and generalizes from his situation to moral and political concerns, though it does not follow that the reader must agree with these judgements, only that the narrator has a definite perspective on this period of his life. Similarly, when writing about the first days in Brazil, the narrator maintains a measure of distance and control, although, perhaps because he is keen for his schoolfriend to experience his anxieties, or more likely because Schneider is keen for his reader to experience them, he sticks somewhat closer to his perspective at the time, notably in short snippets of interior monologue. In recounting the later stages of the visit to Brazil, the narrator is increasingly unable to frame events in the psychologizing and generalizing terms in which he is practised, restricting himself to describing the immediate situation even where his actions beg explanation. The fact that this technique is not especially realistic—since a real person would, on reading a draft of his account, notice the sudden and glaring gaps in the commentary and at least attempt to gloss over them—only highlights its aesthetic function, the unfinished quest for self-understanding being a conventional enough narrative construction that passes on to the reader the task of critical reflection. Moreover, by carefully managing the narrative stance, alternating between controlling distance and helpless immediacy, and by gradually tipping the balance towards the latter, Schneider also transforms the stylistically uniform *Bunte* interviews into a psychological drama, one in which the form reinforces the content, since the narrator's gradual loss of control over his narrative parallels his loss of control over the encounter with his father. An analysis of two passages will illustrate this technique before I consider its implications further.

We join the narrative after a first fruitless exchange of views between the two characters. The father expresses approval of his son's choice of a fiancée who possesses positive 'racial' characteristics, forcing the narrator to recognize that he has failed to make even the slightest dent in his father's ideological armour. The son expresses his helplessness by impulsively placing his hands around his father's neck, but lacks the resolve to follow the action through (that is, to shake him): 'Ich tat nichts dergleichen. Ich sah ihn nur an' ('I did nothing of the kind. I just looked at him'; p. 41).[6] Though equally incapable, at the time of this action, of restraining himself and of asserting himself, the narrator at least remains sufficiently in control of his narrative to judge his gesture as 'lächerlich zitathaft' ('ridiculously imitative'; p. 41), to articulate precisely the motives behind it, and to generalize from the experience. Over the pages that follow even this narratorial control slips from him. Thus, the narrator describes but does not analyse a momentary misapprehension that his father is trying to overpower him (pp. 43–4), leaving the reader to interpret it (for instance as an anticipation of the punishment that he expects for attempting to rebel). In the extended scene that follows, during which the son wanders through the streets of Belem, he offers a series of explanations for his behaviour—'Beides wirkte auf mich wie ein Zeichen' ('Both of these things appeared to me like a sign'); 'Eine Gier [. . .] erfüllte mich' ('I was filled with lust'); and: 'Diese Entdeckung machte mich schamlos' ('This discovery made me shameless'; pp. 46–7)—but these only explain the internal logic of the scene; they do not explain why he chooses to stalk a black woman, or what causes the sudden rush of sexual desire, or why he narrates the scene at all, given that it does not involve his father. The reader is again invited to supply the missing critical distance and to construct a plausible logic, such as this: the narrator seeks escape from his sense of shame at his feebleness vis-à-vis the father by means of what William Collins Donahue calls a 'somatic retreat from reason and judgment', that is, by allowing himself to drift on a tide of unreflected, irrational impulses; and such is the force of his shame that he is unable even at a distance of three years to recuperate his habitual self-critical position.[7]

The final scenes of the story, in which the narrator reports the theft of money from his hotel room, work in a similar way: the narrator is sufficiently distanced to identify impulses that keep events in motion (for example, the fear of wounded pride that makes him reluctant to withdraw his complaint; p. 71), but accounts neither for his dogged pursuit of the hotel owner, whom he suspects of the theft, nor for his lengthy narration of the incident in an account of his relationship with his father. Indeed, in the form in which he narrates it, this episode constitutes the climactic

---

[6] Compare other moments of irresolution that prevent him from confronting his father: 'Bevor ich dies oder etwas Ähnliches sagen konnte' ('Before I could say this, or something like it'; p. 43) and 'Aber bevor ich ihn unterbrechen konnte' ('But before I could interrupt him'; p. 62).

[7] William Collins Donahue, 'Revising '68: Bernhard Schlink's *Der Vorleser*, Peter Schneider's *Vati*, and the Question of History', *Seminar*, 40 (2004), 293–311 (306).

encounter of his trip to Brazil so that it defies narrative sense not to pass comment on its significance and instead to move wordlessly to a laconic description of his return home. Once again, so much studied silence gives the reader plenty to do, most obviously to speculate that the narrator is attempting to obliterate his failure to bring his father to justice by insisting on justice in another matter. Since that matter involves a much pettier crime, and since even this attempt fails, the episode simply accentuates the narrator's ineffectualness. Moreover, if the pursuit of justice is an attempt to free himself, at least symbolically, from his father, then that attempt backfires as he is confronted by his own racist attitudes (p. 72) and by increasingly violent fantasies (pp. 71, 80).

Schneider deliberately establishes the narrator's confidence that he can control the encounter with the hotelier ('Ich war sicher, diese Drohung würde ihn einschüchtern', 'I was sure that this threat would intimidate him'; p. 71) in order then to undermine it: the narrator is wrong-footed when the hotelier accedes to his request to call the police; wishes he could retract his complaint, but feels constrained to pursue it; resorts to helpless insults when he cannot prove his allegations; and mistakenly suspects the hotelier of giving him wrong directions to the police station. Moreover, while the hotelier gives nothing away, the narrator fears that his own hidden intentions are written all over his face.

Even before he reaches the police station, the narrator's sense of purpose is sapped by an access of fatigue: he is overcome by a desire to sit down and 'den Abend, die Jahre [...] verwarten' ('sit out the evening, the years'; p. 73). He blames this on the heat, which means either that Schneider has written the weather to externalize the conflict between his narrator's will and weakness, or that the narrator prefers to attribute his weaknesses to external forces rather than investigate their source in himself.[8] Either way, by having his narrator amend 'den Abend' to the hyperbolic 'die Jahre' Schneider signals a shift into a nightmarish mood characterized not just by the dissolution of time (the figures at the police station are 'in ein zeitloses Warten versunken', 'lost in timeless waiting'; p. 73) but by a disjunction between what the narrator expects of his mind and body and what they are able to do. In particular, he has difficulty reading external reality (he cannot tell whether the people waiting in the police station are suspects or complainants and mistakenly assumes that the duty officer is asleep) and difficulty communicating (he forgets what he wants to say, becomes unable to form and enunciate words, and

---

[8] In the opening passage of the text he claims to be unable to see his father's face because of the dust, though other passages in which he declines to look into his father's eyes (pp. 31, 51) suggest that the problem lies within him rather than in the climatic conditions.

cannot direct the duty officer to write down what he wants to put on record). Eventually he loses the ability to make himself understood at all.

Schneider steps up the tension in this final episode because the narrator does not voluntarily relinquish control as in the stalking scene and also because the loss of control takes a form that threatens his very identity: though his ostensible goal is justice, and though his professional persona is founded on the correct observance of legal practices, the narrator finds himself implicated in police corruption. Two policemen whom he has just watched beat up a suspect appear to be planning to ransack the apartment of an innocent chambermaid as a token retribution. The more the narrator tries to dissociate himself from their methods, the more he is ignored, and since the chambermaid recalls the woman he had stalked he is powerless against the policemen's insinuation that he is only defending her because he finds her attractive. Indeed, given that the narrator had earlier entertained a momentary fantasy of using violence to force a confession from the hotel owner (p. 71), the whole episode evokes the injunction to 'Be careful what you wish for': when similar methods are used in his name he cannot retreat to the safety of the moral high ground.

Given more space, one could analyse all this in greater detail, but there is no point in getting too lost in wonderment at Schneider's ability to write psychological action, which is not in dispute (though other passages are arguably less surely written than these). The question is: What can Schneider hope to gain from humiliating his narrator so mercilessly? More precisely: What can he hope to gain from deploying the narrative trope of the disintegrating male ego, which features in plenty of fiction that has nothing to do with the Third Reich, in a story about the Third Reich? For it must be remembered that this aspect of the text is Schneider's invention. He subjects his lawyer protagonist to a *Heart of Darkness* experience that brings him face to face with the antithesis of his professional principles of justice, liberalism, and a progressive social order; Josef Mengele's son Rolf, though he doubtless had a tough time of it, told no such story. The narrative construction contributes to Schneider's critique of the student radicals: against the story of the typical *68er*, for whom the struggle with the father creates an identity (the narrator claims that his friend 'Du' carries documentary 'proof' of his father's fascist past in lieu of identity papers), Schneider sets the story of a man whose identity is unravelled by the confrontation with the Third Reich. On the face of it this hardly makes him a model figure, but his behaviour points towards a model: his self-defeating attempts to protect his personality from the challenge posed by his father implicitly assign a positive value to a willingness to allow one's secure sense of self to be challenged by the Nazi past and by one's emotional connections to it (though clearly that makes more sense for Schneider's contemporary readers than for later readers).

Two aspects of this construction of the fallible central character repay closer analysis. First, the police-station episode recalls details from Kafka's *Der Proceß*, particularly from the two chapters in which Josef K. visits the inns of court. In the earlier chapter, a haze prevents Josef K. from seeing the courtroom clearly, and from making reliable judgements about guilt and innocence; we cannot be confident that he is reading other people correctly; and he becomes convinced, on the basis of strong and yet not quite conclusive evidence, that the judge is in cahoots with members of the public. In the later chapter, K. is overcome by the airless atmosphere of the court chambers; the more he attempts to take control of his situation, the more debilitated he becomes; he encounters people who are waiting pointlessly for implausibly long periods; and the roles and methods of the officials he meets are curiously opaque.

Once alerted to the Kafkaesque elements of the theft episode, one may begin to see further allusions to Kafka elsewhere in the text, particularly in Schneider's portrayal of the father's body, which, despite an outward appearance of frailty (p. 52), performs sudden and unexpected shows of strength: it is 'unwirklich groß und mächtig' and possesses 'eine entsetzliche Kraft' ('implausibly big and powerful', 'a terrible strength'; p. 43); it can climb the frame of a half-built house 'überraschend gewandt' ('surprisingly nimbly'; p. 58); and force the son to the ground 'mit unglaublicher Kraft' ('with incredible strength'; p. 59). These descriptions recall both *Die Verwandlung* and *Das Urteil*, though the father's affection for his nephew Werner places the story closer to *Das Urteil*, in which the father prefers the friend in Petersburg to his own son. On the other hand, when the father in *Vati*, in what seems an impossibly swift movement, reaches the front door before the son can escape through it (p. 43) this recalls a similar movement by the examining magistrate in *Der Proceß* who, despite standing behind K., reaches the door before him. The main difference in technique is that Schneider stops short of the kind of surreal details that, in Kafka's texts, cannot be explained away by the narrator's subjective perspective, such as the cushions required by the plaintiffs in *Der Proceß* to prevent them from chafing their heads on the ceiling of the gallery.

While it is hardly surprising to find allusions to Kafka in a story that deals with the twin themes of law and the father, there is a tension between Schneider's subject matter and Kafka's. If the narrator's quest for justice becomes—by reference to Kafka—a timeless existential experience of father–son conflict and of the hubris of human reason (which mistakenly assumes that it can secure justice in a world whose sense is impenetrable), then the historical specificity of Mengele's crimes would seem to become irrelevant.

The flawed narrator is also constructed partly by means of the South American setting. The Brazilian environment is made to work hard, perhaps rather too hard, since it must not only elaborate the central themes of biological inheritance (in the scene in the jungle) and justice (in the scene at the police station), but also demonstrate the ways in which father and son construct and process 'foreignness'. The narrator is scathing of his father's unwillingness to adapt to a foreign environment, mocking his crepe-soled shoes as a ridiculous remnant of his life in Germany and sneering at his compulsion to keep things clean in a naturally dusty environment, concluding that his father wants to preserve himself at all costs 'vom Geruch und von der Berührung der fremden Erde' ('from the smell of and from contact with the foreign soil'; pp. 10–11). The same contempt is evident in his comment that the arrival of the father's German friends transforms his house into a 'deutsches Schrebergartenhäuschen' ('a summerhouse on a German allotment'; p. 37).

Yet the narrator's conflicted relationship with his father may colour his reading of him, since a later scene, in which the father speaks in Portuguese to a group of carpenters whose work he has been supervising, suggests that he has in fact adapted successfully to his environment. Moreover, the narrator is unaware that he himself finds the foreignness of Brazil a persistent irritant. In its immediate context, his description of the dogs that roam the street as 'eine Meute schrecklich magerer, herrenloser Hunde' ('a pack of terribly thin, ownerless dogs'; p. 5) may seem unremarkable, suggesting at worst the knee-jerk response of the European traveller accustomed to seeing dogs well-fed and confined, but it is the first in a series of descriptive details that, taken collectively, suggest that the narrator experiences the foreign environment as an unsettling breakdown of normal order. Describing another 'swarm' ('Gewimmel'), this time of children, the narrator notes that they are 'nur mit Turnhose und Unterhemd bekleidet' ('clad only in gym shorts and vests'; p. 9). The sense of the mildly disapproving 'nur' is clarified by the European vocabulary, which suggests an unacknowledged assumption that middle-class European social norms are valid everywhere. To poor Brazilians these are not 'gym shorts' and 'vests' but routine outerwear. Other Brazilians are described as 'halbnackt' ('half-naked'; pp. 9, 45), again implying a sense of propriety imported from a colder climate but which makes no sense in the tropics. The cactuses in the father's garden sound out of place when described by the narrator as 'Büropflanzen im Freien' ('office plants in the open air'; p. 9), whereas they are in fact in their natural climate, if not quite their natural habitat, and it is in European offices that they are out of place. Finally, while his description of the rainforest suggests a culturally generated notion of the natural order—'Hier wuchs kein Baum im nötigen Abstand vom nächsten' ('The trees here didn't grow the necessary distance apart from each other'; p. 59)—in this instance at least he is aware that his gaze is determined by his European experience: 'Ich hatte bisher nur Spielzeugwälder gekannt' ('The forests I had known up to that point were only toy forests'; p. 60).

At first sight it might seem that we can apply the same model—where the reader factors in the narrator's prejudice—to the otherwise super-fluous enumeration of details relating to the police station: it is, we are told, housed in a small wooden shack, equipped with very rudimentary furniture, and overseen by a duty officer who not only wears sandals, shorts, and a T-shirt (i.e. not a uniform) but who also has recent wounds on his calves and arms, appears to be dozing on duty, and takes down the narrator's story without asking any questions. As an evocation of his feelings at the time, these descriptive details suggest that the narrator is irritated by the absence of the characteristics he associates with a European police station; as part of the retrospective narrative it also implies that he sees a connection between the 'foreign' characteristics of the police station and his inability to achieve justice there. And yet, in a poor neighbourhood of a less affluent country than Germany, this might be a normal environment from which justice can perfectly adequately be dispensed, just as the policeman's wounds might have an innocent explanation and his taciturnity be culturally appropriate.

Up to this point, then, it is possible to argue that, by inviting us to see further than the narrator, the narrative confronts us with the shortcomings of an unreflected First World mindset. However, Schneider closes down the possibility of an ironic gap between the narrator's view and a native Brazilian view once he makes the Brazilian police unquestionably brutal and corrupt. For while it is true that, in accordance with his gradual erosion of his protagonist's capacity to read the outside world, Schneider leaves a question mark hanging over certain events (Are the police really in league with the hotelier? Are they really going to ransack the chambermaid's flat?), he nevertheless leaves no doubt that plain-clothes policemen are allowed to beat up a suspect, that this action is an occurrence so normal that it need not be hidden from civilians, none of whom is shocked enough to protest, and that the police employ heavies with sawn-off shotguns to intimidate suspects. However necessary this scandalously routine corruption may be to the text's psychological drama—propelling the narrator towards that heart of darkness where his notions of humane justice disintegrate—it does little for our understanding of Brazil. While nobody with any knowledge of Schneider's work would suggest that he shares his narrator's fear of unfamiliar cultures, he needs Brazilian corruption for his narrative scheme to work, rather as Conrad, even as he deconstructed European values, nevertheless needed his Africa to be 'dark', despite the harmful effects of that European construction of the continent. In *Vati* Brazilian men also need to be sufficiently unenlightened by feminism to be seen 'schamlos grimassierend' ('leering shamelessly'; pp. 45–6) at the woman whom the narrator stalks, in order to facilitate the narrator's regression to an irrational state dominated by primal urges. And the Brazilian hotelier needs to be physically repellent, with his 'schwarzrandige, zersplitterte Nägel' ('split nails, black round the edges'), his 'gelbliche Zahnstummel' ('yellowed tooth stumps'), the rash-like pale patches on his black skin, and his bare 70-year-old's chest, so that the narrator can, simply by noting these details (p. 70), reveal how easily the educated liberal mind can sink into the mire of physical hatred. If Schneider is trying to confront us with our own capacity for prejudice, then this is a risky strategy that depends on awakening our moral sense rather than our aesthetic sense, which might apprehend the manager as a satisfyingly grotesque nemesis for the protagonist, and his foreignness as a conventional element of that role. Even if Schneider is suggesting what Christa Wolf argues explicitly in the story *Störfall*,[9] that, however energetically we project it onto the 'other', the heart of darkness lies within us—in other words, that Brazil's uncivilized ways merely hold up a mirror to the narrator's own capacity for bigotry and violence—he nevertheless needs his Brazil to have uncivilized ways for the sum to add up.

Der Vorleser

Though Schneider's story is not without its drama, Schlink's three-part novel is more conventionally plot-driven, as the careful management of the chapter divisions indicates: typically, the opening or closing line of a chapter is used to announce a new development (the more dramatic the development, the more laconic the announcement) and then Schlink makes the reader wait for the outcome, or at least for the details. Since Michael Berg, in his role as narrator, obliges the reader to adopt the limited point of view of his younger self, we initially share his puzzlement

---

[9] Christa Wolf, *Störfall. Nachrichten eines Tages* (Frankfurt/Main: Luchterhand, 1987), esp. 98–100, 104, 108–9, 116–17.

at the behaviour of his older lover Hanna Schmitz—her anger at his lack of application at school, her alternation between imperiousness and tenderness, and her abrupt departure from his town—though even in part I enough clues are planted to allow the reader to guess that she is illiterate. In part II, Michael, now a law student, encounters Hanna again as she faces trial alongside other former concentration-camp guards. With its combination of present drama and retrospective inquiry, the trial is a conventional enough narrative device; in *Der Vorleser*, it resolves part I's mysteries by filling us in on the years that preceded the characters' first meeting but also has repercussions for their relationship. In a belated epiphany, Michael realizes that Hanna's fear of being exposed as illiterate motivated her recruitment to the SS and her disappearance from his home town, and, in the present, has caused her to tell a lie that scuppers her defence. Her habit of having Michael read to her before they make love, which was described in part I, is cast in a radically different light by witness reports that she obliged women to read to her before their deportation to Auschwitz. This motif is picked up again in part III, when, after the break-up of his marriage and a series of unsuccessful relationships, Michael renews contact with Hanna, now serving a prison sentence, by sending her tapes of readings from world literature. Though she subsequently learns to read and write for herself, Hanna commits suicide on the eve of her release, unable to face reintegration into society. In her suicide note she charges the narrator with delivering her savings to a Jewish survivor who had testified against her. Although the woman refuses to absolve Hanna, she allows the narrator to donate the money to a Jewish illiteracy charity: in this way narrative closure is achieved even if, as the text implies, moral closure is impossible.

Scholarly responses to Schlink's novel have been as polarized as responses to *Vati*. In one corner, and pulling none of their punches, are William Collins Donahue and Heidi M. Schlipphacke. For Donahue, Michael's fretting over moral questions that are peripheral to Hanna's crimes not only blurs the distinctions between victims and perpetrators but also encourages a self-pitying response by suggesting that the Holocaust is an unreasonably taxing moral problem with which Germans battle bravely, but inevitably in vain. Schlipphacke's objections are twofold: that by making Hanna at least partly a victim, Schlink misses a prime opportunity to deconstruct the conventional opposition between the male fascist aggressor and his passive female victim; and that his portrayal of the education of a woman by a man adopts uncritically a misogynistic Enlightenment model of the woman reader. Other critics take a more positive view: Helmut Schmitz sees in the novel a copy-book dramatization of psychoanalytical theory about post-Nazi guilt (an 'inventory of psychological structures of the post-1968 Federal Republic'); for Bill Niven it is a convincing exploration of the workings of a culture of shame and a timely critique of aspects of *Vergangenheitsbewältigung*.[10]

Neither Schmitz nor Niven is uncritical of the text—Schmitz sees its marginalization of the victims' perspective as a weakness, for instance—but both are willing to take it seriously as a representation of historical and memorial processes. They are able to do this partly by reading Michael not as a figure with whom the reader is meant to identify, but as a negative embodiment of the failures of his generation of Germans to deal satisfactorily with the past. (I take issue later in the chapter with this notion of 'generation'.) In a recent article comparing *Vati* and *Der Vorleser*, Donahue responds to those critics who saw his earlier analysis as missing the point of the unreliable narrator, suggesting that, on the contrary, it is other critics who wrongly ascribe a modernist aesthetic (a sustained gap between what is said by the narrator and what is meant by the author) to what is a straightforwardly realist text, reading ambiguity where none was intended. To which Schmitz and Niven might counter that they do not need that gap to construct their readings: the figure of Michael can embody a flawed response to the Nazi past whether his author intends him to or not. In turn, that does not invalidate Donahue's disquiet that *Der Vorleser* has become an enormously popular medium through which to teach the Holocaust despite its at best tangential relationship to the history of the genocide.

The starting point for my analysis is something of a commonplace in scholarly responses to *Der Vorleser*: the unusual degree of stylization and contrivance in the novel. Sally Johnson and Frank Finlay, for instance, have shown that Hanna's fictional illiteracy has little in common with real illiteracy; Juliane Köster points out that there are no known cases of former camp guards educating themselves about the Holocaust as Hanna does in prison.[11] Those who defend Schlink's artifice argue that it is not a cheap concession to popular tastes—though its appeal to popular tastes is self-evident—but a way of pointing the reader towards symbolic readings. If Hanna's illiteracy cannot be read realistically, then

---

[10] William Collins Donahue, 'Illusions of Subtlety: Bernhard Schlink's *Der Vorleser* and the Moral Limits of Holocaust Fiction', *German Life and Letters*, 54 (2001), 60–81; Heidi M. Schlipphacke, 'Enlightenment, Reading, and the Female Body: Bernhard Schlink's *Der Vorleser*', *Gegenwartsliteratur*, 1 (2002), 310–28; Schmitz, *Legacy*, 55–84 (68); Bill Niven, 'Bernhard Schlink's *Der Vorleser* and the Problem of Shame', *Modern Language Review*, 98 (2003), 381–96.

[11] Sally Johnson and Frank Finlay, '(Il)literacy and (Im)morality in Bernhard Schlink's *The Reader*', *Written Language and Literacy*, 4/2 (2001), 195–214; Juliane Köster, *Bernhard Schlink. 'Der Vorleser'* (Munich: Oldenbourg, 2000).

its symbolic function—representing the lack of moral orientation of those involved in Nazi crimes—emerges all the more clearly.

This discussion is worth pursuing. A clearer measure of the plot's artificiality can be taken by comparing it to that of a roughly contemporaneous Italian novel, Paulo Maurensig's *La Variante di Lüneburg* (*The Lüneburg Variation*, 1993).[12] In Maurensig's text an SS officer, a male counterpart to Hanna, likewise forces a camp inmate to indulge his whims, though in this case the guard's passion is for chess, and the man he obliges to play against him is a former rival on the international chess circuit. On the face of it Schlink stops short of this degree of sensation, since Hanna's captive readers are unknown to her. Yet Schlink, like Maurensig, endows SS membership with narrative value, as a secret to be revealed; and Schlink, like Maurensig, engineers a re-encounter between the two main characters in an environment that radically recasts their earlier power relationships. Both authors contrive that an activity in which power and pleasure are intrinsically linked (here the game of chess, there the act of reading aloud) should be performed under quite different circumstances outside the concentration camp and inside it. In both texts we learn of the harmless civilian 'game' before we learn of its sinister re-enactment in the concentration camp (though in Schlink's text the true chronology is the reverse).

Both novels therefore operate with a simplified moral and aesthetic model of the concentration camp in which a single activity simultaneously saves and enslaves the inmates who must engage in it, embodying the inextricability of the benign and the malign exercise of power. This activity, moreover, allows an SS guard to compensate directly for a single, named inadequacy in civilian life. There is some truth in these scenarios: accounts from the camps suggest that the practice of favouritism was widespread, even if it took less richly symbolic forms than in these texts; and, for many guards, power in the SS made up for powerlessness in regular society, even if that powerlessness was more diffuse, less specific, than Schlink and Maurensig portray it. Nevertheless, the danger of this technique of distillation and intensification is that SS brutality becomes a source of aesthetic satisfaction for the reader.

In the case of *Der Vorleser*, the reordering of events is central to this effect: even allowing for the mitigating circumstance of her illiteracy, Hanna's habit of forcing camp inmates awaiting deportation to read aloud to her, if it were related first, would read as a selfish exploitation of the powerless, but since we learn of it only *after* we have heard about her

[12] Paulo Maurensig, *La Variante di Lüneburg* (Milan: Adelphi, 1993), *The Lüneburg Variation*, trans. Jon Rothschild (London: Phoenix, 1998).

using Michael as a reader, we are likely to experience it less as a moral event than as part of a satisfying psycho-narrative pattern. Similarly, a scene in which she hit a camp inmate across the face with a belt would evoke a straightforward moral response from the reader, but no such scene occurs because, apart from the act of selecting and listening to readers, her behaviour in the camp is not described. Instead, her actions as a guard play a silent role in the reading process, as the answer to a narrative puzzle: Why does Hanna hit Michael across the face with a belt and, more generally, act towards him in an aggressive and imperious manner? Since the answer—because she used to be an SS guard, and that is how SS guards act—is not spelt out for us (unusually for a novel that spells out most things) readers have the pleasure of making the link themselves.

Of course, the ordering of events serves an important purpose: we cannot relive Michael's predicament unless we are drawn into Hanna's world *before* we learn her secrets. For him, too, her behaviour is a puzzle to which he finds the key only belatedly, at the trial. Yet that does not alter the fact that Schlink has created this particular enigma and this particular resolution for his protagonist and not a scenario in which, as in *Vati*, for instance, SS brutality is a straightforward fact. Moreover, the doubling-up of the reading-aloud motif is not strictly necessary to the puzzle-and-solution model and its effect is to evoke that pleasurable frisson of horror that occurs when an innocuous event repeats itself in a narrative, recast in malignant form. 'Imagine', the text says to us, 'if something that seemed like a harmless enough love game turned out to have its origins in the concentration camp!'

Schlink's detractors could argue that by sexualizing SS sadism, Schlink panders to the tastes of a contemporary popular readership—which likes its fictional sex to be interestingly deviant but nevertheless assimilable to familiar categories—but adds nothing to the sum of our understanding of SS camp guards. In answer to this it must be said that the text contains its own critique of the cruder popular fantasies about the sexual appeal of jackbooted SS women (pp. 141–2 (p. 146)), but, again, that does not alter the fact that Schlink chooses to link the power dynamics of the concentration camp with sexual power dynamics, not just through the reading-aloud motif, but also more generally, since Hanna's bouts of aggression and imperiousness towards Michael, which are clearly meant to echo her behaviour in the camp, are always followed by conciliatory sex.

In their turn, defenders of Schlink's method might counter that the reading-aloud scenario need not be convincingly motivated, nor historically realistic, because its very artificiality points us towards its figurative meaning: Hanna's compulsion to repeat behaviour learnt in the concentration camp, however unlikely a form it takes, stands for the way in which inter-human relations after the end of the Third Reich were affected, in hidden and unacknowledged ways, by behaviours learnt between 1933 and 1945. Moreover, the argument might run, Schlink does not so much draw a veil over Hanna's actual conduct in the camp as demonstrate the obstacles, real and imagined (assuming an unreliable narrator), that prevent Berg from envisaging and understanding Hanna in her persona as an SS guard. This is Schmitz's view: that the text has little to say about Hanna because it is a symptom of Michael's confused responses to the past that he never attempts to find out about her, and that Hanna's sexual dominance has a legitimate function because it is analogous to the non-sexual power relationships between Hitler and the German people, and between the so-called first and second generations. On the other hand, it is possible to write about non-sexual power relationships using non-sexual metaphors and analogies.

Schlink's conflation of the erotic and the political plays a role in my second line of enquiry. Nearly all critics point to the way in which Schlink takes the conventional relationship between a Nazi-generation parent and a second-generation child, the mainstay of *Vaterliteratur*, and exchanges it for a sexual relationship between a Nazi-generation older woman and a second-generation boy. This is generally acknowledged to be a welcome innovation in a tired genre, but there is no firm consensus about its function. While Ernestine Schlant, for instance, proposes that 'Schlink uses the generational discrepancy that was at the core of the "literature about fathers and mothers" to new purpose when he makes the bond of love between the generations sexual rather than biological', she stops short of naming this 'new purpose'.[13] Others acknowledge that by shifting the relationship to the sexual realm Schlink gains some distance from the child–parent relationships explored in *Vaterliteratur*, rather as Schneider does by choosing an atypical relationship between a major Nazi criminal and his son. From this position, Michael, like Schneider's narrator, is able to criticize the *68er* for denying the bonds of love between parent and child (pp. 162–3 (p. 168)). However, recasting the generational drama with sexual roles has a second effect, transforming it into a drama of social class. Not that class dramas cannot be enacted within the family—clearly they can, where the children of working-class parents become middle-class, for instance—but in the case of Schlink's novel, where the father is a wealthy professional and the son set fair to follow in his footsteps, this possibility is ruled out.

---

[13] Schlant, *Language of Silence*, 210.

Given that Schlink has, not unusually, made his narrator in his own social image, the stark difference in class between Hanna and Michael may be the corollary of his decision to make Hanna illiterate, for the plot, which stretches credibility some way as it stands, would be bordering on the absurd if the woman with a hidden past as an SS concentration-camp guard were not only illiterate but a middle-class illiterate. Moreover, once figured as illiterate, the character is understandably obliged by her disability to stay in low-paid unskilled jobs (though her dissatisfaction with them, her competence, leading to two offers of advancement, and her enthusiastic but undiscriminating passion for literature and film suggest that her natural home is the lower middle class). Nevertheless, having once established a wide social gulf between his two main characters, Schlink can choose what to do with it, and what he does with it is, on the one hand, to play it for dramatic effect, and, on the other, to produce a one-sided, middle-class narrative of how the Third Reich has been remembered.

Class difference is written into Hanna and Michael's affair from the outset: Michael is struck by the lines of washing strung across the court-yard of her apartment block, dangling incongruously above the dirt of a joiner's workshop whose insistent noise contrasts with the quiet of his own house, where a sick boy can be left to convalesce in the fresh air on the balcony. The interior of her flat is also coded working-class, with a windowless lavatory and one main room that does at least triple service, as kitchen, bathroom, and dining room. Michael's home, meanwhile, is given the trappings of 'old' wealth and made the object of Hanna's awed gaze: 'Ihr Blick tastete alles ab, die Biedermeiermöbel, den Flügel, die alte Standuhr, die Bilder, die Regale mit den Büchern, Geschirr und Besteck auf dem Tisch' ('Her eyes explored everything, the Biedermeier furniture, the piano, the old grandfather clock, the pictures, the book-cases, the plates and cutlery on the table'; p. 60 (pp. 59–60)).[14] Though Anthony Minghella's plans to film the novel for Miramax have so far come to nothing, we can be fairly sure that his mise en scène would exploit to the full the mouth-watering desirability of the upper middle-class home.

By using the material differences between their homes to make visible the transgression of class boundaries, Schlink dramatically magnifies Michael's sexual transgression against parental expectations. But while class contributes in obvious ways to the power dynamics of the central relationship and also to the drama of the courtroom (where we enjoy the spectacle of the untutored Hanna challenging the educated judge),

---

[14] Janeway's translation neglects to specify a *grand* piano.

Schlink is in other senses curiously class-blind, declining to reflect on the moral and emotional effects of social background for Hanna's experience and recollection of the Third Reich. Since Schlink withholds details of Hanna's upbringing, her indeterminate lower-class status is elided with her illiteracy, which is the only way we have of explaining her progression from Siemens to the camps. Moreover, because her disability makes her a loner, fleeing environments in which her secret might be discovered, she has no group identity. Without an indication of the values and expectations of her social class, it is impossible to judge whether they have shaped her in any way. This applies equally to her life after 1945: a woman who does not belong in her job as a tram conductress, who keeps others at arm's length, and who, even in the dock, refuses to make common cause with her co-defendants, cannot be read as representative, making it impossible for the text to identify working-class or white-collar discourses about the Nazi past. Thus, while the text suggests that we would gain from listening to those, such as Hanna, who have no way of contributing to the public written record, it remains unclear what we would learn beyond the very general notions that SS guards might have been keen to carry out their jobs efficiently but incapable of picturing the moral consequences of their efficiency (p. 122 (p. 126)) and that a former SS guard might have felt misunderstood after 1945 (p. 187 (p. 196)). Though I take Schmitz's point that Schlink cannot tell us more about Hanna and simultaneously represent the way in which Michael, to his cost, is unable to engage with her past, it is still worth establishing that this silence is not just a silence about Hanna's crimes, but also about the relationship between social background and the crimes committed, and between social background and memory of the Third Reich.

Given that Michael mocks a psychoanalyst girlfriend for inferring unresolved Oedipal issues from his failure to mention his mother sufficiently often, Schlink might mock the kind of critical reasoning that finds significance in what he leaves out of his novel. Nevertheless, the absence I am arguing for has a positive counterpart in the text, in a narrative of how professionals, as a class, have coped with the legacy of the Third Reich. For where Hanna is unrepresentative, the narrator is, as the text makes more than clear, representative. 'Unsere Eltern hatten im Dritten Reich ganz verschiedene Rollen gespielt', the narrator writes of the student radicals:

> Manche Väter waren im Krieg gewesen, darunter zwei oder drei Offiziere der Wehrmacht und ein Offizier der Waffen-SS, einige hatten Karrieren in Justiz und Verwaltung gemacht, wir hatten Lehrer und Ärzte unter unseren Eltern,

und einer hatte einen Onkel, der hoher Beamter beim Reichsminister des Inneren gewesen war. (pp. 87–8)[15]

Though it is likely that there are some working-class or white-collar fathers hidden among the 'Väter im Krieg', this social diversity remains out of focus; instead, the narrator specifies exclusively professional occupations, which are gendered male in the unspoken elision of 'Eltern' and 'Väter'. This rings true at a realist level: the students, as future professionals, are keen to distance themselves from their professional predecessors (who were, on the whole, men) and particularly from those whose professions implicated them in Nazi policy and ideology. Nevertheless, the narrator's retrospective self-criticism, which centres on the way in which he and other students handled the process of 'Aufarbeitung' ('exploring the past'), does not include a deconstruction of this narrowing of the class focus or the implicit downgrading of women's experience of Nazism, which is assumed not to have involved public and professional roles and therefore not to require 'Aufarbeitung'. Schneider uses a similar shorthand when he writes: 'Der mir zugeteilte Vater war nicht etwa Richter, Studienrat, Staatssekretär, Bundeskanzler, UNO-Generalsekretär geworden, sondern der meistgesuchte Mann der Welt' ('My allotted father had not become a judge, say, or a teacher; a high-ranking civil servant, Federal Chancellor, or Secretary General of the United Nations; he had become the world's most wanted man'; p. 29), and when he makes the only other student in the story a man whose father played an unspecified professional role in the Third Reich. Here, too, this may accurately reflect the professional-father fixation of the *Studentenbewegung*, but it does nothing to deconstruct it, even though other aspects of the protest movement are subjected to criticism.

In the plot of *Der Vorleser*, responsibility for dealing with the past is accorded first to the male barristers and judges at court, then to the law students observing them (under the tutelage of their male professor), and ultimately to the legal historian narrator. When Hanna admires Michael's father's study, she is curious to know whether Michael will follow in his father's footsteps and write books. He claims not to know, but he does later write, amongst other things about the legal system of the Third Reich, and we have another, more personal, text about the Nazi past in front of us. The lower-class Hanna eventually becomes a

---

[15] 'Our parents played a variety of roles in the Third Reich. Several among our fathers had been in the war, two or three of them as officers of the Wehrmacht and one as an officer of the Waffen SS. Some of them had held positions in the judiciary or local government. Our parents had included teachers and doctors, and one of us had an uncle who had been a high official in the Ministry of the Interior' (p. 90).

reader, a recipient of writing about the Nazi past, but never a writer. Thus, the construction of the discourse of memory is (with the exception of Hannah Arendt) coded male and professional.

If Schlink endorsed this bias he would grant narrative rewards to the professional male characters; in fact he does the reverse. The male barristers and judges at the trial are shown to have little understanding of Hanna's experience and the narrator's distant academic father is a source of little practical wisdom on the matter, whereas positive roles are accorded to Michael's wife Gertrud, who pursues a successful career as a judge, and to the female governor of Hanna's prison, whose liberal regime has gained her recognition. The Law, it appears, is no longer male and the better for it. The narrator, on the other hand, opts out of legal practice by becoming a legal historian, his maverick law professor becomes increasingly isolated, and a fellow student abandons the Law to become a pub landlord. Yet, even allowing that *Der Vorleser* can be read as the story of the failure of a male professional caste to come through the experience of 1960s 'Aufarbeitung' with its ideals intact and its practical energies preserved, this is nevertheless portrayed, rather self-indulgently, as a failure suffered exclusively by a male professional caste.

It would be quite legitimate to play the unreliable-narrator card at this point, to argue that Schlink wants us to recognize these limitations in the narrator, who, for all his educated soul-searching, understands a good deal less than he thinks he does. Nevertheless, the rhetoric of the text is of a piece with some of Schlink's journalistic writings, in which he likewise speaks of the professional classes in generalizing terms that overlook the non-professional majority, and in which he likewise accords to professionals, and to them alone, the task of shaping and articulating Germany's attitude to the past. In 'Die erschöpfte Generation', an essay on the ineffectualness of Schröder's second-term government, Schlink defines the red–green coalition as the government of his 'generation'. Throughout, Schlink uses the word not in its dictionary sense but synecdochally, to refer to all those who, like him, trained at university for professional careers in the 1960s. Accordingly, he illustrates the general effeteness of his 'generation' by reciting a litany of burnt-out lawyers, doctors, journalists, clergymen, and academics (but not, for instance, burnt-out car-plant workers or nurses). That Schlink uses the male rather than the double-gendered forms for the professions may simply reflect *Spiegel*'s house style but nevertheless obscures women's role in effecting (or, as he argues here, giving up on) social and political change.[16]

---

[16] Bernhard Schlink, 'Die erschöpfte Generation', *Der Spiegel*, 30 Dec. 2002.

'Die erschöpfte Generation' is not directly concerned with the Third Reich, but in another essay, commissioned for a *Spiegel* series on memory of the Nazi past (and reproduced without commentary by the Bundeszentrale für politische Bildung in one of its packs of teaching materials for secondary-school students), Schlink writes of the importance of that past for 'meine Generation':

> Wenn wir in Wissenschaft und Schule, Kultur und Medien tätig sind, war die Vergangenheit früher oder später einmal unser Thema, oder sie ist es noch; wenn wir in Politik, Verwaltung und Rechtsprechung arbeiten, hat sie unser Verständnis von Freiheit, Gleichheit und gerechter Ordnung geschärft; wer in der Wirtschaft oder in den freien Berufen über deren Verantwortung nachdenkt, denkt auch über ihre Verstrickung ins Dritte Reich und den Holocaust nach. Für die meisten von uns war die Vergangenheit des Dritten Reichs und des Holocaust prägend.[17]

And if we work in a call centre? Or on public transport? Schlink does not say, but he goes on to stress that this 'generation' has actively changed public attitudes to the Third Reich by talking openly about it where the previous generation had remained silent. At no point does Schlink acknowledge that the non-professional majority might have helped shape and even liberalize public discourses on the Third Reich, not through their influence in public institutions or their self-expression in the media (though even these are hardly out of bounds to non-professionals), but through their tastes, their consumer and leisure habits, their voting practices, and their family culture, amongst other things.

Sigrid Weigel has identified a similarly exclusive use of the deceptively neutral term 'generation' in early post-war literary discourse and sees the problem as persisting unchecked to the present day.[18] Thus, when the poet Peter Rühmkorf wrote in support of the 'generation' of men who had belonged to the Hitler Youth in the final years of the Third Reich ('a generation that was without blemish but not without experience'), he silently excluded both women and Jews. As Weigel explains: 'Within the notion of "generation" in postwar literature there is hidden the implicit national (German) gender-specific (masculine) matrix of this norm.'[19]

---

[17] 'If we work in academia or education, in culture or the media, the past sooner or later became an issue for us, or still is; if we work in politics, administration, or the judiciary, it has honed our understanding of equality and of a just social order; for those who work in business or the professions, to reflect on their responsibility is to reflect on their complicity in the Third Reich and the Holocaust' (Bernhard Schlink, 'Auf dem Eis. Von der Notwendigkeit und der Gefahr der Beschäftigung mit dem Dritten Reich und dem Holocaust', *Der Spiegel*, 7 May 2001).

[18] Sigrid Weigel, '"Generation" as a Symbolic Form: On the Genealogical Discourse of Memory since 1945', *Germanic Review*, 77 (2002), 264–77.

[19] Ibid. 274.

Similarly, Helmut Peitsch sees in the use of the terms '68er-Generation' and '89er-Generation' a 'biologization of political positions', an attempt to code as natural and therefore unquestionable something that is actually politically constructed, and also a habit that 'exerts consensus pressure to conform and [. . .] invokes the idea of the nation in the image of the one generation being succeeded by the next'.[20] One could argue that Schlink attempts to disguise a political position—that the professional classes alone are responsible for constructing (and, despite some failures along the way, liberalizing) discourses about the Nazi past—as an agreed and uncontroversial fact and also that he makes a questionable rhetorical leap from generation to nation, most obviously in the apposition 'das Schicksal meiner Generation, das deutsche Schicksal' ('the fate of my generation, a German fate'; p. 163 (p. 169)). Weigel sees a similar conflation in early post-war writers' use of the term 'young Germany'.[21] Finally, one might question the uncritical replication of Schlink's own terminology of 'meine Generation' in scholarly studies of the novel.

It may be that the text signals its own insufficiency in this respect. The two occasions on which the narrator is least able to analyse his experiences (the equivalent of the son's encounters, in *Vati*, with the Brazilian woman and the hotel clerk) are both encounters with lower-class figures: when he confronts a man who has given him a lift (accusing him, without firm evidence, of having been an SS guard) and when he mistakenly intervenes in a dispute among working-class regulars of a pub. The lower classes appear in the text as an impenetrable other.

Conclusion

Both Schneider and Schlink exploit their characters' connection with the legal profession to explore the fraught relationship between guilt as defined in the institution of the Law and the more diffuse psycho-logical guilt that haunts the so-called 'second generation' of Germans brought up after 1945. This intellectual sophistication goes hand in hand with popular narrative models of the legal system, Schneider's vision of police corruption being blacker but no less mainstream than Schlink's courtroom drama. Schlink generalizes from the professional classes to

---

[20] Helmut Peitsch, 'Communication, Generations, and Nation: Ulrich Woelk's *Rückspiel*', in Arthur Williams, Stuart Parkes, and Julian Preece (eds.), *'Whose Story?' Continuities in Contemporary German-Language Literature* (Berne and Berlin: Peter Lang, 1998), 317–40 (321).

[21] Weigel, 'Generation', 275.

a whole generation of Germans, an approach that has the effect of obscuring specifically working-class or white-collar experiences of the Third Reich and its aftermath. Through his successful female profession-als he celebrates feminist social advances, but within the logic of the text this success is a marker that excludes women from the key historical experience of 1968. Feminist progress, for which the Pill and the liberal-ization of the divorce laws act as shorthand (pp. 50, 52), is cited in *Vati*, too, as a guarantee that Nazi ideology is dead and buried, but as in *Der Vorleser* 1968, the rite of passage into membership of a 'generation' that defines the nation, happens only to men.

The introductions to British student editions of these two novels conclude on a strikingly similar note. For Colin Riordan, the value of *Vati*, which he has already termed 'a lesson to us all', is that it encourages us to 'learn how to live in a post-Auschwitz world'; for Stuart Taberner, 'what *Der Vorleser* teaches us', by raising questions that are 'still relevant in the [. . .] world in which we live', is that we need to 'learn to live with the ambiguities of the human condition'.[22] To a degree this coincidence reflects a common expectation, possibly on the part of publishers rather than editors, that A-Level students are interested in literary texts primarily for their relevance to themselves, so that German-language texts dealing with German history have to be shown to have universal human concerns. Nevertheless, the statements also reflect a broader tendency in scholarly writing, and I would not want to exclude my own entirely from this, to read texts about the National Socialist past for what they teach us about the workings of German history and German memory. *Vati* and *Der Vorleser* differ from *Das schreckliche Mädchen* inasmuch as critical opinion is divided about whether they are, in fact, instructive, but the dominant critical mode on both sides of this divide is exegesis: textual detail is cited to validate readings of the text's message about the past (whether this is accounted a 'good' message or a 'bad' message), and these readings are corroborated with reference to extra-literary authorities. If I find myself drawn to the more negative critiques of the two novels (for example those by Höfer and Donahue) despite the rather shrill tone of condemnation and despite their tendency to assume that there is a correct way of dealing with the Nazi past, then it is because they are able at least to a degree to move beyond exegesis, in particular by shifting the focus from what the text 'says' to what the text 'does', for instance to the way in which it offers its readers identificatory positions and emotional rewards. Schmitz's study of *Der Vorleser*, though it is first and foremost a

---

[22] Schneider, *Vati*, ed. Riordan, 24, 29; Bernhard Schlink, *Der Vorleser*, ed. Stuart Taberner (Bristol: Bristol Classical Press, 2002), 38.

sophisticated validation of the text by reference to established scholarly knowledge about the 'second generation', nevertheless steps outside the text's message when he writes that 'the figure of Hanna necessarily remains psychologically vague because the text has to keep her at arm's length for the sake of the generation conflict' or that 'the composition of the novel according to psychoanalytical theorems does not allow Michael empathy with the victims' or that 'for this to happen, certain questions about Hanna's personality have to remain unanswered'.[23] My analysis has tried to take for granted that it is possible to extract historical lessons from these texts and to concentrate instead on the ways in which the texts construct their messages—by means of narrative structures and through processes of exclusion and definition—and on the ways in which academic writers construct readings of the texts. For while it goes without saying that the two novels 'teach' us a good deal about the way in which Germans of Schneider's and Schlink's 'generation' have experienced the aftermath of the Third Reich, they also teach us that once novels move away from the model exemplified by *Das schreckliche Mädchen*, that is the exposure of complicity in crimes and the exposure of forgetfulness about that complicity, once they address instead the difficulties of having an emotional connection to the Nazi past, they come under an extraordinarily intense kind of critical scrutiny. Critics sometimes appear to be fighting for the soul of a text, seeking either to recuperate it for the project of 'coming to terms' or to condemn it as an evasion of that responsibility.

[23] Schmitz, *Legacy*, 58, 68, 77.

3 Documentary and Gender
Helga Schubert's *Judasfrauen*, Helke Sander's *BeFreier und Befreite*, and Ruth Beckermann's *Jenseits des Krieges*

This chapter brings together a work of documentary literature, Helga Schubert's *Judasfrauen* (*Judas Women*), and two documentary films, Helke Sander's *BeFreier und Befreite. Krieg, Vergewaltigungen, Kinder* (*Liberators take Liberties*) and Ruth Beckermann's *Jenseits des Krieges* (*East of War*).[1] As non-fiction genres, documentary literature and documentary film pose similar methodological challenges, but my analysis acknowledges that they have discrete traditions and should not be conflated uncritically. On the face of it, the subject of Sander's film—the rape of German women by Allied soldiers in spring 1945—bears only a tangential relationship to the representation of the Third Reich, but the film is of interest precisely because it has been read as part of a wider tendency to use German suffering to divert attention from German guilt.

Notwithstanding Sander's focus on the period of the 'Liberation', the three works share a common concern with the ways in which gender shaped personal experience of the Third Reich and with the ways in which it shapes post-war memory of the Third Reich. The fact that all three are by women might be taken to imply that gender issues are the preserve of women artists, but other chapters in this study suggest otherwise, and show that gender-sensitive readings of male-authored texts and films about the Third Reich are routinely possible, regardless of whether the works address gender explicitly. A weightier objection might be that by grouping these works together I risk reducing the issue of gender and the Third Reich to a set of crude binary oppositions relating to guilt and victimhood. Thus, an opposition could be set up between Schubert's account of female complicity in the Nazi system of terror and Sander's portrayal of women as the perpetual victims of men in wartime. The opposition might then be reinforced with reference to Beckermann's documentation of atrocities committed by male soldiers. In the analyses that follow I take care not to use the texts in this manner and to evaluate individually

---

[1] Helga Schubert, *Judasfrauen* (Berlin and Weimar: Aufbau, 1990; in the text, page references in brackets are to this edition), Helke Sander, *BeFreier und Befreite. Krieg, Vergewaltigungen, Kinder* (Germany, 1992), Ruth Beckermann, *Jenseits des Krieges* (Austria, 1997). The two films went on English-language release under the titles given in the main text.

the artists' own construction and deconstruction of just such oppositions.

Because the three works focus on immoral acts committed by individuals during the Third Reich and immediately after its collapse, and
because all three adopt a laconic tone that invites the reader or viewer
to make connections, they lend themselves most readily to the kind of
approach taken by Reed (assigning value to works for what they tell us
about the historical period) and Ryan (valuing them as works that activate
our moral conscience). My analysis attempts to show how productive
these approaches can be while nevertheless maintaining some distance
from them.

Documentary Literature and Schubert's *Judasfrauen*

The term 'documentary literature' covers a range of forms in which
the 'documentary' and the 'literary' combine in varying proportions. At
one end of the spectrum is journalistic reportage, whose claim to the
title 'literature' is based on the quality of the writing rather than on
aesthetic form; at the other end is the collage text in which excerpts
from historical documents are creatively assembled; somewhere in the
middle lies fictional writing based on historical documents, which is what
concerns me here. Documentary literature enjoyed a heyday in 1960s
Germany thanks to practitioners such as Peter Weiss, Rolf Hochhuth,
Günter Wallraff, and, in the East, Heinar Kipphardt. The peculiarly
bureaucratic framework of Nazi crimes helps explain the prominence
of the Third Reich among the subjects tackled. More particularly, legal
documents (including documents from the trials that brought Nazis to
book after 1945) have proved a strong draw for documentary writers,
doubtless because of their link with the central post-Holocaust questions
of guilt and responsibility. While Weiss's drama *Die Ermittlung* (1965),
based on the protocols of the Frankfurt Auschwitz trials, is probably
the most prominent example, an interesting recent example is Austrian
novelist Ludwig Laher's *Herzfleischentartung*, which, like Schubert's text,
encompasses both the Nazi and post-war justice systems, and documents
attempts to prosecute the commandant and warders of an Austrian
concentration camp.

Based on authentic court records, *Judasfrauen* reconstructs the stories
of ten women whose denunciations of neighbours or acquaintances
during the Third Reich sent those people to their death. These case
studies are contextualized by two essayistic texts: 'Judasfrauen' recounts

the story of Schubert's archival research, while 'Spitzel und Verräter' ('Informers and Betrayers') examines the psychological make-up of the typical informer. Whereas Laher, in *Herzfleischentartung*, tends to stress continuities between the pre-1945 and the post-1945 justice systems, Schubert is interested in the way in which forms of behaviour that are rewarded under one regime may be criminalized by the next. As the women in her stories discover, denunciation is encouraged before 1945 but deemed criminal in retrospect, a legal peripeteia that is neatly summed up by a single narrative statement: 'Diesmal war sie Angeklagte und er Zeuge' ('This time she was the accused and he the witness'; p. 73). This outcome is inevitable, Schubert suggests, because 'jede Ära hat ein Ende' ('every era comes to an end'; p. 101).

When the communist era came to an end, quite unexpectedly, between the completion of the manuscript (in 1988) and its publication, the text took on a new significance: suddenly, the post-regime judicial reckoning that is held up as a warning and a hope in *Judasfrauen* was no longer part of a hypothetical future but a realistic prospect. As Beth Alldred has shown,[2] Schubert and her West German publishers Luchterhand responded to the changed situation by making explicit, in an author's foreword, Schubert's intention to criticize the GDR, and by prefacing the case studies with the two essays: 'Spitzel und Verräter', with its warning that informers must expect to get their comeuppance under a future regime, and 'Judasfrauen', which contains surprisingly frank criticism of the GDR's myth-making about the Third Reich. Alldred contrasts this strategy with that of the East German publisher that held parallel rights to the text: Aufbau used an afterword rather than a foreword and relegated 'Spitzel und Verräter' to the eighth chapter. This should not, however, be taken to mean that Aufbau was attempting to hide something that Luchterhand was boldly exposing: GDR readers were well used to reading between the lines and in this text they barely needed to. Indeed, in retrospect, Schubert has criticized her text for being 'overburdened' ('überlastet') by its all-too-plain political intentions.[3] She has also attested that those who attended her readings from the manuscript before November 1989 (admittedly a self-selecting group likely to have been particularly attuned to dissenting opinions) recognized immediately that the stories were parables of life in the GDR.[4] It is therefore

---

[2] Beth Alldred, 'Two Contrasting Perspectives on German Unification: Helga Schubert and Brigitte Burmeister', *German Life and Letters*, 50 (1997), 165–81.

[3] Helga Schubert in conversation with Christine Tesch, 'Gestern belohnt—heute verfemt', *Wochenzeitung*, 16 Mar. 1990.

[4] Helga Schubert, *Judasfrauen* (Munich: dtv, 1995), 8.

possible that Aufbau, which routinely places extra-textual material at the end of a volume, simply saw no reason for editorial intervention in a text that was, within the GDR literary tradition, self-evidently critical, while Luchterhand, more attuned to the free market, may have been keen to cash in on the sudden interest in the Stasi.

Despite the pleasing sense that, by the time the text was published, Schubert's predictions had been fulfilled, it is important to keep a critical distance from this aspect of the project. As Niven has shown, comparisons between the Third Reich and the GDR are problematical because to conceive of fascism as just one symptom of a worldwide twentieth-century plague called totalitarianism is to obscure Germany's specific historical responsibility for the Holocaust.[5] It is certainly possible to argue that, in her eagerness to use the Nazi past to shame the GDR, Schubert deliberately passes over the differences between the two regimes, not least the fact that informers under GDR socialism did not, with perhaps rare exceptions, send their victims to their death.

The essay 'Judasfrauen', which lends its title to the volume, relates a series of confrontations with individuals, all but one of them women, who were opposed to Schubert's project. A woman academic objects to the suggestion that the Nazi judge Roland Freisler learnt his notoriously aggressive courtroom manner from observing Stalinist show trials. While Schubert reassures her that she understands the difference between Stalinism and fascism, we can infer from her choice of words and from the academic's indignant response that Schubert sees only the origins as different, not the way in which the ideologies were put into practice. Because of the way in which Schubert stages this rhetorical contest—the academic's arguments are dogmatic and brook no dialogue, whereas the author sees her research as an open-ended process from which she might emerge with changed views—arguments against equating the GDR with the Third Reich never stand a chance, and so a more nuanced view of the pitfalls of equationism is never voiced.

On the other hand, we should not confuse the era in which Schubert was writing with the quite different era in which the book was published. At the time of writing, Schubert was fighting a very real enemy: a GDR élite so afraid of equationist arguments that it reacted to them hysterically and refused to acknowledge what was obvious to all, namely that the GDR restricted its citizens' freedoms in ways that were authoritarian and inhumane. Schubert could not have anticipated that this enemy would no longer exist by the time the book appeared in print,

[5] Niven, *Facing the Nazi Past*, 6 and *passim* (indexed under 'GDR, equations of with Third Reich').

nor that equationist arguments would very soon be used by the Right in an attempt to free German national identity of its burdens of guilt. Within Schubert's immediate political horizons, one could argue, a certain amount of hyperbole and pointed dramatization was a legitimate way of making her point. Thus, if Stasi informers are implicitly likened to informers whose denunciations killed, then this is not with the aim of suggesting a moral equivalence between the Third Reich and the GDR, but with the aim of shaming East German informers (and, more broadly, a society that tolerates their existence) by confronting them with an exaggerated version of their own offence.

'Judasfrauen' implies a gender reversal, transforming the male embodiment of betrayal into a woman. Schubert claims to be attacking a widespread tendency to idealize women and, specifically, to suggest that women were the victims of Nazism. By noting the opposition of a series of women to her undertaking, she implies that women share responsibility for creating and sustaining this myth. In interview, Schubert maintains that she was rebelling specifically against feminist thought and writing, and though she names no names the choice of the epithets 'authentisch' and 'subjektiv' point to Christa Wolf, with her aesthetic of 'subjektive Authentizität':

> Ich habe mich immer etwas geärgert über diese Bevorzugung von Frauen in der Literatur von seiten einiger meiner Kolleginnen: daß Frauen besonders authentisch sind, subjektiv, daß nur sie die richtigen Gefühle haben und sie ausdrücken können gegenüber den kalten Männern. Das empfand ich als ausgesprochen einseitig und fast schon präfaschistisch. Das war Mutterkult für mich. Ich wollte Frauen wieder zu normalen Menschen machen. [. . .] Ich wollte Frauen auch in ihrer Destruktivität zeigen, nicht immer als Opfer dieser schlimmen Gesellschaft.[6]

Schubert's deliberately polemical anti-feminist stance is not without foundation. Heidi M. Schlipphacke has noted that feminist portrayals of the fascist father have had negative as well as enlightening effects: 'While such texts shed light upon the deep-rooted psychological underpinnings

[6] 'I have always felt rather annoyed by this privileging of women in literature on the part of some of my women colleagues: that women are particularly authentic, subjective, that only they have the right kind of feelings and can express them to cold men. I found that extremely one-sided and almost proto-fascist. For me that was a mother-cult. And that's what I wanted to challenge. I wanted to turn women back into normal human beings. [. . .] I wanted to show women in their destructiveness, not just as victims of this terrible society.' Helga Schubert in conversation with Ulrike Helwerth, 'Die Täterin ist immer die Diktatur', *Tageszeitung*, 12 Apr. 1990.

of political events, they nevertheless serve to polarize and thus oversimplify the roles of victim and victimizer along gender lines: woman as victim/Jew, man as victimizer/Nazi.⁷ Even so, Schubert's fellow women writers would almost certainly demur at her description of their work, and, leaving aside the question of whether she has fairly represented their intentions, she may not fairly represent her own, for both her combative attitude towards feminism and her narrow focus—in interview and in her various forewords to *Judasfrauen*—on the text's critique of the GDR, have tended to obscure the fact that she is an acute observer of the social basis of gender relations.

A central concern of Schubert's earlier anthology *Lauter Leben* (1975) had been the GDR's relationship culture. While divorce, abortion, single motherhood, and affairs with married partners are presented as common occurrences incurring no obvious moral disapproval, the texts make clear that social permission to fail in one's relationships without the threat of stigmatization hardly makes the GDR an egalitarian paradise. Given Schubert's historical distance from her subject, the picture painted in *Judasfrauen* of the marital and sexual politics of the Third Reich is necessarily less vivid, but Schubert's careful editing of her source material nevertheless invites us to consider how far women's life-choices were determined by the social expectations attached to relationships. In 'Eine Frage ohne Antwort' ('A Question without an Answer'), for instance, a woman becomes suspicious that her husband is having an affair at his garrison in Poland. When the husband refuses to deny or confirm her suspicions, the wife begins a series of affairs with local soldiers and denounces her husband to the authorities for the treasonable offence of wishing Hitler dead. The fact that a local male official asks the leader of the local Women's League to dissuade the wife from her affairs, while representatives of another public organization have stern words with her equally liberated female friend, suggests that sexual behaviour was considered a matter for public regulation: hardly a new insight but interesting inasmuch as it shows that, for all Schubert's energetic insistence on the text's covert critique of the GDR, *Judasfrauen* cannot be reduced to that critique, since this form of regulation had no obvious equivalent in GDR society.

A series of male officials (including a *Sturmführer* in the SA, the *Ortsgruppenleiter*, the judge, and the local police) find the wife's desire for revenge over a cheating husband *more* dishonourable than the husband's

---

⁷ Schlipphacke, 'Enlightenment', 313.

unabashed criticism of Hitler (at a time when the regime was meting out harsh and summary punishment to 'defeatists'). Seen in a positive light, this might suggest that dissenting views were tolerated by some of those in authority even within the Nazi dictatorship; but it also suggests, rather more negatively, that married women were subject to a strong unwritten moral codex. A public expression of disloyalty was evidently deemed so 'unwifely' as to be quite beyond sanction, whereas a male expression of political disloyalty, though strictly illegal, was normal enough to be passed over. To show that conservative views of wifely behaviour were built into social structures that outlived fascism, Schubert cites the couple's divorce proceedings, initiated in 1949, in which the woman is declared the guilty party on two grounds: because she denounced her husband and because she entertained 'ehewidrige Beziehungen mit fremden Männern' ('extramarital [literally 'contra-marital'] relationships with other men'; p. 72). Schubert may be making an implicit comparison here with the more enlightened legal system of the GDR, which abolished the notion of guilt in divorce proceedings (though, as I have suggested, she is in general no champion of GDR sexual politics).

In 'Das vierte Kind' a doctor is sentenced to death for *Wehrkraftzer-setzung* (undermining military morale) after telling a pregnant patient that Germany will lose the war. Documents cited by Schubert refer to the informer (the patient) as 'die Ehefrau Else N.' ('the married woman Else N.'; p. 33). Exactly what role the term 'Ehefrau' plays is difficult to establish from such brief extracts, but since we can safely assume that no man would be referred to in legal prose as 'der Ehemann Herr N.', it points to the (again, not entirely surprising) fact that Third Reich society routinely defined women according to their marital status. Appealing against the judgment, the woman's lawyer concedes 'daß das Verhal-ten des Verurteilten als Arzt gegenüber einer schwangeren Soldatenfrau außerordentlich verwerflich ist' ('that the behaviour of the accused towards a pregnant soldier's wife is exceptionally reprehensible'; p. 34). The lawyer clearly hopes that by yielding ground in this quarter he can stand his ground elsewhere, but whether his outrage is real or feigned, his confidence that it will have the desired effect on judge Freisler suggests that it corresponds to prevailing values. Both the martial values and the reproductive ideology of the Third Reich are evoked in the status accor-ded to the woman as the pregnant wife of a soldier. More fundamentally, the use of the woman's pregnancy to discredit the condemned man (as if anti-government statements were more gravely criminal when expressed in the presence of a pregnant woman) suggests that the stereotypical view of pregnant women as emotionally fragile was sufficiently well anchored in Third Reich society to be used in legal case-making. The woman herself is happy to accede in this scheme of values, declaring in her affidavit that the doctor was particularly dangerous because he imposed his views 'an mir als einer schwangeren Soldatenfrau' ('on me as a pregnant soldier's wife'; p. 39). The motif is repeated a third time, in Freisler's judgment: 'Ein Arzt, der eine mit drei Kindern evakuierte schwangere Frau eines Soldaten [. . .] in Ausübung seiner ärztlichen Betreuung diese Frau seelisch so mißhandelt, begeht auf sie einen nicht weniger infamen Angriff wie jener andere Verbrecher, der eine Frau in der Verdunkelung vergewaltigt' ('A doctor who, in the course of his medical treatment of her, emotionally maltreats in this way the pregnant wife of a soldier who has three children and has been evacuated, commits an assault on her no less disgraceful that that committed by the criminal who rapes a woman in the blackout'; p. 43). Here again, both the woman's supposed vulnerability as a pregnant woman and her special status as a mother and soldier's wife are used to criminalize the doctor's behaviour, a process that is reinforced by spurious comparison with rape. Gendering the crime, as the malicious act of an aggressive man against a defenceless woman, is evidently a convenient (and also publicly convincing) way of giving clear contours to the nebulous misdemeanour of *Wehrkraftzersetzung*.

Even if I have ignored Schubert's direction to see in the text an exploration of women's capacity for evil, not of their victimhood, my analysis nevertheless reads with the grain rather than against it since it is Schubert's stated intention—and the corollary of her laconic style—that the reader should make critical judgements about the values and behaviour of ordinary individuals in Nazi society. The danger of this approach is that it turns us into amateur social historians. To gauge the general validity of my interpretations of the historical evidence I would have to test them out on a much bigger corpus of material from the Third Reich and against established disciplinary criteria. Nevertheless, what one can say with confidence is that Schubert's text helps formulate the kind of questions we would need to pose of that material in order to understand something of women's status and room for manoeuvre in the Third Reich.

Documentary Film

Beyond the well-known, populist series about the Third Reich produced by ZDF and Spiegel-TV lies an extensive body of documentaries bought or commissioned from independent film-makers, both by television companies and by institutions such as memorial sites and museums.

In addition, film archives (notably Chronos Films) make documentaries to exploit their collections commercially. Although this study is not, in the main, concerned with the periodization of the process of 'coming to terms' in German and Austrian fiction and film, I include here a short account of post-war documentary on the Third Reich, since this is missing from equivalent studies and helpful to an evaluation of Sander's and Beckermann's films.

The earlier and more conservative documentaries tend to construct a *Große-Männer-Geschichte* (history as enacted by great men), reflecting the dominance of the top-down approach to explaining the Third Reich in early post-war academic historiography. From the 1970s onwards there is a move towards *Alltagsgeschichte*, in content and in method, as film-makers discover the power of *Zeitzeugen* (literally 'witnesses to the times' and the word used for ordinary people who give oral testimony about the past); this coincides with the belated adoption of oral history practices in the German-speaking world.[8] At about the same time, and in line with the autobiographical turn in German and Austrian fiction, documentary makers begin to put themselves in the frame and to make explicit their personal involvement in the subject matter. A male voice-over is the norm, even for female film-makers such as Irmgard von zur Mühlen, suggesting that the male voice is strongly associated with factual authority, with what Ilan Avisar, writing about Holocaust documentary, disapprovingly calls '"Voice-of-God" authority' (though even the more tentative, questioning voice he praises in Resnais's *Nuit et brouillard* is conventionally male).[9] The predominance, even today, of chronological narrative is in part a function of the grim teleology of the Nazi era, which means that almost any topic comes ready supplied with a dramatic arc of escalation and cataclysm, but doubtless also reflects a perception that viewers need a clear structure.

All documentarists draw heavily on the vast storehouse of photographic material produced during the Third Reich, although talking heads begin to displace original footage and photographs in later documentaries. Examples of outright propaganda are normally flagged up by the narrator of the documentary, but otherwise directors show little critical interest in the circumstances under which photographic images were produced, in the power relationships between photographer and subject, or in the detailed significance of individual images. So strong is the tug of the

---

[8] For an account of Germany's late start, see Paul Thompson, *The Voice of the Past: Oral History*, 2nd edn. (Oxford and New York: Oxford University Press, 1988), 62.

[9] Ilan Avisar, *Screening the Holocaust: Cinema's Images of the Unimaginable* (Bloomington: Indiana University Press, 1988), 17.

narrative flow that it is almost unknown for a documentary to freeze a single frame long enough to examine it critically, let alone to play a film sequence several times in order to guide the viewer through possible interpretations. Nor do documentarists acknowledge the often loose connection between the voice-over and the images.

The relationship between documentary film and oral history is worth pausing on briefly because both Beckermann's and Sander's films use *Zeitzeugen* testimony. There is, of course, a world of difference between a rigorously managed academic oral history project, whose aim is to establish a database of primary sources, and interviews conducted by a documentary maker, which may be no more than a set of journalistic questions captured on film, particularly where the interviewee is a professional speaker such as a historian or politician. Moreover, whereas in the academic context a strict framework governs questions of consent, interview technique, archiving, and so on, the documentary maker is subject to no such professional constraints. One kind of documentary work (pioneered by Claude Lanzmann and employed also by Beckermann) involves chance encounters with ordinary people, usually with members of the majority 'perpetrator culture', who are encouraged by apparently sympathetic questioning to talk about what they witnessed in the Third Reich. Whether the resulting testimony fulfils the academic criteria for historical evidence is questionable. Notwithstanding all this, many documentary makers share the broad aims of the oral historian: to counter the dominance of official historical narratives by allowing those traditionally excluded from history-writing to tell their story in non-written form.

In summary, despite the element of personal engagement that informs many German and Austrian documentary films about the Third Reich, few are technically or aesthetically innovative, and few aspire to the standards of academic historiography; none that I have seen acknowledges the influence of, or takes issue with, other documentary films; next to none reflect critically on their own methodology; and next to none address the gendered construction of social reality, of film, or of the historical record. Nevertheless, many documentaries are valuable by virtue of their social and political ambitions, and it makes little sense to judge a documentary primarily by academic or aesthetic standards when its aim is to make an immediate impact in the public arena. Even the less political documentaries are informative, and taken together illuminate developments in journalistic and historiographical approaches to the Third Reich. Given that it is almost impossible to avoid them altogether, it makes sense to arm oneself with a set of critical criteria for evaluating even mediocre documentary films on the subject of the Third Reich, not least because this empowers one to make better use of their rich fund of visual material than the directors do themselves.

Sander's *BeFreier und Befreite*

Today a noted feminist academic, author, and film-maker, Helke Sander was a key member of the New Women's Movement that grew out of (and in reaction to) the *Studentenbewegung*. She founded the first European feminist film journal, *Frauen und Film*, in 1974, and her directorial work has included both feature films and documentary. With *BeFreier und Befreite* she tackles a subject central to the feminist study of gender relations, rape, investigating the widespread rape of German women by Allied (mostly Russian) soldiers in 1945. Properly speaking, *BeFreier und Befreite* is not a single work, but a composite project comprising a film and a book.[10] In the two-part film archival footage and stills of photographic and printed material are cut together with interviews, in which rape victims, children who are the product of rape, and academics speak to camera. Characteristically for the auteurist documentary of the 1980s and 1990s, Sander maintains a visible presence throughout. In the book *BeFreier und Befreite*, edited jointly by Sander and Barbara Johr, a full script and stills from the film are supplemented by additional interviews and texts, and contextualized by scholarly and journalistic articles. The film has polarized opinions: what for Sabine Smith constitutes 'the vanguard of contemporary feminist film art'[11] is for Atina Grossmann a highly partisan work that serves to absolve a generation of German women of responsibility for the National Socialist regime and, more damningly still, implies an equation between the widespread rape of German women and the German genocide of Jews.[12] My analysis takes issue with both positions.

I criticized above the tendency of documentaries to use pedestrian narrative structures that lead the viewer passively through their material. This is certainly not the case with Sander's film. While there is a broad sequential logic to the bipartite structure (the experience of rape is the

---

[10] Helke Sander and Barbara Johr (eds.), *BeFreier und Befreite. Krieg, Vergewaltigungen, Kinder* (Munich: Kunstmann, 1992).

[11] Sabine H. Smith, *Sexual Violence in German Culture: Rereading and Rewriting the Tradition* (Frankfurt/Main: Lang, 1998), 258–85 (260).

[12] Atina Grossmann, 'A Question of Silence: The Rape of German Women by Soviet Occupation Soldiers', in Nicole Ann Dombrowski (ed.), *Women and War in the Twentieth Century: Enlisted with or without Consent* (New York and London: Garland, 1999), 162–83 (esp. n. 9).

focus of part I, while its post-war consequences occupy part II), in neither part is there an obvious rationale for the visual sequence. Admittedly, the similar and roughly contemporaneous experiences of rape do not invite a sequential approach, but Sander reinforces this simultaneity by employing montage techniques, cutting the *Zeitzeugen* testimony against a disparate collection of clips and stills. Connections between these visual fragments, which are united only by a series of broad themes (war, sexual activity, and gender roles), are only occasionally made explicit by the voice-over. On a few occasions a layered effect is created by framing a discussion group that is, in turn, watching a bank of televisions screening other interviews or clips. A complementary form is employed in the book, where excerpts from texts about rape interrupt the transcript.

The success of this montage strategy is open to question: the one-time viewer of the film may well come away with a general sense of wrongdoing and victimhood, but unable to rehearse any of the potentially very complex arguments about wartime rape in 1945. On the other hand, the approach clearly has the potential to activate the viewer, forcing him or her to make connections. This is especially the case because Sander, unlike most documentarists, does not employ visuals as a self-explanatory backdrop to a documentary script, but rather offers them to the viewer as texts that can be read, or, as Smith puts it, as 'transmitters of constructed and constructing truths'.[13] To take just one example, a clip of a demurely dressed American singer entertaining the troops and making a coy, wordless joke about her jiggling breasts might seem frustratingly irrelevant to the subject of the rape of German women in 1945, but invites us to reflect that a soldier's sexuality is constructed long before the moment of rape, amongst other things by the regulated (though clearly not entirely regulable) sexual dynamics of officially sanctioned military entertainments.

Grossmann's attack on Sander is weakened by her summary dismissal of this technique: she criticizes Sander for attempting to 'gain macabre comic relief' from the 1945 rapes 'by editing in clips of U.S. Army anti-venereal disease films'.[14] Yet the clip in question (it is, *pace* Grossmann, a single clip) is linked to the one featuring the singer because both show a few frames of an audience of soldiers (one group listening to the singer, one watching the information film) and so foreground the soldier's psycho-sexual formation through institutionalized group experiences. Indeed the two clips enter into an interesting dialogue: whereas the singer's sexuality is unspoken (absent from the song lyrics, suppressed

[13] Smith, *Sexual Violence*, 275.   [14] Grossmann, 'Question of Silence', 165.

by her dress, and only hinted at in her gestures), the information film provides its audience of soldiers with an explicit vocabulary for male sexual activity. Even if one cannot generalize in any kind of scholarly way from these uncontextualized fragments (and even if there is a mismatch between the accumulation of American footage at this point in the film and Sander's contention that it was mainly Russian soldiers who raped), Sander nevertheless points to where the answers to the question of why soldiers rape would need to be sought: in the multi-layered and conflicting sexual discourses with which soldiers engage in the lead-up to war.

Despite its imaginative use of montage, *BeFreier und Befreite* suffers from a problem peculiar to history documentaries: that it is impossible for the director to contextualize the historical visuals adequately in the time conventionally allowed for the voiced-over commentary (which is, almost without exception, the time in which the frames run, once, at normal speed). In *BeFreier und Befreite* this problem is exacerbated by Sander's decision to write her voice-over text in a drastically pared-down style, rather than in the more reasoned scholarly discourse of the book. This leads to obvious oversimplifications, some of which are curiously self-defeating given that they are contradicted by the more complex picture drawn in the project as a whole. One such laconic statement runs: 'In jedem Land waren die Frauen Schuld an den Geschlechtskrankheiten' ('In every country it was women who were responsible for sexually transmitted diseases'). At this point we have just seen the information film mentioned above, followed by two posters warning GIs of the dangers of casual sex; now we are looking at a bureaucratic array of photographs of German women, each holding in front of her chest a board inscribed with her address. As with the earlier sequences, this one sets rape within the broader context of prevailing sexual attitudes, inviting the viewer to consider the possibility of a causal connection between the brutal treatment of women and contemporaneous public discourses that framed women as a diseased threat to male health. On closer inspection, however, the link between the voice-over and the commentary is not as smooth as Sander's programmatic statement would like to suggest. Granted, the narrator of the information film has just said: 'If the woman has gonorrhoea or syphilis' and added sarcastically: 'which she probably has'; but the poster that follows, with its caption reminding men of their wives back home, makes men responsible for their sexual behaviour: 'She is true to you. Are you being true to her?' The photographs of infected women, meanwhile, appear to criminalize the women because of their resemblance to police mugshots, but one would need to know the circumstances in which they were taken and the ways in which they were deployed to be able to judge whether this is more than a generic coincidence. If, for instance, they were filed by hospital officials as the medically most efficient way of keeping track of the spread of potentially life-threatening diseases at a time of considerable social chaos, then that would be one thing; if they were taken by policemen or other officers of the law and publicly displayed to shame women, then that would be quite another. Since the book offers only the summary comment 'Fotos, Plakate. Warnung vor Venereal Disease' ('Photos, posters. Warning about venereal disease'), we have no way of establishing the facts.

Grossmann implicitly questions the most prominent example of Sander's telegraph style, one of the film's opening statements: 'Alle wußten davon, doch niemand sprach darüber' ('Everyone knew about it, but nobody talked about it'). Grossmann argues that while there are indeed grounds for describing the rapes as a taboo, especially from the 1950s onwards, and especially in the Soviet Zone and GDR, Sander ignores evidence that rape was the subject of a lively private mythology and that rape experiences were articulated publicly in a range of writing and film. In fact, Sander's film does refer, at least implicitly, to the tradition of rape testimonial—three women in the film read from their own writings about rape—and in the book Sander and Johr quote extracts from the same well-known rape narrative as Grossmann, only more extensively. In other words, there is less ground separating Grossmann and Sander than Grossmann's polemical formulations suggest.[15]

While acknowledging that writing has been one constructive female response to rape, Sander notes in her book that German women did not use the public sphere to articulate their experiences to the same extent as male ex-soldiers (who published much more widely and organized themselves into veterans' associations). Given the obvious affinities between feminism and oral history—the desire to empower the weak and particularly those with restricted access to public discourses—it is understandable that Sander's film is made up largely of witness testimony. Moreover, as Smith points out, allowing witnesses to speak on their own terms is doubly valuable in the case of rape testimony, not, as one might think, because of the taboos surrounding rape, but because the forums in which rape *may*, by convention, be discussed (the courtroom, the confessional, the hospital, the talk-show) impose standardized linguistic and social codes on the victim and force her into dialogue with figures

---

[15] Sander has defended herself against Grossmann's attack: Helke Sander in conversation with Sabine H. Smith, 'Interview with Helke Sander: Reception of *Liberators Take Liberties*: I would have hoped for a different discussion…', in Ingeborg Majer O'Sickey and Ingeborg von Zadow (eds.), *Triangulated Visions: Women in Recent German Cinema* (Albany: State University of New York Press, 1998), 251–60.

of authority who construct rape according to the models peculiar to their field. For Smith, then, simply allowing victims to speak freely to camera about rape is a merit in itself. Nevertheless, I do not share Smith's confidence that Sander's documentary operates without such codes, representing a value-free space in which the rape victim 'is not limited to articulating her experience in culturally scripted and accepted ways'.[16] Sander has admitted in interview to controlling the direction of the interviews,[17] and in the film itself pointed questions indicate that she is guiding interviewees towards aspects of their story that have been rehearsed. Moreover, she stages the interviews in settings of her own devising. Though interesting artistically, this is hardly consistent with the principle of gathering testimony on the witnesses' own terms. Introducing the first interview from one end of a table, with the camera placed at the other end to emphasize its length, Sander declares: 'Frau Hoffmann, ich möchte dieses Thema mal an einem Vorstandstisch behandelt wissen' ('Frau Hoffmann, I would like for once to see this subject discussed at a boardroom table'). By setting the woman's private memory in an iconic locus of public power Sander has found an arresting way of reminding us that speaking out about rape is pointless if it is not spoken about in the still largely male spaces where social policy is made. Yet the cleverness of the conceit has no obvious relevance to the unassuming and slightly bemused woman whose testimony is used to make the point.

On her way to interview female Soviet war veterans, Sander tells us that she is going to ask them 'ob sie vielleicht als Soldatin zu einem Mann gesagt haben, "Mann komm"' ('whether as soldiers they ever said to a man, "Man come"'). This is the gender inverse of 'Frau komm' ('Woman come'), the phrase used by Soviet soldiers with only rudimentary German-language skills to select women for rape. Sander's statement of intent is purely rhetorical, since she does not ask this question of any of her interviewees; the question itself is tendentious, since she already knows the answer; and the whole concept does not stand up to too much scrutiny since it is debatable whether the same sexual codes applied to male and female soldiers, even supposing that they were on an equal footing in all other respects. On the other hand, this deliberately polemical formulation serves to denaturalize wartime rape by suggesting that, since women who find themselves in the rare position of having the power to rape do not, men also have a choice. Possibly, a more illuminating foil would have been the sexual culture of male armies or sections of armies that did not rape.

[16] Smith, *Sexual Violence*, 264.   [17] Sander in conversation with Smith, 258.

All of this may seem to have taken us a long way from the Third Reich. I have shown how the film invites reflection on what makes wartime rape possible; and I have problematized the presentation, in film, of rape testimony; but as yet I have said nothing about the fact that the women raped were German and, more importantly, Germans who had, at least to some degree, participated in the twelve years of Hitler's rule and who now found themselves attacked by men whom Hitler had encouraged them to hate and, in the case of the Russian soldiers, to despise as racially inferior. Grossmann would argue that this validates her most fundamental objection to the film: that it universalizes to a degree where the historical context for the rapes, and specifically Germany's shameful responsibility for the war in which the rapes took place, disappears from view. 'The film's essential (and essentialist) message', writes Grossmann, is such that 'even as it deals with a particular historical moment, it posits the horrific universality of rape. The universal soldier [. . .] rapes and pillages innocent women; women as universal victim are the booty of every war, the unrecognized and uncompensated targets of war crimes.'[18] Grossmann bases this criticism partly on another of Sander's epigrammatic comments, tagged onto the end of her assertion that the rapes were not publicly acknowledged: 'Wie in Kuwait, wie in Jugoslawien' ('Just like in Kuwait, just like in Yugoslavia'). These references to the Iraqi invasion of Kuwait and to the Bosnian War do indeed momentarily put the rapes in Germany in 1945 on an equal footing with rapes committed during more recent conflicts. The transhistorical comparison is strengthened by the inclusion, in the book, of a newspaper report discussing the possibility of creating a separate legal category of asylum rights for women. Moreover, Sander's focus on American attitudes to sexuality and Russian attitudes to rape shifts the emphasis from the national culture of the victims to the national cultures of their attackers. Finally, Sander's use of the term 'Geschlechterkrieg' ('war of the sexes'), which builds a rhetorical bridge between wartime rape and the director's late twentieth-century feminist politics, might be taken to imply that these women were raped *qua* women, not as German women in a historically specific conflict.

It is possible, however, to construct at least a partial defence of Sander's approach. Grossmann argues that the rapes 'cannot [. . .] be usefully understood by quick comparison to Kuwait or Yugoslavia',[19] but this rather unfairly suggests that Sander stops at this relativistic position. In fact, the film does try to suggest that the victims were socially constructed as much as their attackers. Sander includes plenty

---

[18] Ibid. 164–5.   [19] Grossmann, 'Question of Silence', 165.

of *Zeitzeugen* testimony about the differences between sexual attitudes then and now, and shows a newsreel clip from 1945 in which each of several women interviewed uses the word 'bestialisch' ('bestial') of the rapists. Though Sander leaves us to interpret this for ourselves, the context suggests that the women are influenced by a racist ideology that stamps all Russians as sub-human 'Bestien'. Doubtless an exploration of sexual codes in the Third Reich could go further, as Grossmann's own work has shown, and I think Sander misses a trick in not asking her interviewees whether 'bestialisch' was a word they themselves used at the time and whether they could remember using it in other contexts before the rapes. On the other hand, it would be an extremely skilled interviewer who could gain the trust of her speakers even while probing them for evidence that their understanding of their rape was shaped by Nazi discourses that they had internalized in the preceding years.

The historical specificity of Nazism plays a role elsewhere in the film, though in a problematical way. Marie-Luise Gättens is puzzled by Sander's interest in the ethnic mixing brought about by the wartime rapes, a topic with which she says Sander is 'strangely obsessed'.[20] Though 'obsession' is too strong a word for a few scattered references, Gättens's irritation probably derives from the fact that Sander, so explicit in some parts of her film, is vague in respect of this theme. Sander appears to want to enact a kind of intellectual revenge on Nazism by demonstrating that its aim of racial purity was undermined by the birth of many thousands of children of mixed German and Slav or other non-'Aryan' parentage. To highlight this paradox she sets the testimony of a woman who suspects that her mother's rapist may have been Asian in a mock desert (a scene for which Sander was criticized, although it corresponds to the woman's testimony that she fantasizes about an 'exotic' father). There may be a sense of poetic justice in this but it can hardly be a consolation to the children of rape that their conception defied Nazi racial ideals.

Beckermann's *Jenseits des Krieges*

By the time she made *Jenseits des Krieges*, Beckermann was already known for her documentary films exploring pre- and post-Holocaust Jewish identities, such as *Wien retour* and *Die papierene Brücke*. *Jenseits des Krieges* is her first cinematic engagement with the majority, non-Jewish culture of Austria and its relations to the Nazi past, and like

---

[20] Marie-Luise Gättens, 'Helke Sander's *Liberators Take Liberties* and the Politics of History', in Majer O'Sickey and von Zadow, *Triangulated Visions*, 261–71.

Sander's project it comprises a film and a book.[21] The film, a compilation
of interviews with visitors to an exhibition in Vienna, has no narrative
voice, so that the book functions as Beckermann's commentary on the
project, which she articulates in the form of a short essay, an interview,
and a production diary. In addition, the book contains an essay by the
Austrian-Jewish writer Robert Menasse, transcripts of the interview clips
that make up the film, and full-length transcripts of two of the more
interesting interviews. In this way, the book both provides a partial
interpretation of the film and complicates its meanings and effects in
significant ways.

Jenseits des Krieges is an important element of the reception of
the German exhibition *Vernichtungskrieg. Verbrechen der Wehrmacht
1941–1944 (War of Annihilation, Crimes of the Wehrmacht 1941–1944)*,
popularly known as the *Wehrmachtsausstellung* or Wehrmacht Exhibition, which was put together by the privately funded Hamburger Institut
für Sozialforschung (hereafter HIS) as part of a wider study of violence
in the twentieth century, and which opened in 1995. The exhibition
made headlines with its provocative, but by no means new, thesis that
members of the regular German army, and not just the SS and its
adjuncts, had facilitated and even carried out racially and ideologically
motivated killings in the war zones of Eastern and Southern Europe.
The exhibition became something of a national event, provoking heated
discussions in the public and private spheres, violent clashes between
extreme right-wing and left-wing factions, and a formal debate in the
Bundestag. Accusations of inaccuracy and manipulation, later largely
disproved, only increased the exhibition's notoriety and led to its temporary withdrawal in 1999. A substantially revised version, with the barely
revised title *Verbrechen der Wehrmacht. Dimensionen des Vernichtungskrieges 1941–1944 (Crimes of the Wehrmacht. Dimensions of the War
of Annihilation, 1941–1944)*, still popularly known as the *Wehrmachtsausstellung*, opened in 2001 and toured Germany and Austria until
March 2004. While an analysis of the exhibition is beyond the scope of
this book,[22] one aspect—the deployment and interpretation of photographic evidence—deserves brief mention because it plays a role in my
reading of Beckermann's film. Much of the impact of the first exhibition
derived from the display of photographs showing Wehrmacht soldiers
as witnesses to, or participants in, the persecution and murder of Jews,

[21] Ruth Beckermann (ed.), *Jenseits des Krieges. Ehemalige Wehrmachtssoldaten erinnern sich* (Vienna: Döcker, 1998). Further references appear in brackets in the main text; where I have cited participants in the film, I have followed the transcript of their words in the accompanying book.

[22] See instead Niven, *Facing the Nazi Past*, ch. 6.

partisans, and other non-combatants. As I have argued in more detail elsewhere, the HIS's silence about the photographers whose images it used and about the wider context of photographic practice in the 1940s, coupled with its dissemination of scholarly speculation about the psychology of those who photographed atrocities, has led to a certain fetishization of the soldier photographer, whose gaze has become a symbol of amorality.[23]

Beckermann's film, shot when the exhibition visited Vienna, shows little interest in the photographs and those who took them. Where more mainstream documentarists would have capitalized on the conventionally televisual images of violence and death, Beckermann and her cameraman studiously avoid training the camera on the exhibition boards, instead taking close-ups of the visitors' faces, or framing them seated at a table a little apart from the exhibits. Photographs do appear, fragmented and blurred, in the background, as is clear from the shot used in publicity for the film and reproduced on the cover of the video (Fig. 3), in which a black-and-white image of a Wehrmacht soldier, photographed in half-profile from the left, is aligned horizontally with the figure of an *ex*-Wehrmacht soldier who is visiting the exhibition, filmed in half-profile from the right. When extracted as a still it creates the impression of an old man juxtaposed with his younger self, a nice marketing device that encapsulates the social impact of the exhibition but is not representative of Beckermann's aesthetic: the shot is generated by chance when the man moves and the cameraman is obliged to follow him, and the camera movement means that the viewer does not register it as a single image.

While the technical strategies open to Beckermann were limited by her last-minute decision to film at the exhibition, which obliged her to use a Hi-8 video camera and a single technician, it was nevertheless open to her, at the editing stage, to insert stills from the exhibition into the film. Whether her strategy of excluding the photographs is to be considered a merit or a deficiency is a matter for debate. On the one hand, the men's reactions to the exhibition remain, to a degree, without referent (a problem that will increase over time); on the other hand, the technique suggests that Beckermann's concern was with making an immediate impact, not with posterity, and the omission could be read as a refusal to compound, through filmic reproduction, what already amounts to a

[23] Chloe Paver, ' "Ein Stück langweiliger als die Wehrmachtsausstellung, aber dafür repräsentativer": The Exhibition *Fotofeldpost* as Riposte to the Wehrmacht Exhibition', in Anne Fuchs, Mary Cosgrove, and Georg Grote (eds.), *German Memory Contests: The Quest for Identity in Literature, Film, and Discourse since 1990* (Rochester, NY: Camden House, 2006), 107–25.

Die „Wehrmachts-Ausstellung" und ihre Besucher:

JENSEITS DES KRIEGES

Eine Anhörung von Ruth Beckermann

Fig. 3. A still from Ruth Beckermann's *Jenseits des Krieges,* used as publicity material by the distributors, suggests a confrontation between a veteran and his younger self

double humiliation of the victims: the primary humiliation recorded in the photographs and the secondary humiliation constituted by the act of photographing the victims in a state of abject powerlessness.

Support for this view is provided by 'Das Photo der jungen Frau' ('The Photo of the Young Woman'), the opening text of the book *Jenseits des Krieges*. The subject of this brief photo-analysis, a single photograph to which Beckermann felt compelled to return each day she spent at the exhibition, depicts neither a gallows nor a grave pit: the superficially peaceful, if disorderly scene shows a group of Jewish citizens crowded together in advance of their execution (Fig. 4). Supposing (wrongly, as we shall see) that the photographer is a soldier taking a snapshot,

Das Photo der jungen Frau

„Die jüdische Bevölkerung vor Ihrer Erschießung, Lubny, 16. Oktober 1941", sagt die Legende unter einer Photoserie in der Ausstellung über die Verbrechen der Wehrmacht.

Frauen, Männer und Kinder, die gedrängt beisammen stehen und warten. Ein Photo und auf diesem Photo eine Person, ein Gesicht, ein Blick sticht heraus, zieht mich bei jedem Vorübergehen an, erwartet schließlich meinen täglichen Besuch. Der Blick der jungen Frau, die inmitten der Männer, Frauen und Kinder steht und wartet und noch nicht weiß, daß sie an jenem 16. Oktober 1941 auf ihre Erschießung wartet.

Die junge Frau schaut in die Kamera. Den Körper halb abgewandt, dreht sie den Kopf zur Kamera. Die Lippen geschlossen, die rechte Augenbraue fast bis zu der sorgfältig ondulierten Haarsträhne, die unter dem Kopftuch hervorschaut, gehoben.

Ein Blick aus den Augenwinkeln. Ein Blick tiefster Verachtung.

7

Fig. 4. A photograph of a young Jewish woman awaiting execution is the subject of a photo-analysis by Ruth Beckermann in the book *Jenseits des Krieges*

Beckermann finds a metaphor to express the military dominance that empowers him to photograph the captives without their demur. The eye that looks through the viewfinder is 'das bewaffnete Auge des Feindes' ('the armed eye of the enemy'; p. 8). However, she thinks she perceives a contained anger in the crowd that represents a form of passive resistance and that is concentrated in the withering look which, on her reading, a young woman is directing at the photographer. Beckermann's erroneous assumption about the photographer (who is identified in the exhibition catalogue as a propaganda corps photographer) might add weight to Miriam Arani's criticism that the HIS took too little care to distinguish between professional and amateur photography in the exhibition.[24] Certainly, the professional reportage to which the photograph of the young woman belongs was treated carelessly in the first exhibition, which so muddled the order that it was unclear that it constituted a single, very methodical, project. Even so, Beckermann's mistake is scarcely credible, given the obviously professional quality of this and other portraits in the series, and seems therefore to confirm the attractiveness, as a clearly identifiable moral target, of the iconic soldier-photographer, who sees, and possibly even takes pleasure in the act of seeing, but does not protest. Beckermann's creative reanimation of the girl and of her relationship to the photographer corresponds to Marianne Hirsch's concept of 'postmemory', which she defines as a memory that connects to the past 'not through recollection but through projection, investment, and creation', and which she likewise illustrates with examples of the imaginative appropriation of Holocaust photographs by artists and writers.[25] Beckermann goes on to say that she abandoned the idea of using the photograph of the young woman as a closing still for the film for fear that the young woman would be at the mercy of the ex-Wehrmacht soldiers who make up the majority of Beckermann's interviewees. However subjective Beckermann's fear (given that the mere contingency of two photographic subjects does not imply a relationship of power between them), it shows her to be aware of ethical issues involved not just in photography but also in the deployment of photographic reproductions. Of course, I am also implicated in these issues because I have reproduced the picture here, to illustrate my argument. I have, however, deliberately reproduced it as it appears framed in Beckermann's text, to avoid the widespread tendency, criticized by Hirsch, to decontextualize Holocaust-related photographs.

Notwithstanding the memorable image of the 'bewaffnetes Auge' in Beckermann's introductory essay, her general lack of interest in the soldier as photographer is still worth remarking on. Though she repeatedly asks the men at the exhibition what they *saw*, she never once asks them whether they photographed similar scenes, or even (given that that question would most likely elicit a simple 'No') whether they owned a camera at the time and in what circumstances they used it. Beckermann's response to my criticism might be to quote, as she does in her work-diary,

[24] Miriam Y. Arani, ' "Und an den Fotos entzündete sich die Kritik". Die "Wehrmachtsausstellung", deren Kritik und die Neukonzeption. Ein Beitrag aus fotohistorisch-quellenkritischer Sicht', *Fotogeschichte*, 85–6 (2002), 97–124.

[25] Marianne Hirsch, 'Projected Memory: Holocaust Photographs in Personal and Public Fantasy', in Mieke Bal, Jonathan Crewe, and Leo Spitzer (eds.), *Acts of Memory: Cultural Recall in the Present* (Hanover, NH: University Press of New England, 1999), 3–23 (8).

Holocaust historian Raul Hilberg, who told her in interview that the nit-picking over who exactly committed the crimes (the SS, Wehrmacht soldiers, or others) is a preoccupation exclusive to the majority culture; for the victims it is irrelevant by whom their fellows were killed (p. 86). As the daughter of Holocaust survivors, and faced with the reality of Wehrmacht atrocities visible in the photographs, Beckermann may well feel that it is of little concern to her whether the photographer owned a Voigtländer or a Zeiss, whether this not yet ubiquitous personal possession earned him the respect or envy of his fellow soldiers, and whether the photographic studio that developed his prints ever commented on his gruesome choice of subject matter. On the other hand, such insights into the social norms of amateur photography, however tangential to the moral issues at stake for Beckermann, could have fed into her exploration of the social norms of war.

Having thus begun, perhaps unfairly, by considering what Beckermann's film does not do, I have arrived with this last statement at one of the many worthwhile things that it does: it explores the range of conduct that was open to Wehrmacht soldiers on the Eastern Front. In particular, it seeks to denaturalize the supposedly immutable 'nature' of war as expressed in the cliché 'Krieg ist Krieg und Krieg ist schrecklich' ('War is war, and war is terrible'). Beckermann rejects the self-confirming logic of this axiom (variations on which are used, unprompted, by several speakers in the film) and deplores its use to excuse wartime excesses. Far from being natural, she insists, war is a human activity and the form it takes a matter of choice: 'Denn Krieg ist eben nicht Krieg. Krieg ist eine gesellschaftliche Situation, in der von der Gesellschaft bestimmt wird, was erlaubt ist und was nicht' ('Because war is not war, that's precisely the point. War is a social situation, in which society determines what is allowed and what is not'; p. 20). In the film, Beckermann relies on her editing to expose the fallaciousness of the 'war-is-war' position, relativizing assertions that soldiers had no choice (e.g. pp. 45, 58, 69) by cutting them against testimony which suggests that, on the contrary, a range of behaviours was possible within the Wehrmacht, including declining a role in non-combative killing operations (pp. 35–6, 38, 40–1). Similarly, the testimony of those who say they saw nothing of crimes (pp. 27, 74, 84) is cut against the testimony of those who saw crimes (pp. 28–9, 35–42, 63, 68–9), and further undermined by the testimony of two men who speak of acquaintances having seen crimes of which they later deny all knowledge (pp. 53, 82–3).

It would be unfair, however, to reduce Beckermann's editing to an elementary strategy involving the contrivance of easy contrasts between clearly opposing positions. Were this her aim, she would not include testimony where no single clear-cut position is expressed. Thus, one man relates how he refused to get involved in unspecified behaviour involving a concentration camp and condemns the 'charakterlose Leute' (the 'unprincipled people') who volunteered (pp. 54–6). The same man, however, also attempts to discredit the exhibition, which he calls a 'Dreck-lawine' ('an avalanche of filth') unjustly unleashed on the Wehrmacht, whose Austrian battalions, in particular, were 'anständig' ('decent'). Though he is not the only interviewee to align himself with the forces of morality in order then, from this socially correct position, to con-demn the exhibition (see also pp. 73–4), the man further complicates his response by discrediting the Wehrmacht, condemning the cruelty of its punishment battalions. From his apparently paradoxical position, then, both the exhibition's critical portrayal of the Wehrmacht *and* the Wehrmacht itself threaten the concept of soldierly decency with which he identifies, and which is tied to his sense of national identity. A different but comparable case is that of a witness whose testimony is recorded in full in the book (pp. 99–122). He recalls a variety of ways in which he expressed his disagreement with the regime's war-conduct, including an attempted desertion. Looking back, he concludes that the attempt, which foundered on his fear of the Soviet artillery, would probably never have succeeded because of the language barrier. By leaving this passage in the transcript (which could easily have been cut off before this point), Beckermann acknowledges that even her 'witnesses for the prosecution', so to speak, offer some support for the contention (favoured by apo-logists for Wehrmacht crimes) that opportunities for resistance in the Wehrmacht were circumscribed.

From these examples it is already clear that, like all the works explored in this study, Beckermann's film has a double focus: how the Third Reich was lived, and how it is remembered. Oral historians understand that interviewees' statements are mediated through a normative social discourse that evolves and stabilizes over a period of years and that acts to regulate the way in which the past is spoken of: 'We compose our memories so that they will fit with what is publicly acceptable.'[26] Both Beckermann and her guest-essayist Menasse recognize the way in which social pressures shape what interviewees feel that they can and cannot say about the Third Reich. Menasse argues that most *Zeitzeugen* couch their statements, at least initially, in socially expedient terms: 'Es hat sich ein "gesellschaftliches Wissen" darüber herausgebildet,

---

[26] Alistair Thomson, quoted by Bernice Archer in ' "A Low-Key Affair": Memories of Civilian Internment in the Far East, 1942–1945', in Martin Evans and Ken Lunn (eds.), *War and Memory in the Twentieth Century* (Oxford and New York: Berg, 1997), 45–58 (45).

welche Betroffenheitsadjektive eingeflochten, welche Distanzierungs-
floskeln ausgestellt werden müssen' ('A kind of "social knowledge" has
developed about which adjectives connoting dismay one should work
into one's discourse and which hackneyed expressions of critical distance
one should put on public show'; p. 12). As the sarcastic tone suggests, he
views this as a negative process of accommodation to liberal norms that
leaves underlying attitudes untouched. Though he gives no examples,
one might cite the woman who acknowledges the illegal basis of the
war with the help of a standardized expression heard at several points
in the film—'Gut, es war ein Angriffskrieg, ja' ('Yes, sure, it was a war
of aggression'; p. 71)—but whose next words amount to a wholesale
dismissal of the exhibition's message: 'Aber es war nicht so, wie es hier
dargestellt wird. Sicher nicht' ('But it wasn't like it's depicted here, that's
for sure'; p. 71). Another example is the man who begins by evoking the
'normal' moral stance on the events depicted in the exhibition: 'Daß das
alles ein Verbrechen war, bestreitet kein Mensch. Kein Mensch… Einer
der normal ist, wird das nie bestreiten' ('Nobody denies that all this was a
crime. Nobody… A normal person isn't going to deny it'; p. 73), but who
goes on to offer various facts in mitigation of the Wehrmacht that, taken
together, diverge quite radically from the 'normal' moral stance: that he
himself, as a personal friend of Jews, is living proof that not all soldiers
were anti-Semitic; that the exhibition tars everybody with the same brush
and over-emphasizes the atrocities; that all this had happened before,
for instance in the age of slavery; that 'war is war'; that the exhibition
simply rehashes well-worn material; and that the concentration camps
were far worse (pp. 73–4).[27]

It is clearly possible for individuals to apprehend the prevailing codes
(Menasse's 'social knowledge' about post-Holocaust discourse) partially
and imperfectly. Thus, for instance, a man who gives one of the two
full-length interviews recorded in the book nervously seeks permission
to tell Beckermann about his involvement in the National Socialist youth
movement in the days before the *Anschluss*, even though this turns out
to be a fairly innocuous anecdote of youthful revolutionary fervour, but
seeks no permission to make disparaging remarks about 'der Russe'
(literally 'the Russian', but implying a disparaging generalization not
appreciable in the English (p. 137)), nor to reveal (p. 147) exactly how

---

[27] Cf. Beckermann: 'Indem sie die Judenvernichtung als "entsetzlich" bezeichnen, also der
Verurteilung des Schlimmsten zustimmen, gewinnen sie die Freiheit, alles andere mehr oder
weniger zu entschuldigen oder gar zu verteidigen' ('By calling the extermination of the Jews
"terrible", that is, by concurring in the condemnation of the worst outrages, they earn the freedom
more or less to excuse everything else, or even to defend it'; p. 88).

many Jews he would consider an acceptable number for the city of Vienna. One speaker even sneers at the liberal code, deriding the verb 'hinterfragen', a word that means 'to enquire critically what lies behind a phenomenon' and which is used to reprove those who lived through the Third Reich for not seeing beyond the surface of Nazism to its murderously racist core. 'Ich hatte keinen Grund,' says the man, 'das zu hinterfragen, um so einen blöden Ausdruck zu verwenden, der jetzt immer verwendet wird' ('I had no reason to look behind the scenes, to use a stupid expression that's always being used these days'; pp. 47–8).

One could continue in this vein at some length, reading the film along the lines suggested by Beckermann and Menasse in the accompanying book, inferring from the particular utterances of the interviewees the collective mechanisms of repression and impenitence that still function within Austrian society, particularly but not solely among its older members. I have two caveats, however: first, that most of us are no better qualified than Beckermann and Menasse to extrapolate sociological truths from witness testimony; and second, that this approach is the critical equivalent of making a Meccano model by following the instructions on the box. In particular, because Beckermann, as I think we may safely assume, has selected the most provocative statements from her forty-six hours of filmed material, it is tempting to content oneself with enumerating the many hair-raisingly illiberal, racist, and revisionist views voiced by some of the film's participants. Yet this kind of moralizing simply aligns us with the (perfectly commendable, but by no means mandatory) moral positioning of the film-maker. Even if much of the film's value lies precisely in Beckermann's having captured so much shocking self-incrimination in such a concentrated space, we need also to keep a critical distance from the project.

Unlike Sander's film, *Jenseits des Krieges* is not explicitly informed by a feminist politics. Nevertheless, it does address gender issues in various ways, and the fact that the exhibition is concerned with an exclusively male sphere of activity invites a gendered reading of its reception. In her work-diary, Beckermann notes the low ratio of women to men in the exhibition halls and quotes approvingly an old woman who deplores the widespread belief among women that the exhibition is irrelevant to them (p. 89). Beckermann counters this misapprehension by over-representing women in her film (though they remain in the minority), giving space to women's testimony even though women inevitably had almost no direct contact with Wehrmacht operations. Given that the two most categorical rejections of the exhibition come from female visitors (pp. 57–9 and 71), the clips of female interviewees have certainly not been chosen with the intention of contrasting women favourably with men. While acknowledging that women suffered as émigrées, as rape victims, and, on the Russian side, as combatants, Beckermann is not afraid to implicate women in immoral behaviour and attitudes.

The film also suggests that soldiers use gender boundaries to map the limits of military roles and behaviour. It is clear from Beckermann's questions that she does not set out to explore this topic; nevertheless, the fact that she includes the testimony in her edited selection suggests that she recognizes its value and invites her viewer to reflect on it. One man relates, in a rather confused narrative that points to a continued emotional disorientation, his horror at encountering a battalion of Russian women soldiers: 'Ich meine, daß eine Frau ... das war so ganz gegen unsere Ordnung und gegen unseren soldatischen Begriff' ('I mean to say, the idea that a woman ... that was completely contrary to our principles and contrary to our notion of soldierly behaviour'; p. 65). That he is particularly horrified by the view of women's bloated corpses suggests that the soldierly 'order' entails the preservation of the healthy female body intact, a taboo that is perhaps the psychological bargain struck to legitimize the maiming and killing of the male body. In other words, the death of women on the battlefield destabilizes the consensus that deaths on the battlefield are acceptable: this might explain why German soldiers violate one Russian woman soldier's corpse (an action that the witness seems to consider logical, even if not desirable).[28] Another former soldier argues that soldierly discipline is the sole criterion by which soldiers should be judged:

> Mein Ziel war es—das war mein absoluter Wille—, daß ich den Beruf, den ich hatte, anständig ausführe. Dazu gehört auch z.B., daß man sich nicht an Frauen vergeht. Man muß es ordentlich machen. Jeder muß seinen Job, den er macht, mit einer gewissen Disziplin und einer gewissen Ordnung durchführen. Aber sonst... (p. 50)[29]

While this could be dismissed as a crude exculpation of German military excesses, which are implicitly contrasted with the supposedly more barbarous behaviour of the Red Army, it is nevertheless revealing. The

---

[28] In his study of male violence, Klaus Theweleit describes the unwillingness of members of the *Freikorps* to shoot at female demonstrators and identifies one motivation for male combat as the desire to exclude the feminine: 'Der heroische Tötungsakt anstelle des Liebesakts ist eine Angelegenheit unter Männern [...]. Die Existenz des Weiblichen wird in der mann/männlichen Verschlingung als Selbstzeugung weghalluziniert' (Klaus Theweleit, *Männerphantasien*, ii (Reinbek bei Hamburg: Rowohlt, 1980), 31–9, here 276).

[29] 'It was my aim—this was my absolute resolve—to carry out my job decently. And that includes, for instance, not molesting women. You have to do things properly. Everybody has to perform his job with a certain discipline and a certain order. But apart from that...'.

fact that the interviewee believes that it takes discipline not to rape women would seem to suggest, beyond a crude misogyny, that he is working with a model of war in which the citizens of defeated territories are understood to be at their conquerors' mercy (rather than, say, a model of war in which people in occupied territories are automatically incorporated into the soldiers' home nation and enjoy similar rights to other fellow citizens). And the fact that he praises this particular effort of self-control as a guarantee of soldierly respectability suggests that a strict sexual code may have been used to create a self-image of 'decency' that freed soldiers to act in politically and militarily 'indecent' ways (just as, in Beckermann's view, some people permit themselves to hold racist and nationalist views by constructing a self-image in which they deplore the Holocaust).

A rather more systematically gender-critical perspective, such as is adopted by sociologist Gaby Zipfel in an article on the Wehrmacht Exhibition, can usefully supplement Beckermann's understanding of her own work and my extrapolations from it.[30] Zipfel argues that the exhibition helped perpetuate the myth that war is a male affair from which women remain detached, sheltered from the action in an apolitical 'female hinterland' ('weibliches Hinterland'). According to a different but related myth (which is no less mythical for being liberal in its intentions), women living in wartime are empowered by this marginal position to throw a critical light on the conduct of war.[31] In reality, Zipfel maintains, no element of war is entirely free of female influence, and if female *Zeitzeugen* buy into the myth of women's critical view from the sidelines, then this is often a diversionary manoeuvre that obviates the need to examine their own or their families' complicity in the values of the Third Reich. Moreover, female witnesses to the era often continue uncritically to fulfil the unacknowledged function of the 'female hinterland', which is to mirror and reinforce male soldierly values. To Zipfel's own examples, likewise drawn from interviews with visitors to the exhibition, one could add several from *Jenseits des Krieges*. A woman who denounces the exhibition as an insult to her male relatives' courage in battle and who goes on to cite the stories she was told as a child about the dangers of disobedience in the army, before deferring to a male interviewee who experienced the Eastern Front at first hand (pp. 57–8), adopts a position similar to that of a soldier's wife quoted by Zipfel, not just deferring to

[30] Gaby Zipfel, 'Vom weiblichen Blick auf den männlichen Krieg', in Hamburger Institut für Sozialforschung (ed.), *Besucher einer Ausstellung. Die Ausstellung 'Vernichtungskrieg. Verbrechen der Wehrmacht 1941 bis 1944' in Interview und Gespräch* (Hamburg: Hamburger Edition, 1998), 141–60.
[31] Ibid. 142.

male narrative authority but actively defending it against a perceived attack. In fact, nearly all the women who speak to Beckermann (even one who expresses liberal views) refer at some point to the stories told by their male relatives, as if they could not engage with the subject without reference to this male narrative.

One woman who offers a particularly confused and agitated riposte to the exhibition might be seen to illustrate the workings of Zipfel's 'female hinterland'. Though she does not deny the crimes of the Wehrmacht, she insists that they must be set against the positive values of the Third Reich, citing as proof of these her work in the Nazi girls' organization the BDM, her fifty-year marriage, and the successful careers of her children. In this retrospective biographical construction, the BDM is not part of a wider nationalist and racist ideology, but a realm of charity and public spirited-ness, one, moreover, that forms a solid foundation for the subsequent fulfilment of the roles of wife and mother. That this notion of a woman's roles might itself have been instilled in her as part of a conservative ideology, in which, amongst other things, a male monopoly on military activity is unquestioned, is beyond the interviewee's comprehension, but Beckermann, working here as elsewhere with a model of unwitting self-incrimination, evidently hopes that her viewer will reflect on the woman's words from just this kind of critical perspective.

As one might expect, interesting cultural cross-currents result from filming Austrian responses to a German exhibition that documents a shared Austrian and German past. The film highlights the distinct traditions of Germany and Austria before 1938 by including testimony from men who opposed Hitler as monarchists (pp. 44, 55), whereas opposition in 1930s Germany is associated with social democratic and communist politics. Even if we did not have access to Beckermann's work-diary, in which she deplores the fact that no Austrian politician deigns to attend the exhibition, whereas the Minister of Defence (unnamed by Beckermann but identifiable as Werner Fasslabend of the ÖVP) has attended the right-wing remembrance ceremony at the Ulrichsberg, which honours the war dead but excludes the victims of Nazism (p. 85), we would know from her edited selection of testimonies that she is critical of Austria. We have already seen that some interviewees imply that Austrian soldiers were more humane than their German counterparts, yet their own and others' testimony gives the lie to the myth of Austrian innocence. A particularly damning testimony comes from a Jewish *Zeitzeuge* forced into exile after the *Anschluss*, who relates how, in 1948, an Austrian judge prevented him from regaining possession of his murdered parents' Viennese apartment, favouring instead the Nazi Party member who had benefited from their dispossession (p. 77). Since this testimony has nothing directly to do with the exhibition, it is clearly included to imply that Austria's post-war rehabilitation permitted anti-Semitism to continue unchecked. Though both Beckermann and Menasse draw understandably gloomy conclusions from the interviews about modern-day Austria and the generation that built it, it must be said that in the film itself there are at least eight instances in which visitors to the exhibition interrupt and reprove those they believe are speaking inappropriately, suggesting a healthy degree of democratic responsibility, at least amongst the self-selecting group that visits the exhibition.

One significant merit of Beckermann's film not noted by the director herself is that, by allowing ordinary people drawn mostly from one region of Austria to articulate their experiences in their local accent and/or dialect, it helps to regionalize the Second World War, restoring a local identity to those who fought.[32] This is important because much narrative film about the Third Reich, perhaps as an inevitable consequence of using trained actors (or, in the case of dubbed films, trained dubbing artists), gives the impression that the era happens in *Hochdeutsch* and therefore in a kind of supra-regional no-man's-land. In one sense, of course, war veterans have a strong regional identity in Austria, because of the prominent role played by veterans' associations (*Kameradschaftsbünde* or *Veteranenvereine*) in local, especially rural life. However, the diverse social roles played by these associations (many of which were founded in the nineteenth century by veterans of earlier wars) mean that the connection between their members and the actual facts of the war are largely obscured. Indeed, one witness (in his full-length testimony in the book) comments on the way in which the largely economic function of the veterans' associations (p. 122) secured their continuity in the post-war years, regardless of the conduct of the soldiers during the war. The film, then, succeeds in reconnecting veterans who have a clearly audible regional identity with the events and social behaviours of the war in the East.

As with Sander, the choice not to construct a linear narrative may have been made for Beckermann by her subject matter (a disparate group of people talking about similar and roughly contemporaneous events whose order is not decisive), but it is nevertheless to her credit that she does not employ the quest-for-the-truth narrative typical of academic and pseudo-academic documentary, instead forcing her viewers to make sense of what they see. This is not to say, however, that there is no structure at all. Though it is impossible to know in exactly what order the

---

[32] Judging by their accents, the majority of speakers are from Vienna or the neighbouring areas. The effect is lost in the transcripts, which eliminate dialect terms for ease of understanding.

scenes were filmed, a certain amount of ordering has clearly taken place during editing. For instance, Beckermann chooses to end the film with a scene that was filmed, so her work-diary informs us, half-way through production. This is a disagreement between an ex-soldier who insists on having seen atrocities before being drafted into the Wehrmacht, and another ex-soldier who insists that all those at the front saw nothing. The latter sums up his opinion of the former thus: 'Sie sind verwundet worden und reden noch so einen Blödsinn' ('You were wounded and you still talk such rubbish'; p. 84). It may be that the cameraman was forced to cut the sequence at just this point because the two men stopped talking, but in the finished work Beckermann increases the sense of a dramatic punch line by making these the final words of the film. Beckermann suggests in interview that she deliberately framed the film with disagreements about what was seen and what was not seen to avoid any suggestion of a movement towards conciliation and enlightenment (p. 25). In fact, if one listens carefully to the dispute, it rests on a misunderstanding, since the experiences of the two men are not incompatible, and it is in that sense rather trivial (I do not read it as Beckermann does, as proof that those who saw crimes now lie about it). However, the apparently illogical suggestion made by the second man, that those who have been wounded in battle should speak only positively of the army in whose service they were injured, implies the existence of narrative codes within the military that serve to mitigate the potentially alienating effects of personal injury by binding the injured soldier more strongly to the army. This sense of the army as having a distinct culture is one of the positive outcomes of Beckermann's film, though the insights are fleeting and tentative, and often a by-product rather than an objective of Beckermann's questioning, which focuses narrowly on the question of seeing and not seeing crimes.

In the book Beckermann pursues the same strategy of avoiding a conciliatory progression, choosing to end with a full-length interview given by an unrepentant and openly racist interviewee, rather than with the other full-length interview, given by a likeable man who highlights possibilities for resistance within the Wehrmacht. Moreover, she ends the final interview just as the interviewee advances the view that there were at least 80,000 too many Jews in Vienna before the *Anschluss*. Of course, one would need to see the film of this dialogue in order to be absolutely sure that the man is not provoking Beckermann. His otherwise humourless responses suggest not, however, and one would expect Beckermann to indicate, as elsewhere, if his words were accompanied by laughter. It is also impossible to know whether or not the original interview broke off here, but it seems unlikely that the man's inhumane calculation provoked no response at all from Beckermann. Either way, the decision to end the book here lends the words an obvious dramatic value. The ending challenges the reader to accept not only that attitudes that allowed fascism to thrive in the Thirties are alive and well in Austria, but that at least some of those who hold them have no awareness that their views might offend against majority values.

In the only detailed study to date of Beckermann's film, Dagmar Lorenz comments on the congruence of Beckermann's sparing aesthetic and the functional appearance of the exhibition hall, concluding: 'All in all the Alpenmilchzentrale, which bears a certain resemblance to the bathrooms, surgical facilities, and torture chambers in concentration camps, turned out to be the ideal setting for the exhibition and Beckermann's film.'[33] This seems to me to illustrate the danger, from which I claim no special immunity, of over-identifying with the moral message of works dealing with the crimes of the Third Reich. Lorenz emulates Beckermann's moral engagement by offering an interpretation of the exhibition space that reinforces the admonitory gesture of the exhibition and film, either by making graphic the connection between Wehrmacht crime and the wider Holocaust or—more radically—by symbolically placing members of the majority culture inside the space in which the victims were tortured and killed. A more empirical approach would take account of the social and cultural context of the Alpenmilchzentrale building. Part of the trend for regenerating disused factory buildings, this former dairy has been subdivided into loft-style offices that are leased to media and design companies; the remaining, undeveloped floorspace played host in the 1990s to exhibitions and performances of contemporary art. This was neither the first nor the last time that the Wehrmacht Exhibition was displayed in such surroundings: in its first incarnation it began, and in its second incarnation it ended, at the Kampnagel arts centre, a former factory in Hamburg. Thus, whatever Viennese visitors to the Wehrmacht Exhibition felt about the exhibition space, as distinct from the exhibition's content, it is likely to have been determined primarily by their attitudes towards, and levels of experience of, this kind of fashionably hybrid commercial/cultural, renovated/unrenovated space. Visitors to the exhibition are thus as likely to have associated the tiled walls with other arts venues that proudly display their industrial past as they are to have associated them with concentration camp buildings.

---

[33] Dagmar Lorenz, 'Austrians and Austria in Ruth Beckermann's *Jenseits des Krieges*, the Film and the Book', *Modern Austrian Literature*, 32/4 (1999), special issue: *Austria in Film*, 323–33 (325).

Conclusion

In terms of the film history that I rehearsed earlier, the films by Becker-mann and Sander represent an important step forward for documentary-making on the subject of Germany's troubled twentieth-century past inasmuch as they allow women's voices to be heard, not just as *Zeitzeu-gen* (in which capacity they have more than proved their worth since the 1980s) but also as critical film-makers with an interest in gendered exper-ience. The two film-makers are, however, arguably stuck in a double-bind in which their work, however positive, strengthens the perception of a male/female divide that ultimately works to the disadvantage of women: for as long as Guido Knopp, the king of German television documentary about the Third Reich, continues to engage only male narrators to deliv-er his historical certainties, women's voices such as Beckermann's and Sander's may be associated with a more exploratory, communicative, and correspondingly less authoritative, approach. The narrative mode will doubtless continue to be the norm for documentary, but there is no reason why the scripts should not be read by women nor, indeed, any reason why men should not make documentaries that are informed by gender studies and/or employ a feminist aesthetic. Knopp's main com-petitor, Spiegel-TV, has made at least two documentaries on the Third Reich in which men and women not only share the narration, but do so without recourse to stereotypical distinctions between male and female domains (the woman, for instance, narrates military events, while the man reads from a woman's rape testimony). This may point the way for other documentary makers.

The question of authority is related to that of genre. All three works discussed in this chapter occupy a space at the intersection of art, journ-alism, and academic scholarship, a hybridity that leads to interesting tensions, both within the works and in our critical relationship to them. Gättens, for instance, notes that Sander's film stakes a claim to serious historiography even as it uses filmic means to ironize and relativize the historian's endeavour.[34] To construct a historical or sociological argu-ment out of these works' documentary material is arguably to realize the authors' own intellectual ambitions. Yet, as we have seen, this is prob-lematical, since the evidence is not collected in a rigorously scholarly way. On the other hand, to seek such scholarly rigour in the works and then find them wanting is to undervalue their creative thinking and pop-ular appeal; and not to interpret their fascinating collections of evidence

---

[34] Gättens, 'Politics of History', 266.

at all, for fear of making untenable generalizations, would be a regrettable waste. In all three cases the authors imply that a knowledge of the construction, internalization, and negotiation of social norms (whether martial, marital, or sexual) would allow us to get a handle on what appears, from the vantage point of the early twenty-first century, to be thoroughly *ab*normal behaviour. The three works are therefore valuable not so much for telling us 'how it was' in the Third Reich (which, as my Introduction suggests, was a measure of value used by scholarship in the 1970s and 1980s) as for highlighting what kind of knowledge one would need to have about the Third Reich in order to understand it better.

4 Sound Effects and Language Barriers
Marcel Beyer's *Flughunde*, Michel Tournier's *Le Roi des Aulnes*, and Volker Schlöndorff's *Der Unhold*

Marcel Beyer's *Flughunde* has been seen as a new departure in German-language fiction about the Nazi past: written by an author 'not one, but two stages removed from biographical involvement in National Socialism', it moves on from questions of guilt, denial, and intergenerational conflict and attempts to recover the voices of the perpetrators that fell silent after 1945.[1] And yet Beyer's 1995 novel *Flughunde* has much in common with a novel published twenty-five years earlier by the French author Michel Tournier: *Le Roi des Aulnes*.[2] Set largely in the Third Reich after 1940, both novels give us privileged access to the Nazi élite: Tournier smuggles us into Goering's hunting lodge, Beyer into Goebbels's family circle and Hitler's bunker. Both endow their protagonists with unusual powers of sensory perception, a keen sensitivity to smell in the case of Tournier's hero, Abel Tiffauges, and to sound in the case of Hermann Karnau, Beyer's protagonist. Both Tiffauges and Karnau are characterized as pacifists in a militaristic society, yet both are drawn by their highly idiosyncratic intellectual systems into association with Nazi race scientists. Preferring the company of animals to that of adult human beings, both reject parents and parenthood but nurture a special love of children, a fact that does not prevent them from leading a group of children to their death. In each case this deadly climax is timed and placed to coincide with the rout of Germany's eastern troops in spring 1945.

One should therefore be cautious of hailing Beyer as the pioneer of a definitively new form of fiction about the Third Reich. This is not to say that Beyer must have modelled himself on Tournier,[3] but rather

---

[1] Schmitz, *Legacy*, 125. See also Sandra Schöll, 'Marcel Beyer und der Nouveau Roman. Die Übernahme der "Camera-Eye"-Technik Robbe-Grillets in *Flughunde* im Dienste einer Urteilsfindung durch den Leser', in Marc-Boris Rede (ed.), *Auskünfte von und über Marcel Beyer* (Bamberg: Universität Bamberg, 2000), 144–57.

[2] Marcel Beyer, *Flughunde* (Frankfurt/Main: Suhrkamp, 1995; repr. 1996), *The Karnau Tapes*, trans. John Brownjohn (London: Vintage, 1997); Michel Tournier, *Le Roi des Aulnes* (Paris: Gallimard, 1970; repr. 1996), *The Erl-King*, trans. Barbara Bray (London: Methuen, 1984). Page references appear in brackets in the main text.

[3] This is not, however, out of the question. Beyer's first novel, *Das Menschenfleisch* (1991), testifies to an interest in intertextual writing and a range of intertexts have been identified in *Flughunde*:

that Tournier's aesthetic approach chimes with post-1989 views of the Third Reich, which may explain why a film version, directed by the veteran German film-maker Volker Schlöndorff and entitled *Der Unhold*, reached German cinemas a year after the publication of *Flughunde*.[4] Schlöndorff's film not only repays analysis as a cinematic representation of the Third Reich; it also provides a case study in *Literaturverfilmung* (adapting a literary source for the cinema), while raising questions about what now constitutes German film. Is a film still German if it is a German–French–British co-production, based on a French novel, co-scripted by a Frenchman and a German, acted by French, American, British, German, and Russian actors, with the help of Polish extras, performed almost entirely in English (though later dubbed into French and German), and filmed in Poland, Berlin, and Paris? In other words, is the single fact of the director's nationality enough to qualify it as 'German cinema'? Film has always been less bound by geographical and cultural borders than literature, but contemporary European cinema is increasingly crossing national boundaries, largely for practical and commercial reasons, and films about the Third Reich are inevitably caught up in this trend. In the latter part of this chapter the multinational character of *Der Unhold* is used both to decentre Germany and Austria's cultural discourses about the Nazi past and to open up a discussion of monolingualism and multilingualism in literature and cinema that draws us away from the more usual discussions of moral messages and national psychopathology.

Beyer's *Flughunde*

In my opening remarks I identified the sound technician Hermann Karnau as the protagonist of Beyer's *Flughunde*; in fact, he shares the task of focalization with Helga Goebbels, eldest daughter of Hitler's Propaganda Minister. However, where Helga's childish viewpoint is circumscribed by the narrow horizons of her family, Karnau is characterized by considerable social and geographical mobility as well as wide-ranging intellectual concerns, and it is his actions that drive the

see Schmitz, *Legacy*, 138–41, Ulrich Simon, 'Assoziation und Authentizität. Warum Marcel Beyers *Flughunde* auch ein Holocaust-Roman ist', in Rede, *Auskünfte ... Beyer*, 124–42, and Roman Pliske, '*Flughunde*. Ein Roman über Wissenschaft und Wahnsinn ohne Genie im Dritten Reich', ibid. 108–23. I deal below with a further intertext, by the media theorist Friedrich Kittler.

[4] Volker Schlöndorff, *Der Unhold* (FRG, France, and UK, 1996). Distributed in English as *The Ogre*; in French as *Le Roi des Aulnes*.

plot forward. Although Helga Goebbels is a historical figure and Karnau's name borrowed from a historically documented person (a guard stationed in Hitler's bunker), Beyer shows scant respect for the historical record, inventing for his fictional Karnau a highly contrived story that is as implausible as it is entertaining. Having recommended himself to Goebbels by masterminding the sound transmission at a rally, Karnau accepts the Minister's request to house his five eldest children while their mother is recovering from the birth of the sixth. Though Beyer goes some way towards acknowledging the outlandishness of this childcare arrangement by having both Karnau and Helga remark on its unexpectedness, he makes no real attempt to justify it. This merely underlines its aesthetic purpose: to bring Karnau (and therefore the reader) closer to Goebbels and to yoke Karnau's fate to Helga's in a way that forces us to compare and contrast the two figures. Beyer subsequently sends his hero on a series of narrative missions to geographically and socially disparate locations in pursuit of interesting encounters between the central theme of sound and significant aspects of the Third Reich. On the pretext that sound technicians are needed to gather taped evidence of resistance, Karnau takes part in the operation to stamp out the French language in the newly conquered territory of Alsace (the so-called *Entwelschung* campaign). At the Eastern Front, Karnau makes the reader a witness to the physical horrors of war, again with the excuse that his technical skills necessitate his presence there. The third mission takes us not to a particular location but into the gruesome world of Nazi race science: Karnau is invited to join SS scientists in conducting medical experiments on human beings. Finally, Beyer secures employment for his hero in the key locale of the final days of the war, Hitler's Berlin bunker. This reunites us with the six Goebbels children just prior to their murder, in which Karnau, it is hinted darkly, probably has a hand.

The fact that Beyer neither makes special efforts to justify the improbability of this plot, nor flagrantly parades it (in the form of magic-realist flights of fancy, for instance), might suggest that the Third Reich, freed at last from the constraints of its historical actuality, can henceforth be 'raided' for interesting moments and motifs. On the other hand, Beyer's episodic narrative owes something to the centuries-old tradition of picaresque writing, with its overtly artificial plot-twists and its technique of sending the hero to a variety of socially and historically interesting locations. Grass's *Die Blechtrommel* drew on the same tradition more than three decades earlier, contriving to position its hero in the very building where the first close combat of the Second World War took place and to send him to Normandy's coastal defences just prior to the Allied invasion. Moreover, as critics have been at pains to show, Beyer's text is based on extensive historical researches, so that while little in the action actually happened, much of it could conceivably have done so, given what we know of the Third Reich.[5]

Unlike Christoph Ransmayr's *Morbus Kitahara*, the subject of the next chapter, *Flughunde* offers a stylized plot based in historical reality rather than a radically alternative history. One measure of this stylization is that, unusually for the hero of a novel, Karnau exists in a sexual and familial vacuum: no mention is made of relationships with women; he has neither children (p. 234 (pp. 176–7)) nor siblings (p. 60 (p. 43)); and though Beyer is obliged to mention the character's parents in his descriptions of children's socialization through sound, they remain depersonalized and without social context (reduced, for instance, to the sexless synecdoche 'die Elternhand' ('[the] grown-up hand', p. 43 (p. 28)). Karnau must of necessity be the product of particular social circumstances, yet he stylizes himself as a man without a biography (p. 18 (p. 9)). His lack of family ties sets him in stark contrast to Helga, whose brief life is played out almost entirely within the physical and mental confines of her family circle. By configuring the characters in this way, Beyer creates at least two effects:

First, he draws attention to contradictions at the heart of the National Socialist ideology of the family. While Magda and Josef Goebbels conform to government policy by producing a large brood of children, they value them little enough to risk their lives in the bunker and then to murder them. Moreover, their public shows of family harmony are undermined both by Josef's affairs and by Magda's illnesses, caused at least partly, it is suggested, by her frequent pregnancies. Karnau, meanwhile, negates the principle of building a National Socialist future through reproduction, remaining in a state of permanent sexual immaturity betokened by his still unbroken voice. On one reading, the high-pitched adolescent voice stands for Karnau's refusal to enter fully into the adult world of power relations (especially as exemplified by militaristic Nazism); on another it symbolizes the sterility of National Socialism which, for all its grandiose talk of self-perpetuation, contained only the seeds of its own hasty destruction, in less than the generation that would have been necessary for Helga to become a mother: the autopsy on her corpse (pp. 298–9 (pp. 225–6)), which reveals that she had just reached sexual maturity, draws attention to the possibility of motherhood ruled out by her death.

Secondly, by creating a man with neither social past nor future, and by making the secondary focalizer a child whose own past and future

---

[5] See e.g. Simon, 'Assoziation', 125 and *passim*.

do not reach beyond the Third Reich, Beyer distances himself from the conventional literature of 'coming to terms', which concentrates on the social roots of Nazism and/or the problematic relations between successive generations of Germans after 1945. Admittedly, Beyer does include one short post-war episode (chapter 7), but it does not flesh out Karnau's still bare biography. A report dated 1992 of a grim discovery in a Dresden cellar (a laboratory where experiments on live subjects have recently been carried out) is followed by a passage of interior monologue from an unrepentant, though troubled Karnau, still repressing the knowledge of his involvement in the children's deaths. This stylistically anomalous chapter allows Beyer to suggest that fascism is still latent in post-unification German society and that the task of remembering remains problematical, while nevertheless distancing himself, by means of the grotesque unlikelihood of the events, from the realist intergenerational confrontations of *Vaterliteratur*. The sentiments are conventional, in other words, even if the form is not. In fact, Beyer comes very close to mainstream *Vergangenheitsbewältigung* in his reflections on how Germans repressed their past after 1945 (pp. 229–32 (pp. 172–5)), although he approaches the question from a new angle by narrowing the analysis to sound and voice. In the final chapter, too, in which Karnau tries to reconstruct the deaths of the children with the help of historical documents, Beyer's approach is fairly conventional, demonstrating the unreliability of witnesses implicated in Nazi wrongdoing and suggesting that only personal conscience (here, Karnau's willingness to unlock his own repressed guilt) can compensate for the gaps in evidence about the crimes of the Third Reich.

The juxtaposition of Karnau and Helga is a juxtaposition of narrative voices, but it is not enough to say that Beyer contrasts these voices. Both points of view are sufficiently flexible to dramatize a range of positions vis-à-vis the Third Reich and each moves freely between identification and distance, so that the reader is denied a comfortable position from which to engage with the action. Schmitz has suggested that by endowing Karnau with considerable but not unlimited intellectual powers Beyer is able to use him both as a credible mouthpiece for his own views on sound-related matters and as an embodiment of the kind of over-inflated intellectual ambition, unfettered by moral conscience, that was allowed to thrive under Nazism.[6] Beyer also endows both narrators with a limited amount of critical distance from their surroundings, though in the case of Helga this gradually grows, while in Karnau's case it gradually diminishes.

---

[6] Schmitz, *Legacy*, 144.

Karnau, for instance, is able to mock Goebbels for his fixation with male heirs (p. 47 (p. 32)) while at the same time assisting his cause through his work as a technician.

The counterpart to the critical viewpoint is a 'view from within' that sees what goes on in Nazi Germany as normal. This is created partly by means of interior monologue: Helga and Karnau relate their experiences for the most part as they happen or immediately after they happen.[7] Even this 'view from within' is not straightforward, however, distancing us from the Third Reich even as it creates a sense of living through it. In her study of how authors use the child's view to recreate the Third Reich, Debbie Pinfold argues that

> there is great power to defamiliarize in the gaze of one who finds the Third Reich 'normal' [. . .]. Those who have read countless books, watched films, and learnt about the period in history classes run the risk of [. . .] habitualization; they 'know' about the Third Reich and it thus risks losing any kind of impact on them. [. . .] Moreover, encountering a viewpoint that appears to take the values of this society for granted forces the active, responsible adult reader to fill in the moral gaps left by that perspective.[8]

While one might stumble over Pinfold's 'active, responsible reader', a critical construction presented as a commonsensical given, even a passive, irresponsible reader cannot help but register the gap between how the Third Reich is spoken of today and how Beyer's characters speak of it. Helga brings her extraordinary family to life as no history book can because she considers it entirely normal. Pondering the mystery of when her father finds time for a haircut, she guesses 'Beim Tagebuchdiktat?' ('While he's dictating his diary?' p. 95 (p. 70)). She takes for granted that people dictate their diaries to a secretary; the reader who knows that a diary is a private, amateur form will be struck by Goebbels's extraordinary vanity.

As Pinfold's comments suggest, no fiction about the Third Reich can completely eliminate its readers' or its author's retrospective understanding of the period, and Beyer consciously works elements of hindsight into his text, most obviously in Karnau's reflections from his standpoint in 1992 (in chapters 7 and 9), but also elsewhere. Ulrich Simon has analysed the way in which Beyer works with the reader's knowledge of the Holocaust, for instance by putting into the mouths of the children unwitting

---

[7] The technique is uneven, and no realist context is given for the monologues, but the reader is likely to accept the format unquestioningly, given that it communicates the action.

[8] Debbie Pinfold, *The Child's View of the Third Reich in German Literature: The Eye among the Blind* (Oxford: Oxford University Press, 2001), 26–7.

allusions to the regime's atrocities.[9] The children's nanny provides a further example. Waking her charges in the middle of the night for the move to Karnau's house, she tells them: 'Ihr werdet abgeholt' ('You're going to be collected'; p. 33 (p. 20)). Though the nanny uses 'abholen' in its standard sense of 'to pick up, fetch', its secondary meaning, as a euphemism for 'arrest', resonates clearly because the scene recalls the practice of night-time raids on the homes of Jews designated for deportation. Indeed, the idea of taking the children from their beds (otherwise unmotivated since they are safe in the care of the household staff) must have been contrived solely to set up this resonance. It suggests that the children's safe, privileged lives can only be viewed without sentimentality against the backdrop of the horrors that they never had to face but which their father and his political peers visited on Jews and others.

Beyer also draws extensively on broader intellectual developments from the half-century between 1945 and 1995, with the result that he conceives of the Third Reich in a way that it could not have conceived of itself. In that sense his novel lends itself, unexpectedly, to the kind of approach practised on an earlier generation of writers by an earlier generation of scholars (Reed, among others), one that seeks in novels an understanding of the social reality of the Third Reich rather than, for instance, evidence of a process of mourning. The 1986 study *Grammophon. Film. Typewriter* by media theorist Friedrich Kittler has provided Beyer with insights into the connections between technology and war,[10] technology and physical disability,[11] and technology and death.[12] It also directs Beyer to Rainer Maria Rilke's essay 'Das Urgeräusch', the subject of Karnau's nightmare in chapter 7. Other aspects of Beyer's retrospective understanding are of a more abstract nature. When Karnau decides to investigate those elements of human sound that have hitherto been neglected by specialists in the human voice because they lie outside the realm

---

[9] Simon, 'Assoziation', 126–8.

[10] Friedrich Kittler, *Grammophon. Film. Typewriter* (Berlin: Brinkmann & Bose, 1986). Compare Karnau's description of the development of audio technology for use at the Front (p. 100 (p. 74)).

[11] Kittler argues that physical disabilities played a vital role in helping pioneering technologists to understand normal (i.e. able-bodied) sight, hearing, and sound production (Kittler, *Grammophon*, 39–40). Beyer uses the disabled in an analogous way: their disabilities threaten to upset the careful choreography of the Nazi rally (pp. 11–14 (pp. 3–6)), helping us to understand the rigorous bodily discipline required for staged Nazi gatherings.

[12] Arguing that early media technologists were preoccupied with death, Kittler cites Edison as saying that his phonograph could be used to record people's dying words (p. 23). Similarly, Karnau uses the new medium of pre-magnetized tape to record the death rattles of soldiers at the front. Kittler also cites an associate of Goethe who experimented on voice boxes taken from corpses (p. 116); Karnau conducts similar experiments on live subjects.

of language (cries of pain, for instance), he challenges the way in which the members of a scholarly discipline establish by unthinking consensus arbitrary boundaries to their object of study, often replicating ideological processes of marginalization and exclusion in the process. At the same time, Karnau is obliged to concede that he can never entirely step outside the boundaries set by the human brain (because there are sounds that he cannot hear). This critique owes much to post-structuralist thinking.

One advantage of the child/adult constellation is that it allows Beyer to explore the induction of children into an adult order based on consensus, regulated behaviour, and unequal distributions of power. Authors often do this by contrasting a child, still only partly socialized, with fully socialized adults, but, as Pinfold suggests, such an approach is problematical in the case of depictions of the Nazi era because children were socialized so early and so vigorously into the ideological order that few had anything approaching an outsider's view.[13] If authors writing about the Third Reich continue to use the device of the child-outsider, Pinfold argues, this is because the aesthetic benefits outweigh the loss of realism. Beyer uses a less conventional approach, contrasting an almost fully indoctrinated child with an adult who, having resisted the forces of socialization, is keenly and critically aware of their operation. In line with the novel's strict thematic focus, socialization is related primarily to the human voice. Karnau's refusal to enter willingly into adulthood is, as already mentioned, indicated in vocal terms by the failure of his voice to break, and in a key passage (pp. 74–5 (pp. 53–5)) he describes the way in which children begin to discipline their voices to conform to accepted social practice. As elsewhere, he is interested less in spoken words than in the non-verbal aspects of vocal expression: children learn how to cough in an acceptable manner, how to control the volume of their voice, not to repeat words compulsively, not to imitate others' voices without licence, and so on. Later they learn to make the noises of reassurance, agreement, and approval that make civilized human interactions possible (p. 75 (p. 54)). By siting this passage just ahead of Karnau's departure for Alsace, Beyer encourages the reader to understand the National Socialist regime's proscription of the use of French as a distortion of the normal and necessary process of voice-discipline into a form of totalitarian control. Beyer also connects the disciplining of the voice with a more general disciplining of the body, most explicitly when he has Karnau comment that the so-called 'Father of Gymnastics', Friedrich Ludwig Jahn, was as interested in the purity of the German language as he was in physical

---

[13] Pinfold, *Child's View*, 6.

education (p. 84 (p. 61)), and suggests that the dominated voice has its counterpart in a dominating voice or 'Herrenstimme' ('masterful voice'; p. 11 (p. 3)), which manifests itself in a particularly militaristic form in the Third Reich, screaming orders in a 'Befehlston' or 'Kasernenhofton' ('imperious [tone]' or 'barrack-square tone'; p. 28 (p. 17)). These ideas are brought together in the figure of the Hitlerjugend officer who attempts furiously to discipline the naturally wayward bodies of a group of blind men by booming out the orders 'Heben. Senken. Heben. Senken' ('Up! Down! Up! Down!') to force them to rehearse the raised-arm salute (p. 13 (p. 5)). The 'Herrenstimme', Karnau speculates, functions by holding out to children the promise of access to the same masterful tone of voice in later years, in exchange for present compliance with its orders. Orders barked in German, such a lazy cliché of English-language films about the Third Reich, are here subjected to serious analysis. Moreover, because Karnau sees the 'Herrenstimme' as a feature not just of Nazism, but also of the societies that preceded and followed it (pp. 43 (28), 232 (175)), Beyer invites us to consider the extent to which social control is misused even in non-totalitarian societies.

Flughunde is an obvious candidate for inclusion in a study like this because it is self-evidently 'about' the Third Reich, and yet its concerns at least partly go beyond that subject. It would be an interesting exercise, for instance, to analyse *Flughunde* in relation to texts that have no thematic link to the Third Reich but that deal with the socialization of the human body or with the relation between the body and technological advance.

Tournier's *Le Roi des Aulnes*

Like Beyer, Tournier employs a highly artificial plot structure, periodically moving his character to new settings to bring him as close as possible to the historical action. Where Beyer sends his hero from Germany to occupied France, recalling him to the more interesting war-torn Reich once the French location has served its purpose, Tournier sends his from France to Germany, and, within Germany, from one classic National Socialist locale to another. After a childhood spent at a boarding school, Tiffauges works in Paris, outwardly conforming but living largely in his head and keeping the company of children. Falsely accused of rape, he escapes prison only by being enlisted in the army on the eve of the Second World War. After a short interlude in a signals regiment (which allows Tournier, some time before Kittler, to explore the connections between war and technology),[14] he is captured and transported to East Prussia. From a POW camp there Tournier sends Tiffauges first to the nearby hunting lodge of Hermann Goering and then to an élite Nazi school or Napola. There, Tiffauges secures the favour of his captors by press-ganging boys, with increasing use of force, from the local villages. Tournier peoples the Napola with a representative range of ideological figures: a dyed-in-the-wool Nazi officer, a Nazi race scientist, and an aristocratic member of the plot to kill Hitler at nearby Rastenburg on 20 July 1944.

Like Karnau, Tiffauges is a deeply equivocal figure. Endowed with a fine critical sense, wide cultural knowledge, and a mistrust of authority and received ideas, his clear-sighted critiques of 1930s French society and his acute observations of Nazism draw the reader in. At the same time, the reader is repelled by his extreme individualism, especially by his self-stylization as a mythical ogre protected by Fate, which gives him licence to ignore social norms and values.[15] Tournier contrives an element of progression in this push-and-pull effect, with the push eventually becoming stronger than the pull, for, like Karnau, Tiffauges aligns himself gradually with Nazism despite an instinctive distrust of its activities and beliefs. While the title of chapter 4, 'L'Ogre de Rominten', refers to Goering, the title of chapter 5, 'L'Ogre de Kaltenborn', refers to Tiffauges. Like the ogres of legend, who devoured human flesh, and like the King of the Alders in Goethe's ballad 'Der Erlkönig', who abducts children, Tiffauges has a morbid fascination with bodies, animal and human. This eccentricity is apolitical, but Nazism allows him to indulge it to the full, first as a huntsman on Goering's estate and later at the Napola, where he hunts for boy recruits and makes selected pupils the powerless objects of his scientific study.

Though he begins by passively serving the Nazi doctor Blättchen, Tiffauges later assumes his mantle, delighting in the procurement of identical twins, whose physical characteristics and symbolic significance he analyses in detail. For maximum effect, Tournier synchronizes the most advanced stage of Tiffauges's decline with the end of chapter 5. In the course of this chapter, Tiffauges's intellectual energies, which had earlier ranged across such diverse subjects as capital punishment and the meaning of the hunt, begin to focus on the human body. At first fairly

[14] See esp. the conflict between the 'filistes' (telephone engineers) and the 'sans-filistes' (radio operators) (pp. 181–6 (pp. 120–2)).

[15] Even more clearly than Karnau, Tiffauges marks himself out as existing in a social and familial vacuum: 'Vieux comme le monde, immortel comme lui, je ne puis avoir qu'un père et une mère putatifs, et des enfants d'adoption' ('Old as the world, and as immortal, I can have none but putative parents and adopted children'; p. 12 (p. 12)).

generalized, his reflections gradually home in on the bodies of the boys in his care. One by one, he deconstructs the meaning of the boys' naked bodies as they bathe, their sleeping positions, their buttocks, and their penises. Finally, in a rare moment of purely sensual, non-intellectualized delight, he marvels at the taste of their earwax. Taken out of context, all this sounds like a clear expression of paedophilic intent, but by this time Tournier has carefully established for Tiffauges a sexual profile that is non-active and pre-adolescent, that is, childlike rather than paedophile. Whether or not readers actually heed Tournier's directions, there is no doubt that Tournier presents Tiffauges's fantasies as increasingly predatory and invites his readers to feel a frisson of horror at the danger enveloping the unsuspecting children.

A similar effect is created in the final two chapters of *Flughunde*, where Beyer is careful to remind us that the same Karnau who now seems, to the increasingly nervous children imprisoned in the bunker, the only friendly and trustworthy adult, has shown himself capable of all manner of inhumanity. Thus, when Helga asks Karnau to keep a secret about a birthday present for her sister, his reply—'Kein Sterbenslaut wird über meine Lippen kommen' (p. 259 (p. 195))—ensures that, just as Helga's trust in him reaches its peak, the reader is reminded of his sinister fascination with the dying cries ('Sterbenslaute') of soldiers.[16] At the same time the words anticipate the final moment in the children's lives, when the sound of their dying will be recorded, most probably by Karnau himself. Read in a different way, Karnau's words could be a hint that, like Tiffauges, Karnau is, or sees himself as, immortal. Here the two novels come close to fairy tale, in which children are victims of violence at the hands of adults representing eternal forces of evil. But since both Tournier and Beyer are concerned to explore, in quite some realist detail, the nature of relationships between children and adults in the Third Reich, they seem to me to avoid offering the passive thrill of watching innocence walk into the clutches of evil.

One criticism that might be levelled at both writers is that by choosing as protagonist an atypical, socially isolated, and intellectually ambitious man they suggest that evil is the province of extraordinary individuals and preclude reader identification with their immoral actions. In other words, the two novels contradict Hannah Arendt's famous dictum about the 'banality of evil'. However, to advance this argument is perhaps to

---

[16] Brownjohn's use of an equivalent idiom, 'My lips are sealed', inevitably loses the literal sense: 'Not a dying sound will pass my lips.' The expression is normally 'kein Sterbenswörtchen' ('not a dying word'); the substitution of 'Laut' is consistent with Karnau's privileging of pre-verbal sounds over words, and encourages the reader to make the link with his sound experiments.

apply realist criteria in too pedestrian a fashion to explicitly non-realist texts. One can be fairly sure that there was not a single Frenchman in the 1930s who, having constructed an intricate intellectual system based around the obscure concept of 'la phorie' ('carrying'), proceeded to test out his theories in an élite Nazi school; just as one can be fairly certain that 1940s Germany contained not one man who, having constructed an intricate intellectual system based around the human voice, proceeded to test out his theories by mutilating the voice boxes of political prisoners. Yet by means of imaginative exaggeration the novels do throw a light on Nazism, implying that it thrived partly by giving licence to enthusiastic, self-inflated amateurs to live out their intellectual fantasies. The protagonists also demonstrate the close relationship between rationalism and irrationalism in Nazism, while their peculiar intellectual systems offer a parallel with the closed, self-justifying, unassailable structure of Nazi ideology.

Schlöndorff's *Der Unhold*

The methodological questions raised by *Der Unhold* are of a different order to those raised by *Das schreckliche Mädchen* because Schlöndorff's film is based, not on the life-story of a real person, but on a literary source. In formulating an approach to the film we can draw on a body of theory and criticism relating to the practice of *Literaturverfilmung*.[17] In the early days of scholarship in this field, academics tended, consciously or not, to use the now discredited critical model of 'Fidelity Criticism'. Taking as read that the literary source-text was superior to its screen adaptation, Fidelity Criticism focused on what the film version omitted, distorted, or was unequal to conveying. Later critical practice sometimes retained this system of hierarchical value judgements, but in inverted form, arguing that the film director, as original creative force or *auteur*, produced something of self-evidently superior value to his or her textual source. Current best practice in the study of film adaptations attempts to maintain a value-free approach to the comparison of the source and its adaptation and to shift the investigative focus to the respective historical, cultural, ideological, and industrial contexts of the two genres, literature and film. While the following analysis of Schlöndorff's film may not avoid the pitfalls of Fidelity Criticism altogether, because it is difficult

---

[17] My brief summary of the theory of film adaptation draws on Sally Faulkner, *Literary Adaptations in Spanish Cinema* (London: Tamesis, 2004).

not to present the novel as an altogether richer and subtler product, I attempt nevertheless to re-direct attention towards questions of cultural context and towards the practicalities of film production, relating these to the specific difficulties of screening the Third Reich. What happens when a German director films a French text about the Third Reich? What meanings might be accessible to a German audience but not to a French audience, or vice versa? How does the performative context of film create problems of language use that do not exist for literature, and why are these particularly acute for filmic representations of the Third Reich?

Schlöndorff and fellow screenwriter Jean-Claude Carrière have extensive experience of *Literaturverfilmung*, both individually and as a team. In adapting *Le Roi des Aulnes* they fully exploit Tournier's plot but, given the time constraints of film, there is inevitably a process of selection and compression. A host of minor characters are omitted and the screenwriters compress that part of the action that takes place in France: this comprises just under half of the novel but only the first twenty-five minutes of the 115-minute film. Schlöndorff makes no comment in interview on this abridgement, but it may result from a commercial decision to focus on the marketable topic of the Third Reich rather than on the society and politics of 1930s France, whose appeal would largely be limited to French nationals. Another possibility is that Schlöndorff and Carrière simply responded to the difficulty of transferring a largely reflective section of the text to the screen by cutting it to a minimum.

In the case of the episode set in a French signals regiment at the opening of the Second World War Schlöndorff makes a virtue out of the necessity for compression. From an early draft of the script (available at the Hochschule für Film und Fernsehen Konrad Wolf) it is clear that Schlöndorff and Carrière had originally conceived a series of sixteen short scenes to act out Tournier's thirty-page chapter 'Les pigeons du Rhin', but the sequence was drastically reduced in production. In a single scene of less than two minutes, a military pigeon-handler extols the merits of carrier pigeons to a distracted captain more concerned with his lunch. By using the birds to transmit war intelligence, the pigeon-handler argues, the army will be guaranteed the most up-to-date information, keeping them abreast of any movement of the enemy. At these words, the camera adopts the viewpoint of the officer and the pigeon-handler, showing the three men on the other side of the lunch table raising their arms in response to an event out of shot behind the camera (Fig. 5). As the officer and the pigeon-handler turn around to follow the men's gaze, the camera abandons their perspective and places them in the frame, a ploy that delays the revelation a second longer and focuses attention on their reactions. In the next shot the words 'Guten Appetit' and 'Hände

Fig. 5. In Volker Schlöndorff's *Der Unhold*, a French soldier proceeds, in a single motion, from pouring wine to surrendering

hoch' are spoken off-screen and the points of two rifles appear in the foreground. While the pigeon-handler's promise of advance knowledge of the enemy's whereabouts is thus heavily laden with irony, the comic effect is not created solely through dialogue and action: the scene offers a copybook example of how the diverse elements of film—visual, aural, generic, and symbolic—can be combined. These include:

- the acting (the captain, for instance, responds to the pigeon-handler's exposition by raising a glass in his direction and nodding as he swills a mouthful of wine appreciatively around his mouth, suggesting that his mind is on grape varieties and vintages rather than military strategy);
- the film in the camera (black-and-white film recalls both Second-World-War newsreels and early slapstick film);
- the camera angles and editing (whose effects I indicated in brief above);
- the music (a light-hearted French popular tune, added post-production and reinforcing the sense of an army still in civilian mode, is timed to reach its playful ending at the precise moment of surrender);
- the appeal to the viewer's knowledge of the comic stereotype of the gourmet Frenchman; and, finally:
- the extreme contraction of the scene, which leads the French army from the planning of its war strategy to defeat within a mere minute and a half.

The scene will, of course, have different effects on different national audiences, since it is only for a French audience that it represents a satirical affront to national pride. This is in keeping with Tournier's more extensive description of this period of the war; the satire is, however, likely to have had less bite in the 1990s than it did in the 1970s, when France's conduct in the war was more central to its national self-definition. The effect for German viewers may be more complex, given that the swift defeat of the French is attributable largely to the formidable military prowess of the armies of the Third Reich, a fact of which German viewers can scarcely be proud, making it a rather odd subject for comedy.

Whereas Tournier refers to his hero throughout as Tiffauges, the film script identifies him as 'Abel', and I use that name to distinguish the film character from his literary counterpart. A basic problem in any transfer from book to screen is point of view, since the camera cannot easily reproduce that sensation of being inside a character's head that characterizes much modern fiction. The problem is particularly acute in the case of *Le Roi des Aulnes*, where the hero's eccentric self-conception is central. Unable to give us access to Abel's thoughts, Schlöndorff establishes point of view by other means. The first of these—the use of a voice-over to narrate Abel's thoughts—may seem a feeble compromise, but Schlöndorff uses it sparingly to provide a link between otherwise disconnected episodes. Moreover, the distinctive voice of his lead actor, John Malkovich, carries the technique convincingly, at least in the original English version (his French and German dubbing doubles are less distinctive). The second method makes better use of the capabilities of cinema, using camera angles and physical action to establish Abel's view of the Third Reich as a view from below, the perspective of a powerless man on the powerful. On several occasions, Malkovich adopts a crouching or kneeling position in relation to more powerful figures: he crouches and then lies prostrate as he rolls out a red carpet for Goering; he bends low as he gingerly approaches Goering's pet lion and bows to Goering's guests when they applaud his daring; he kneels to polish Goering's car; and again to proffer a bowl of jewels to the seated Goering. Kneeling also puts him on a level with children, as we see at a passing-out parade where Abel kneels beside a protégé. The symbolic effect relies not just on the actor's pose and on Malkovich's position relative to others but also on the camera angle. In the first example, the camera shoots from below him on the hunting lodge steps and his employer, the Chief Forester, appears in shot above him. In the second the camera points past the cowering Abel to Goering's guests, standing upright behind him. In the third Malkovich has to raise himself to the level of the car window to see Goering seated inside. And so on. While this technique certainly evokes the extreme imbalances of power in a totalitarian society, it can only symbolize a point of view, not reproduce it. It can tell us that Abel 'looks up at' the Nazi élite from the bottom of the social hierarchy, but it cannot make us see Nazism as Tiffauges sees it in Tournier's novel, at first with a certain amount of repulsion and later with increasing fascination, but always in complex intellectual terms.

But before we step onto the slippery slope of Fidelity Criticism, let us interpret this apparent deficit more positively: rather than attempt to convey Tiffauges's complex intellectual fascination with Nazism, something his medium cannot readily do, Schlöndorff finds an approach that actively exploits the filmic medium, investigating Nazism's propagandist use of visual aesthetics. This takes two forms: he recreates on set the carefully choreographed mass ceremonies used to arouse positive national feelings and to bind the individual to the *Gemeinschaft* (community); and, modelling himself on Leni Riefenstahl's *Triumph des Willens* and *Olympia*, he recreates the cinematic means used to frame this pageantry in such a way as to maximize its political effect. Schlöndorff himself has called a sequence depicting a sports exhibition at the Napola, which draws attention to the strength and grace of the boys' bodies and celebrates their faultless teamwork, 'die Riefenstahl-Passage'.[18]

In this and another sequence, boys sing songs that were used to indoctrinate the young. The fact that Schlöndorff has his sound editor dub the sound of a boys' choir over the voices of his young actors, while allowing the viewer to believe that he or she is hearing the actual voices of the massed ranks of boys visible on screen, shows that Schlöndorff is not interested in a realist portrayal of life at the Napola (where not every boy would have sung in tune), but in a strictly controlled, aestheticized version. Agnieszka Holland's film *Hitlerjunge Salomon* which, like *Der Unhold*, is concerned with cross-border experiences and with the political training of the young, likewise uses a hyperrealist sound to recreate the emotional power of massed ranks singing (first at a communist, then at a Nazi school). Though she does not credit a particular choir, Holland has either selected her extras for their singing abilities or has used sound editing to improve both the acoustics and the quality of the voices.[19] Similarly, one has only to look at a photograph of the real-life 'Hitlerjunge Salomon' with his schoolmates at a Hitler Youth academy to see that the uniforms of the historical Hitler Youth were

[18] Volker Schlöndorff in conversation with Brigitte Desalm, 'Eine Sache des Instinkts', *Kölner Stadtanzeiger*, 13 Sept. 1996.

[19] Agnieszka Holland, *Hitlerjunge Salomon* (FRG, France, and Poland, 1990).

not always as smart, ironed, indeed 'uniform' as those that are looked after by a wardrobe-mistress:[20] in Holland's film and in many others, the image of the uniform owes more to the Nazis' own self-presentation (in ceremonies and in the official photographic record of those ceremonies), than to reality.

The danger of a copycat method is that it results in pastiche which, when used in relation to the Third Reich, is arguably not just an aesthetic shortcoming but also politically and morally suspect. Schlöndorff argues that only a view from within can show how Nazism was able to enthral so many,[21] and at the same time that implicit in his reuse of Riefenstahl's techniques is a critique of them: 'Ich wollte diese Bilder offensiv ausstellen, sie als Mythen behandeln und damit entmystifizieren' ('I wanted to display these images aggressively, to treat them as myths and so to demystify them').[22] It is difficult to see exactly how the film treats Nazi images as myth, given that it gives us no insight into how these images are constructed, unlike, say, Beyer's behind-the-scenes description of the Nazi rally, which shows exactly how much anxiety, discipline, and coercion goes into the synchronizing and choreographing of naturally disorderly human bodies. In the film *Mutters Courage*, Michael Verhoeven tells his audience directly that the Babelsberg studios at which the film is being made are tainted by their past associations with Nazism, thereby cautioning the viewer to be suspicious of cinema's manipulative powers.[23] Schlöndorff's film, too, was made partly at Babelsberg (indeed, Schlöndorff was running the studios at the time), but such defamiliarization would have been at odds with his chosen method of exposing Nazism from within its own horizons. In mitigation it can be said that Schlöndorff does break the Riefenstahl effect at least momentarily by having Malkovich act the clown in some of the sporting scenes. Besides, it can be argued that he works with the time-gap between Riefenstahl's films and his own: images of boys doing gym, however beautiful the boys and however beautifully shot the images, are no longer likely to inspire misty-eyed wonderment and national pride, but more likely a slight discomfort or distaste, so that an automatic distance arises between image and viewer.

As is often the case with literary adaptations for the cinema, the divergence between the source and its realization in film is particularly

[20] Sally Perel, *Ich war Hitlerjunge Salomon*, rev. edn (Munich: Heyne, 1993), 101.

[21] Volker Schlöndorff in conversation with Angie Dullinger, 'Vielleicht hat mich ja der Teufel geritten', *Abendzeitung* (Munich), 18 Sept. 1996.

[22] Volker Schlöndorff in conversation with Ralph Eue, 'Sind Sie ein Germane, Herr Schlöndorff?', *Tagesspiegel*, 12 Sept. 1996.

[23] Michael Verhoeven, *Mutters Courage* (FRG, Ireland, UK, and Austria, 1995).

apparent in the film's ending. In Tournier's novel, the denouement is preceded by a lengthy encounter between Tiffauges and a Jewish child, Éphraïm, who opens Tiffauges's eyes to the Holocaust. Far from showing remorse, Tiffauges is typical of a particular brand of literary hero who, in the words of Lorna Milne, ' "colonize[s]" historical events by collapsing the distance between history and their individual existence, reducing external phenomena to the status of peripheral occurrences that revolve around the centralizing consciousness of the protagonist, and whose only meaning is to mirror or to serve him'.[24] Though affected by what he hears, Tiffauges assimilates the Holocaust to his world view by interpreting it as confirmation of a system of mirroring to which he alone holds the key (rather than as an event with concrete social and political causes to which he has in some way contributed). Tournier maintains a distance from Tiffauges's egocentrism by having his narrator speak of 'la déduction tiffaugéenne des camps de la mort' ('the Tiffeaugean deduction of the death camps'; p. 477 (p. 306)) and it is therefore with a sense of Tiffauges's moral limitations that the reader experiences the novel's ambiguous final moments. While the half-blind Tiffauges is able, with Éphraïm on his shoulders acting as a guide, to evade capture by the Russian army, it is unclear whether either or both of them survive their passage through a marsh. A reference to alder trees recalls both Goethe's ballad 'Der Erlkönig' and an incident earlier in the novel in which the skeleton of an ancient German tribesman was discovered in just such a marsh and was christened 'Roi des Aulnes' because the skeleton of a child lay alongside it. It is therefore open to us whether we read the final scene as the ultimate expression of Tiffauges's *Erlkönig* persona, once more leading a child to its death (though in this case the waters will also swallow him, as they did the tribesman), or as a re-enactment of the novel's other foundational myth, the legend of St Christopher.

While Tournier leaves open the question of whether Tiffauges deserves the same redemption granted to St Christopher for his service in carrying the child Jesus, Schlöndorff and Carrière seem to resolve the ambiguity in favour of redemption, the logical consequence, one critic has suggested, of turning Tournier's sinister, self-aggrandizing Tiffauges into the more harmless simpleton Abel.[25] Abel's response to Éphraïm's (much curtailed) revelations is not to rearrange his philosophical system to

[24] Lorna Milne, 'Olfaction, Authority, and the Interpretation of History in Salman Rushdie's *Midnight's Children*, Patrick Süskind's *Das Parfum*, and Michel Tournier's *Le Roi des Aulnes*', *Symposium*, 53/1 (1999), 22–36 (31).

[25] Urs Jenny, 'Erlkönigs Wiederkehr', *Der Spiegel*, 2 Sept. 1996.

accommodate them, but to acknowledge the error of his ways—in a passage of voice-over in which a soft-spoken Malkovich invites our sympathy. This colours our reading of the final scene. While Schlöndorff attempts to preserve some of the ambiguity of the original (Abel never gets to the other side of the marsh, which stretches on towards the horizon as the credits roll, and Malkovich's voice-over breaks off mid-sentence), the film ends only once Abel has successfully negotiated a patch of deep water and the voice-over refers us explicitly to the legend of St Christopher, while suppressing the counter-narrative of the *Erlkönig*.

This is where the practitioner of Fidelity Criticism would stop, having compared novel and film and found the film wanting. But both endings are problematical in respect of their treatment of the Jewish child. In their evocations of the St Christopher legend, both author and film-maker equate Éphraïm and the Christ-child. This is typical of a tendency to Christianize the Holocaust by framing it within the narrative of Christian redemption that has been analysed amongst others by Niven.[26] That Tournier's text is written from within and for a Christian majority is clear from his comments in interview on why he chose the name 'Éphraïm': 'J'ai cherché un nom juif qui ne soit past trop commun. Je ne voulais pas l'appeler Jacob ni Abraham—des choses trop lourdes. Dans l'esprit des gens, des lecteurs ordinaires, Éphraïm, c'est joli, c'est très juif, mais cela ne signifie pas grand-chose' ('I was looking for a Jewish name that wasn't too common. I didn't want to call him Jacob or Abraham—anything too heavy. In people's minds, in the minds of ordinary readers, Ephraim is pretty, it's very Jewish, but it doesn't mean a great deal').[27] It is clear that, for Tournier, 'les lecteurs ordinaires', whose status as the norm is reinforced by their equation with the universalizing term 'les gens', are Christian. He shows no interest in what a Jewish reader (for whom the name Éphraïm is neither 'très juif' nor empty of meaning) would associate with this or other names. Given, however, that his novel explores the ways in which both individuals and cultures use legends and myths to construct personal and national identities, the non-Jewish French reader is at least encouraged to understand the Christian redemption narrative as one such myth, no more or less valid than, say, the folkloristic legend of the *Erlkönig*.

---

[26] Niven, *Facing the Nazi Past*, 16–19. A Jewish victim is the subject of a similar narrative of Christian redemption in Jan Hrebejk's film *Musíme si pomáhat* (Czech Republic, 2000).

[27] Michel Tournier in conversation with Cornelia Klettke, in Klettke, *Der Postmoderne Mythenroman Michel Tourniers am Beispiel des 'Roi des Aulnes'* (Bonn: Romanistischer Verlag, 1991), 285–308 (303).

Gender

Another contentious element of both works is gender. Tournier's novel is dominated by Tiffauges's aggressively male perspective. As well as rejecting what he sees as a female construction of virility designed to subjugate men (p. 19) and yearning nostalgically for the time before God created women (pp. 30, 112), Tiffauges relinquishes his passion for young girls after an accusation of rape, convincing himself that boys are superior (p. 174). His capture and imprisonment by Nazi forces is a passport to an exclusively male world that corresponds exactly to his masculinist philosophy: no women feature in the POW camp, he registers none at Goering's hunting lodge, and the only woman at the Napola, the matron, Frau Netta, has a conventional, mothering role. While Tournier clearly does not share Tiffauges's viewpoint uncritically, nor does he necessarily give us the tools with which to take it apart, tending to reproduce rather than deconstruct the patriarchal structures of Nazi society. For his part, Schlöndorff appears to give the matter no thought at all, creating no new or more complex roles for women, as one might expect given the time lag of twenty-five years—twenty-five busy years for feminism—between the publication of the book and its filming. Because film embodies characters in a way that written narrative, however detailed, cannot, we are more aware (and therefore potentially more critical) of the extreme masculinity of Abel's surroundings, especially at the Napola. At the same time, the camera is less selective than the pen and so cannot help but show us women, particularly in the party scenes at Goering's hunting lodge. The unarticulated experiences of these mute women may well arouse and frustrate the viewer's curiosity, an irritation absent from the novel, where the corresponding women are simply passed over in silence. One could justify this in terms of Tournier's and Schlöndorff's shared aim of giving a 'view from inside' Nazi Germany; equally, one could point out that inside Nazi Germany women constituted every second citizen and led active, visible, and complex lives, so that a 'view from inside' would have to take account of their experiences.

In comparison, Beyer's use, in roughly equal measure, of a male and a female narrative focalizer, rises above Nazi patriarchal bias, giving a prominent voice to the sex that was, in most public capacities, silenced under Nazism (at the same time as giving a voice to a child eclipsed by its dominating and historically prominent father). Even so, the more mobile, active role is, as I have shown, reserved for the man. Indeed

Beyer needs the older figure in his double-gendered adult/child pairing to be the man if he is to dispatch him to the interesting sound-centres of the Reich: even Beyer would not have stretched the already considerable implausibility of his plot to the point of inventing a female technician who manages to get herself posted successively to Alsace, the Russian front, a medical institute, and Hitler's bunker. Helga is, of course, by no means immobile, but while travel is an important feature of her privileged lifestyle, Beyer is more interested in the fact of this freedom to travel (between the family's various homes, in their father's sports car, by train and plane, and in chauffeur-driven comfort) than in the destinations, with which Helga barely engages. It might be argued, then, that while Beyer clearly has an interest in the experiences of the female half of Third Reich society, he chooses a narrative model which, though unrelated to Nazism, nevertheless replicates its gender imbalance. More positively, Ulrich Schönherr argues that Beyer gives the more moral voice in the text to the female character as a deliberate 'narrative counterweight to the barbarism of the male-dominated National Socialist culture' (p. 331).[28] This needs some qualification. There is a respectable feminist tradition that presents women as a force for moral resistance, by virtue not of their biological sex but of their marginal position in male-dominated societies. As a privileged member of the national élite, Helga does not quite fit this category, and Beyer accordingly demonstrates that she has a strong investment in the dominant ideology. At the same time, he demonstrates, particularly through the game 'Vater Mutter Kind' (pp. 60–1) and through the father's unequal treatment of Helga and Helmut ('der einzige Junge darf sowas. Wir anderen sind nur Mädchen'; 'Helmut can get away with murder, being the only boy. The rest of us are just girls'; p. 79 (p. 57)), that even privileged women occupy a secondary position within their own élite class. This gives Helga a vantage point from which to observe, with increasing clarity, the duplicities of her surroundings, reaching a climax when she reflects on her parents' propensity to lie (p. 207 (p. 156)). However, the scene in which she and another sister, mimicking a well-known act of Nazi brutality, force their younger siblings to clean the floor with toothbrushes (continuing even when the younger children become frightened), makes clear that the girls are not biologically disinclined towards aggression and domination: their society simply does not reserve this role for them in later life.

---

[28] Ulrich Schönherr, 'Topophony of Fascism: On Marcel Beyer's *The Karnau Tapes*', *Germanic Review*, 73 (1998), 328–48 (331).

Franco-German Perspectives

Finally, it is worth comparing Beyer and Tournier/Schlöndorff's interest in Franco-German relations in the context of the Third Reich. Confined in Beyer's novel to a single, but powerful episode, this interest informs a large part of Tournier's text. In his description of the *Entwelschung*, Beyer draws attention to a grave criminal injustice against the French now largely forgotten in Germany, perhaps because it pales into insignificance against the far larger crime of the Holocaust. Though he is drawn to the subject because of its association with sound rather than by a particular interest in Franco-German relations, the very studied, rhetorical style of the passage in question (pp. 79–83 (pp. 57–60)) betrays a clear moral indignation at this act of linguistic imperialism, an indignation that it is difficult to attribute to the opportunist Karnau, the nominal narrator of the scene. As critics have pointed out, the repeated use of passive forms ('Es wird gestrichen', 'Es wird geätzt', etc.) can be read as an expression of Karnau's inability to acknowledge his agency and therefore his responsibility for what he observes, but the very repetition of these formulae, combined with the recurring motif of the 'Grünstift' ('green pen', the bureaucratic tool for erasing French), the highly figurative use of language, and the studied accumulation of detail, seem calculated to arouse the reader's disgust at the inhumanity and stupidity of the campaign.[29]

Tournier's novel is, by his own account, informed by a deep affection for Germany,[30] and while it never lets the French reader forget the political realities of the Nazi era (and therefore the reasons for Germany's loss of sovereignty over East Prussia after 1945), the lovingly detailed descriptions of the East Prussian landscape are tinged with nostalgia for an irretrievably lost German cultural realm. Moreover, the choice of 1945 as the end-date automatically constructs a narrative of loss, whereas a plot that extended into post-war Poland could tell a story of renewal, diversification, and at least partial continuity. The novel as a whole warns against the dangers of romanticizing landscape (as Tiffauges does when he sees in East Prussia a substitute for his dream-land of Canada, yet fails to see the murderous social and political realities playing out around him), but the reader still engages in the nostalgia inasmuch as he or

---

[29] A possible intertext is the chapter 'Glaube, Liebe, Hoffnung' in Grass's *Die Blechtrommel*, particularly its final few pages, which express, in similarly stylized form, a deep anger at the German people's susceptibility to Nazism.

[30] See Michel Tournier, *Le Vent Paraclet* (Paris: Gallimard, 1977), in which he looks back on his early writing career (pp. 117–18).

she shares Tiffauges's viewpoint. In the French context, such nostalgia is at least politically harmless; in the German context it is associated with the construction of Germans as victims. Perhaps in response to this danger, Schlöndorff's film is rather less indulgent in its presentation of the East Prussian landscape than Tournier's novel. Though he has chosen to film in locations of great natural beauty, there are few shots of the landscape that are not contextualized by the presence, action, and dialogue of the characters. In one scene Abel and the Chief Forester ride onto a promontory overlooking a lake, on the far side of which stands a magnificent medieval castle. While the camera placement is chosen to show the castle to best effect, the view is accompanied by the Chief Forester's explanations of the castle's function as a school for the new German élite. The Chief Forester's optimism for Germany's future collides with the viewer's historical hindsight, making the castle, as framed by the camera, morally tainted and politically doomed.

There will be more to say on the subject of Tournier's French–German narrative axis in the last section of the chapter, in which I analyse the treatment of the English, French, and German languages in Tournier's novel and Schlöndorff's film. This more general discussion requires a short excursus on multilingualism and the Third Reich in literature and film.

Language, Film, and the Third Reich

Since narratives about the National Socialist territorial expansion and its culmination in war and holocaust are by definition international, involving confrontations between different language communities, any film director is faced with the problem of how to represent this linguistic diversity on screen. Multilingualism poses less of a problem for literature, which is, at least in the Western tradition, an almost exclusively mono-lingual discursive form. The convention by which an author uses his or her own language to record the speech and thought of other language communities has been internalized to the point where it is not felt to be artificial. In film, the twin elements of sound and performance make it much more difficult to pass off as natural the dominance of a single authorial language in a cross-cultural storyline. The film *Charlotte Gray*, based on the novel of the same name by Sebastian Faulks and set during the Second World War, shows what happens when a director attempts a straightforward transfer from book to screen without taking account of the constraints of each genre.[31] In keeping with Faulks's novel, the

---

[31] Gillian Armstrong, *Charlotte Gray* (FRG, UK, and Australia, 2001).

heroine, played by Cate Blanchett, speaks Scottish English, yet for long stretches of the narrative the action requires that she speak French; indeed, it is the unusually high standard of her spoken French that fits her for work as an undercover agent in the Resistance. In the monolingual novel this poses no problem and the linguistic transitions are barely marked; the monolingual filming is less successful. Blanchett continues in the 'French' scenes to speak Scottish English (if a little unevenly) and the changed linguistic situation is marked by the heavy French accents and occasional French interjections of other characters. The effect is unintentionally comic.

It is possible that as cross-cultural experiences become increasingly mainstream the plundering of literature for screenplay material will become more problematic. It is difficult to imagine, for instance, how a novel like Stevie Davies's 2001 novel *The Element of Water*, whose theme is British–German (more specifically Welsh–German) cross-cultural experience in the immediate aftermath of the Third Reich, could be transferred to the screen without falling into the same trap as *Charlotte Gray*, particularly since the awkwardness of the cross-cultural encounters in *Charlotte Gray* may have less to do with the artificiality *per se* of monolingualism than with the particular pairing Scottish English/French-accented English, which has been used too infrequently to have become unremarkable. The no less artificial pairing of officer's English/German-accented English, which quickly established itself as a norm in the popular genre of British and American Second World War films, now barely registers as artificial even if the actors are notionally communicating in German. The 1951 film *The Desert Fox*, in which most of the American and British cast use their own accents to play German characters, demonstrates that the device was not a given, but had first to be established as a convention.[32] This was achieved partly by using German actors to play German characters, but by the 1990s the convention was sufficiently anchored in the imagination of film audiences for Steven Spielberg to require that British actors, in their roles as Germans in *Schindler's List*, adopt a German-flavoured accent that refers back to earlier film portrayals rather than to the real-life pronunciation of Germans speaking English.

Partly thanks to this device, by which accents act as a marker of nationality and therefore of 'side' in the War, US and British films about the war years of the Third Reich (the years 1933–9 rarely feature) have remained almost exclusively monolingual, though by convention non-essential background speech, and particularly orders, are spoken

---

[32] The character of Hitler is the single exception, but even his, rather shaky, German accent has not yet taken on the standardized form that developed in later decades.

in German, to give a flavour of foreignness and therefore antagonism. In theory, German and Austrian films made about the Third Reich face the same language problem as English-language films, but in reverse. German characters present no problem, but how to deal with the English, American, French, Polish, Russian, Czech, Hungarian, Yugoslav, Greek, or Italian characters? And how to perform the experience of Central Europe's Yiddish-speakers?

Some films avoid the problem by focusing on all-German situations. The choice to stay in Germany is inevitably a choice in favour of the majority 'perpetrator' perspective, since displacement is central to the victim perspective; nevertheless the experience of the majority is a legitimate concern of film-makers, and a monoglot and monocultural focus is only questionable if it forms part of a conservative strategy of 'normalization' that factors out altogether the displacement of victims from Germany and Nazi Germany's many and various crimes against non-German-speakers. This is arguably the case in Gordian Maugg's *Der olympische Sommer*, in which the protagonist not only misses out on the international showcase for Nazism that was the Berlin Olympic Games because a love affair distracts him but is also spared witnessing the escalation of anti-Semitism and the ravages of the Second World War by virtue of being imprisoned, unfairly, from 1937 until his death in 1944.[33] The hero's hibernation through the major historical events of the twentieth century is so grotesquely unlikely that it may provoke the viewer into supplying the missing history; on the other hand the film can be read conservatively, as evidence that it was possible to live an unpoliticized life under Nazism and that Germans could themselves be victims of the Nazi regime.

Other films adopt an unapologetically monolingual approach to cross-cultural experience. Verhoeven's *Mutters Courage*, set amongst Hungarian Jews and their mostly Hungarian captors, is spoken entirely in German. Strictly speaking, *Mutters Courage* is not monolingual because, in an increasingly common bid to maximize international marketability, Verhoeven casts a British actress, Pauline Collins, in the lead, and she and some of the other actors, including some German actors, perform their parts in English. However, Verhoeven uses post-production dubbing to even out the language differences, which are, of course, at cross-purposes with the German–Hungarian narrative.[34]

[33] Gordian Maugg, *Der olympische Sommer* (FRG, 1993).
[34] In his 1981 film *Lili Marleen*, which concerns the career of a singer during the Nazi era, Rainer Werner Fassbinder deliberately plays with dubbing practices to create a distancing effect. Robert and Carol Reimer note that the film 'was originally shot in English, then poorly dubbed into German

Though rarely used, a naturalistic approach involving multiple languages works best where language is thematized, as it is in Rolf Schübel's *Das Heimweh des Walerjan Wróbel*.[35] Framed in conventional manner by courtroom and custody scenes, the main body of the film traces a teenager's journey from his home village in Poland to a farm in North Germany where he is to provide forced labour, and documents his resulting loneliness and depression, which culminate in his setting light to a barn in the hope of being repatriated. After being lost in the justice system for some time, Wróbel's case is eventually decided according to a blatantly ideological interpretation of the statutes, and he is sentenced to death. Based on a true story, *Walerjan Wróbel* records injustices so staggering that it can barely help but be didactic (and accordingly features regularly in educational programmes), but it is saved from crude didacticism by an intelligent exploration of the relationship between language and power. This justifies its analysis before I return to *Der Unhold*.

Artur Pontek, the lead actor, speaks his part mostly in his native Polish but also, where the plot requires it, in heavily accented German, an authentic expression of his limited linguistic abilities. Wróbel's vulnerable position as a slave worker in a culture that considers Poles to have forfeited their basic rights because of their racial inferiority is skilfully encoded in the alternating use of German and Polish. Before he leaves home, his father recommends that he memorize the German words 'Arbeit' and 'Jawohl', assuming that the tactical use of the dominant language to express compliance will keep the boy from harm. On arrival in Germany, Wróbel duly adopts this submissive linguistic strategy, repeating words spoken to him and responding 'Jawohl' even to statements that he has not understood. The gentle humour of this stock situation, in which a foreigner flounders amiably in an unfamiliar language environment, may be intended to lull the viewer into a sense that Wróbel's lack of competence in German is harmless. If so, this throws subsequent developments into sharp relief. Without the chance to communicate with his German hosts, a farming family who address only blunt orders to him, Wróbel is prevented both from quelling his chronic homesickness and from developing more sophisticated language strategies, such as might give him some control, however limited, over his situation. His crude litany 'Ich krank, ich Polen' ('I ill, I Poland') communicates nothing of his unhappiness to his hosts, who are in any case little inclined to investigate its meaning, and after expressing his homesickness through the only

and released in English-speaking countries with the German voice track and subtitles' (Reimer and Reimer, *Nazi Retro-Film*, 36).

[35] Rolf Schübel, *Das Heimweh des Walerjan Wróbel* (FRG, 1991).

route left open to him, that of non-verbal communication (fire), he finds himself in police custody, subject to an authority that expresses itself in a register of German even less accessible to him than the colloquial German of the farming family. The detective's question 'Wer hat dich angestiftet?' ('Who put you up to it?') meets with blank incomprehension. During a subsequent interrogation the presence of an interpreter affords Wróbel a brief opportunity to express himself frankly in Polish, but his request to return to Poland elicits only laughter. The naïvety of his request is linguistically constructed, at least in part: without access to the German language he has no way of comprehending Nazi racial and labour policy and so no way of planning realistic survival strategies in a hostile ideological environment.

Schübel then shows Wróbel standing semi-naked in a hospital room while a German doctor dictates his case notes to a secretary. The doctor does not address the boy, and Pontek's blank, distracted gaze speaks eloquently of his (and therefore also his character's) incomprehension (Fig. 6). The German viewer, obliged by the language gap to occupy the dominant, knowing position, understands that the doctor is declaring him an 'Osttyp' ('Eastern racial type'), a diagnosis that absolves the State of the necessity to send him to a normal prison and permits his incarceration in a concentration camp. Once there, he learns that the

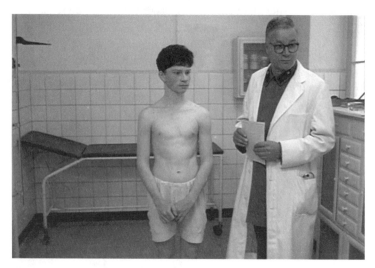

Fig. 6. In Rolf Schübel's *Das Heimweh des Walerjan Wróbel*, a doctor dictates details of Wróbel's 'racial' characteristics in German, a language that neither his patient nor the actor playing him understands

strategy of linguistic compliance advocated by his father now takes a more drastic form: a fellow Pole advises him to master quickly the knack of reeling off his prison number in flawless and unfaltering German, or to fear summary execution. Thus, he can save his life only at the price of losing his personal and national identity. When he is finally returned to the judicial process, a court official asks in German whether Wróbel wants the charge against him read out, and, receiving no answer, records in his notes that the accused declined to have the charge read. As in the scene with the doctor, the dictatorship does not consider it necessary that Wróbel understand the processes acting upon him. Finally, Schübel has the full judgment read out in a lengthy voice-over which, though visually and aurally undramatic, nevertheless dramatically expresses how inaccessible to Wróbel is the language in which the decision about his life is taken.

A monolingual German performance that evened out the linguistic differences in favour of German (however sympathetic to the plight of the young Pole) would re-enact the linguistic domination over the Poles to which the film, as it stands, eloquently testifies. At the same time, Schübel's choice of a dual-language, part-subtitled model not only limits the film's marketability within the German-speaking countries, it also effectively excludes it from the wider international market: the confrontation between the two language communities would be largely lost if viewed with subtitles by an audience with no knowledge of either German or Polish, and entirely obliterated in a monolingual dubbing of the material. Given that the film's bilingualism is simultaneously an audience-loser and integral to its effects, *Walerjan Wróbel* represents a rare triumph of artistic integrity over the commercial interests of cinema. This becomes doubly clear if one considers that Schübel's approach is diametrically opposed to that of Czech director Jan Sverák in his film *Tmavomodrý svet* (*Dark Blue World*), which depicts the contribution of Czech pilots to the RAF during the Second World War.[36] Where Sverák takes advantage of a bilingual plot to cast well-known actors from the more powerful English-language film culture, thereby broadening his film's market appeal, Schübel courageously draws his lead actor from an even more marginal film culture than Germany's, that of Poland.[37]

---

[36] Jan Sverák, *Tmavomodrý svet* (Czech Republic, UK, FRG, Denmark, and Italy, 2001).

[37] This is not to imply that Sverák's motives are baldly commercial: his earlier film *Kolja* (Czech Republic, 1996) is acted in Czech and Russian, a language pair which, like that in *Walerjan Wróbel*, embodies an uneven power relationship (the Czech Republic was occupied by Soviet forces from 1968 until 1989), and shows a genuine interest in cross-cultural relations. He cannot be blamed for the fact that no such acute imbalance of power existed between Britain and Czechoslovakia in 1940, making the alternation of Czech and English within the later film unremarkable.

In retrospect, this courage may have seemed like foolhardiness, and Schübel abandoned his experiments in multilingual narrative before his next, blatantly commercial, film about the Third Reich, *Gloomy Sunday. Ein Lied von Liebe und Tod*.[38] Though set in Hungary before and during the Nazi occupation, no Hungarian is spoken. The blanket use of German effaces all linguistic boundaries and with them all linguistic power relations.

By comparison, the use of languages in *Der Unhold* may seem uninteresting: Tournier's monolingual French novel is filmed monolingually in English, confirming (as if confirmation were needed) the dominance of English in First World cinema, and then dubbed monolingually into German and French respectively. Nevertheless, it should be clear from the foregoing discussions that Schlöndorff's decision to make a monolingual film about a cross-cultural experience during the Third Reich is not a neutral one. The casting of a lead actor who stands outside the French–German axis of the narrative also repays analysis.

Schlöndorff took the commercial decision to cast a big-name Hollywood actor in the lead; Malkovich was his second choice, after Gérard Depardieu turned down the part. I see three potential difficulties with the choice of a non-German lead to perform a German screenplay: first, the script must be translated, with a possible loss of nuance; secondly, the rest of the cast must either perform in the same language as the lead, even if it is not their own, or else multiple languages must be used on set and evened out through post-production dubbing, either of which solutions can have negative consequences for the acting; and thirdly, the performance must be dubbed back into German for the 'home' audience, with the associated loss of realism, as the voices become disconnected from their on-screen bodies. None of these difficulties is, however, insurmountable. Most screen dialogue is sufficiently straightforward as to run little risk of stylistic flattening by clumsy translators. The fact that Schlöndorff was able to use a translation agency, A. Whitelaw & Associates, rather than a literary translator, is indicative of this.[39] Schlöndorff and his casting director had little difficulty finding French and German actors who could perform their parts in accented but acceptable English (a practice that

---

[38] Rolf Schübel, *Gloomy Sunday. Ein Lied von Liebe und Tod* (FRG and Hungary, 1999).

[39] An extreme example of the ready translatability of screenplays is the script of *Heaven* (Germany, Italy, USA, France and UK, 2002), directed by Tom Tykwer following the death of its original director. A *Guardian* critic reports that the script was 'translated [. . .] from Polish into French by some co-producers, then into English by other co-producers, then into German by Tykwer himself, then back into English, from which Tykwer and producer Anthony Minghella drafted the final version. In gibberish' (Peter Bradshaw, 'Wet Blanchett', *Guardian*, 9 Aug. 2002). Bradshaw might have added that the English was part-translated into Italian before filming.

fits the conventions of English-language film). Finally, the 'disembodied' quality of dubbed voices, already partially mitigated by improvements in dubbing technology, is in any case culturally relative: though an irritant to viewers in the English-language market, for whom real-language film is the norm, it is barely experienced as artificial by German-language viewers, for whom dubbed film is the norm.

Where the choice of Malkovich does become problematical is in the representation of the transition from French to German linguistic space. In Tournier's novel, this transition is principally a psychological experience: having been rejected, so he believes, by France, Tiffauges sees in East Prussia a fulfilment of his childhood dream to live as a hunter in a wild, wooded landscape. The need to learn German in order to establish himself in this landscape is twice briefly mentioned, but the first real moment of linguistic confrontation in the novel's dialogue, when Tiffauges meets Goering's Chief Forester, is not marked as such: the Forester's words 'silently' metamorphose into French on the page, and Tiffauges is able to converse with him more or less normally. This monolingual approach is adopted for the remainder of the novel, although a liberal sprinkling of German proper names gives a flavour of the setting. The presence of a Polish-speaking minority in East Prussia is given no linguistic expression, though its existence is acknowledged in a single passing mention that hints, as I suggest below, at connections between language and power (p. 380 (p. 246)).

Despite the absence of real confrontation between the French and German languages in the text, Tournier is concerned, at an abstract level, with what speaking German means to Tiffauges. Twice he suggests that the use of a non-native language keeps Tiffauges at a distance from the behaviour he encounters. The narrator comments on Goering's extravagant entertainments: 'Cette exhibition eût été insupportable au Français, si la langue allemande n'avait dressé entre ces hommes et lui un écran translucide, mais non transparant, qui amortissait leur grossièreté' ('This exhibition would have been unbearable for the Frenchman if the German language had not interposed between him and the rest a sort of translucid but not transparent screen, which took the edge off their grossness'; pp. 271–2 (p. 177)). In this way, Tournier uses the act of speaking a foreign language, absent in practice from his text, to justify his protagonist's lack of moral outrage at the excesses of the Nazi élite. His concern, however, is arguably less with the real experience of language acquisition than with the exigencies of his plot model: if Tiffauges is to continue to spy on the Nazi world for the reader, then it is important to delay his awakening to the evil around him for as long as possible.

No criticism of Tournier is intended here. Because French prisoners of war, unlike the Polish slave labourers depicted in *Walerjan Wróbel*, were classed as enemies of the Reich within the framework of the normal rules of war, and not as racial inferiors within the framework of a murderously racist ideology, their relations with their German captors rarely reached the same extremes of power and powerlessness (some were, for instance, allowed a limited freedom of movement, as Tiffauges is) and for this reason it is perhaps inevitable that there is less to say about language and power in the French–German context than in the Polish–German. Moreover, if he has limited interest in the practical difficulties of being uprooted to another language community, Tournier is nevertheless centrally concerned with uprooting his French readers and placing them in an alien German cultural space. This is a complex process, which can only be outlined here. On the one hand, a wealth of encyclopaedic detail makes the French reader feel that he or she has been transported into German (and specifically Nazi) culture and is seeing it from the inside. At the same time, of course, Germany is not entirely unknown to Tournier's readers, and he deliberately draws on a French stereotype of Germany as the land of romantic landscapes, fairy tales, and legends. To an extent the novel indulges that stereotype, but by associating myth-making and a rootedness in landscape with Nazism, it also discredits it. Moreover, by involving a Frenchman, however atypical, in Nazi practices and malpractices, Tournier brings the evils of Nazism uncomfortably close to home, implicating the French reader, who is invited to question how far the French are susceptible to the power of myths and aesthetics.

Schlöndorff follows Tournier's monolingual approach, with slight variations. In keeping with cinematic convention, any speech associated with the National Socialist characters but not vital to the plot—orders, songs, newsreel broadcasts—remains in the original German. In a scene in the POW camp, Abel whispers to his pigeons in German and a fellow prisoner remarks on his linguistic efforts: 'You speak German? You think they're gonna win the war?', to which Abel replies 'Natürlich!'. In the German dubbed version, of course, this is impossible to reproduce (because the 'Frenchman' Malkovich is already speaking German), so the line is replaced by: 'Warum fütterst du die Brieftauben durch? Glaubst du, sie finden nach Frankreich zurück?' ('Why are you feeding the carrier pigeons? Do you think they are going to find their way back to France?'). In the English and French versions, at least, the snippet of German is enough to suggest that Abel is adapting linguistically to his new environment (even if, for the purposes of the film, he continues to speak English or French respectively in all situations).

The draft screenplay mentioned earlier suggests that Schlöndorff, possibly with Depardieu in mind, planned to use more than one language in the film and to suggest in real, not just in abstract terms, the transition from French to German. Since the screenplay reportedly went through twenty versions,[40] it is impossible to know which this particular one represents, but there are significant discrepancies between the screenplay and the finished performance.

The screenplay stipulates that the Chief Forester 'demands sternly in German' to know what Tiffauges is doing in the cabin where they meet. This suggests that Tiffauges had previously spoken something other than German, and that German is spoken now for the first time. Furthermore, 'Abel speaks with difficulty, groping for words' and is confused by the word 'poacher': 'He doesn't seem to know the German word'. He is forced to use the rudimentary syntax of a language-learner—'Me driver!'—and struggles to find the German word for 'blind'.[41] In the filmed version, in which all the actors perform in English, these brief instances of hesitation and misunderstanding have to disappear, although the director apparently forgets to delete the difficulty over the word 'blind', leaving the viewer baffled as to why Malkovich is unable to recall the word in his own language. Thus, while the screenplay contains indications that Schlöndorff had at least a passing interest in portraying the experience of crossing linguistic boundaries, this comes to little in the filmed and dubbed versions. Whatever the reason for this slippage between written screenplay and on-screen performance, it is clear that the choice of an English-speaking actor makes a nonsense of any attempt to portray the transition from French to German linguistic space.

A special case is that of the Jewish boy Éphraïm. Tournier is careful to mark him out as multilingual: 'Il s'exprimait dans un yiddish melé de mots hébreux, lituaniens et polonais dont Tiffauges ne comprenait que les éléments allemandes. Mais ils disposaient pour se comprendre d'un temps indéterminé et d'une inépuisable patience' ('He spoke in Yiddish mixed with words of Hebrew, Lithuanian and Polish: Tiffauges could understand only those of German origin. But they had unlimited time and inexhaustible patience for getting to understand one another'; p. 471 (p. 302)). That Tiffauges, despite his linguistic limitations, is then able to understand, with no evident struggle, complex stories about Auschwitz is less than likely, but this very implausibility suggests that the boy serves some special purpose here. The fact that he speaks at

---

[40] Ralph Eue, 'Das Spiel mit dem Feuer', *Tagesspiegel*, 25 Aug. 1996.
[41] Volker Schlöndorff and Jean-Claude Carrière, 'The Ogre', unpublished screenplay, pp. 42–3.

least four languages *other* than German points up the sudden realization with which Tiffauges is confronted: that a world exists beyond that constructed and projected by the Germans through the medium of their own language. Whereas earlier he had been contemptuous of two Slav-speaking peasants for pretending not to speak German (a tactic of linguistic subversion that fails to save their children from the *Erlkönig*'s clutches), he is now in a situation in which German has no power. The child's multilingual abilities, which may allude to the tradition of Jews as gifted translators, later save Abel's life: Russian soldiers allow them to pass unscathed through the battle-line because Éphraïm shouts to them in their own language that Abel is a French prisoner of war. While in the novel Tournier can get away with positing a linguistic diversity of which he is not required to offer proof, in the spoken medium of film performance this is a more difficult trick to pull off and Schlöndorff and Carrière are obliged to compromise. In the screenplay, the solution is that 'The child speaks in German and Yiddish',[42] though no decision has been taken at this point as to which words should be spoken in which language. In the filmed version, German and Yiddish become English and Yiddish, although the acting is not entirely coherent, since the child veers between sound and faltering English. The child, played by a Russian actor, also speaks a series of lines in Russian. In both novel and film, then, the ability to communicate beyond one's own native tongue is given a redemptive, almost magical quality, one which holds up a critical mirror to Abel's merely conformist acquisition of German. However, this last meaning may be less accessible to a German viewer, who, as I have shown, is not alerted to the fact that Abel is learning German.

What Schlöndorff cannot hope to reproduce is Tournier's national perspective: his attempt to address France's relationship with Germany from a French point of view. Of course, one could argue that since Schlöndorff's German viewers in the 1990s experienced the narrative at considerable distance from the historical events it depicts, they underwent an equivalent process of displacement into an unfamiliar realm. Nevertheless, the French view of Nazi Germany as a land of sinister romanticism and beautiful but gruesome fairy tale may have made little sense to a German audience schooled in straightforward condemnation of the Third Reich. Schlöndorff himself adduced this as one of the reasons why the film had so little success in Germany (only 162,000 viewers had seen the film in Germany three months after its release, as against the million anticipated

---

[42] Schlöndorff and Carrière, 'The Ogre', p. 97.

by Schlöndorff).[43] It may be that the attempt to produce internationally oriented cinema simply leads to a confusion of meanings.

Conclusion

Recent years have produced other culturally hybrid film adaptations of literary fictions about the Third Reich in which, in contrast to *Der Unhold*, the source text is German but almost every other aspect is not. The 1999 film *Jakob the Liar*, based on Jurek Becker's 1969 novel *Jakob der Lügner*, was directed by Hungarian-born Frenchman Peter Kassovitz, in a French, Hungarian, and American co-production, with American actor Robin Williams in the lead and other cast members drawn from England, Germany, and Hungary.[44] Kassovitz's son Mathieu starred in another such hybrid, *Amen*, adapted from Rolf Hochhuth's 1963 play *Der Stellvertreter*.[45] This French, German, and Romanian co-production was directed by Greek film-maker Costa-Gavras, co-scripted by Costa-Gavras and Frenchman Jean-Claude Grumberg and performed in French and English by a French, German, and Romanian cast. In line with my approach to *Der Unhold*, the student of such film adaptations should not ask 'Which elements of the literary source have been lost in the transfer to film?' (a question that locks one into the value judgements of Fidelity Criticism), but rather 'Why does the German source material appeal to non-German film-makers producing films for an international market several decades after the source was written?' and 'What happens to the German narrative once taken out of its German context?' Germany and Austria have never 'owned' the subject of the Third Reich in the way that they own purely domestic events; however, until recently German-language fiction about the Third Reich was, with rare exceptions, filmed by German-speaking directors. Taken together with Anthony Minghella's so far unrealized plans to film Schlink's *Der Vorleser*, Kassovitz's and Costa-Gavras's films suggest that German and Austrian writers' take on their own past is now considered international property.

Finally, the partial use of Eastern European locations, cast, and crew in *Jakob the Liar*, *Amen*, and *Der Unhold* (as well as in other Third Reich films such as Steven Spielberg's *Schindler's List* and Werner Herzog's

---

[43] Hanns-Georg Rodek, 'Gebt Schlöndorff sein Lächeln zurück! 500 Nachwuchskritiker zum *Unhold*', *Die Welt*, 18 Jan. 1997. The Lumière database confirms the final statistic for 1996 as 163,877. Almost as many cinemagoers saw it in France that year (120,006), but only 852 in Austria.

[44] Peter Kassovitz, *Jakob the Liar* (France, Hungary, and USA, 1999).

[45] Costa-Gavras, *Amen* (France, FRG, and Romania, 2002).

Invincible) is indicative both of the competitive price of Eastern European labour in the post-communist years and of the relative abundance, in Eastern Europe, of unspoilt heritage sites that can serve as historically accurate and visually appealing backdrops for films set in the Nazi era. In Schlöndorff's case this produces an interesting irony, since he uses young Polish extras for the group scenes involving the Napola boys, filmed at Malbork. While in the film dialogue the Nazi doctor Blättchen preaches the need for recruits with Aryan characteristics, the film's casting director fills the roles of those recruits with Polish nationals who would, fifty years previously, have been the objects of these racial politics. A deliberately defamiliarizing approach such as is practised by Verhoeven would have allowed Schlöndorff to let the audience in on this irony. As it is, the film suppresses the Polish nationality of the extras, who appear disguised and silenced, an unintended performance of an equivalent suppression in Tournier's novel, which, in its construction of a French–German narrative axis, overlooks the experience of the Polish minority living in East Prussia before 1945 and of the Polish majority that settled the region after 1945. It would be easy to construct other parallels, with the silencing of the French in the *Entwelschung* campaign, for instance, and with Karnau's fantastical plan to operate on the voice boxes of the defeated peoples of Eastern Europe so as to make them forget their native tongues and emit only German sounds. However, before we accuse the unfailingly liberal Schlöndorff of linguistic imperialism, we should at least listen to the voices of his 'victims': interviewed on set by a journalist, the Polish extras spoke of the fun they were having and of the welcome opportunity to earn pocket money.[46] In recalling the totalitarian attitudes towards language that were explored by Beyer, my intention is not to tar Schlöndorff with the same fascist brush but to make the point that language use in film about the Third Reich is a value-laden, political choice, not a neutral or background feature.

---

[46] Katarzyna Bijas, 'Den Jungs von damals hat das auch gefallen', *Rheinischer Merkur*, 29 Mar. 1996.

5 Memorial Landscapes
Mauthausen, Ebensee, and Christoph Ransmayr's *Morbus Kitahara*

This chapter returns to the literal roots of Nora's term *lieu de mémoire*, that is, to the ways in which memory attaches itself to place. National Socialist crimes have, of course, always been associated with place names and remembered *in situ*, but over the last twenty years German and Austrian memory has been increasingly dispersed, with memorial activity moving outwards from the sites of major crimes to the sites of relatively lesser crimes, from the mostly isolated sites of SS torture and murder to the city-centre sites of Gestapo torture and murder, from sites of execution to sites of judicial or bureaucratic support for execution, from the confines of the concentration camps to the etiolated routes of the death marches, from the centralized prison camps at which forced labourers slept to the scattered industrial sites at which they worked, and, finally, from the sites where victims died together in their hundreds and their thousands to the infinitely more scattered sites at which, before the crimes began, they lived, worked, and studied. Terms such as 'topography of terror' and 'memorial landscapes', Brian Ladd's 'ghosts of Berlin' and Andreas Huyssen's 'urban palimpsests' all express this shift towards a more catholic classification of the sites of memory.

The opposition between the centralization and dispersal of memory plays a role in my case study of two memorial sites, the former concentration camps of Mauthausen and Ebensee. Their Austrian location makes it possible to apply and evaluate techniques developed in studies of German memorial sites, notably by Niven and by James Young,[1] without simply duplicating their analysis, and also to bring into focus some of the specifics of Austrian memorial culture. Because it is run by the Austrian Bundesministerium für Inneres (Ministry of the Interior), with all the bureaucratic rigour of a civil-service portfolio, Mauthausen's history as a memorial is uniquely well archived. Nevertheless, a study that focused exclusively on Mauthausen would reinforce the artificially centralized model of commemoration adopted by the Austrian state after 1945, in unthinking imitation of the camp system, under which

---

[1] James E. Young, *The Texture of Memory: Holocaust Memorials and Meaning* (New Haven and London: Yale University Press, 1993).

Mauthausen was the 'mother camp' to all other camps on Austrian soil. In making at least some room for Ebensee in the limited space available, I acknowledge the tensions between state and local memory.

Although Mauthausen and Ebensee provided the models for a key locale in Christoph Ransmayr's 1995 novel *Morbus Kitahara*, which is analysed in the second half of the chapter,[2] my intention is not to offer a naïvely literal presentation of the real camps behind Ransmayr's fictional versions: that would make little sense as an approach to *Morbus Kitahara*, which actively discourages the reader from viewing the fictional world as a replica of a specific historical or geographical reality. Rather, the novel is considered here because it mounts a critique of the culture of commemoration that is the broader topic of the chapter and because it shows a concern with the way in which historical trauma leaves traces in the landscape. The novel's fanciful reinterpretation of the Allied occupation after 1945 also means that it is not 'about' the Third Reich in a conventional sense. It therefore helps counter the mechanism of self-selection that operates in studies like this, with their tendency to analyse only works in which the Third Reich is the principal focus.

Mauthausen

Studies of memorial sites take broadly similar approaches: most are researched through a combination of fieldwork and archival work; most combine a history of the genesis and development of the memorial site, including any public debates that accompanied it, with a critical reading of the curated space and its artefacts. The dimension of social practice (visitor behaviour, the enactment of ceremonies at the site, etc.) has received less attention, and it would require a social studies training to undertake a systematic study. The following model analysis identifies some of the critical and evaluative issues at stake.

The KZ-Gedenkstätte Mauthausen, or Mauthausen Memorial as it styles itself in English, was established in 1949 and comprises the physical remains of Mauthausen concentration camp—including a number of camp buildings and the quarry in which inmates worked—burial grounds, memorials, exhibitions, and, since 2003, a Visitors' Centre.[3]

---

[2] Christoph Ransmayr, *Morbus Kitahara* (Frankfurt/Main: Fischer, 1995), *The Dog King*, trans. John E. Woods (London: Chatto and Windus, 1997). Page references to the German and English editions appear in brackets in the text.

[3] See http://www.mauthausen-memorial.gv.at/.

Aware that an exhaustive history of the Memorial is awaiting publication as I write,[4] I confine myself here to illustrating how such a historical narrative might be constructed from different primary sources, and what it achieves. In studies of memorial sites, historical narrative is most often used to identify changing attitudes towards commemoration of the Third Reich under different post-war regimes (communist or democratic, conservative or liberal), and in particular to tease out Cold War and post-Cold War discourses about the past. This is a particularly fruitful approach to Mauthausen because its role as a state memorial makes it an important locus of diplomacy.

For instance, Austrian government files from 1964–5 show that permission for what is today known as the 'GDR monument' was granted only because the East German survivors' organization was responsible for it, not the East German state, which Austria still refused to acknowledge even fifteen years after the country had constituted itself. Accordingly, government memoranda speak of the 'sogenannte DDR' (the 'so-called GDR'), and a draft letter that omits the epithet is duly corrected; a press article about the negotiations refers to the GDR as the 'deutsche Sowjetzone' ('German Soviet Zone').[5] Nervous that the GDR would use the monument and its unveiling to force acknowledgement of its statehood, the Austrian government refused to allow any national emblems on the monument and banned the hoisting of the GDR flag at the unveiling ceremony. In 1970 the government also appears to have made difficulties over the granting of visas to the GDR delegates, insisting that different men came each year, even though there were only seventy survivors from which a delegation could be formed.[6] Yet in 1955 the Austrian state had marked the withdrawal of Soviet troops by erecting a monument to Soviet POWs at Mauthausen and in 1963 representatives from the Ministry of the Interior and the Ministry of Defence attended the unveiling of a Soviet memorial. This suggests that Austrian attitudes towards the communist states were not of a piece but determined by diplomatic expediency.

Not surprisingly, the US defined itself, in memorial matters as in others, in opposition to the whole of the Eastern Bloc. In 1965, a Ministry of the Interior memorandum reported on US negotiations to erect

[4] Bertrand Perz, *Die KZ-Gedenkstätte Mauthausen 1945 bis zur Gegenwart* (Innsbruck: Studienverlag, 2006). Like Perz I draw partly on documents held in the Archiv der KZ-Gedenkstätte Mauthausen at the Bundesministerium für Inneres in Vienna, hereafter referred to in the text as the Mauthausen Archive. Where archived documents are explicitly cited a reference to the relevant file is given, in the form MA V/1/98.

[5] MA V/1/102/1; Anon., 'Manöver um Mauthausen-Opfer. Sowjetzone will durch KZ-Mahnmal Anerkennung erreichen', *Die Presse*, 27 Jan. 1965.

[6] MA V/1/78.

a memorial: 'Das Department of State erklärte bei dieser Gelegenheit, daß man die Anbringung von Gedenktafeln in Mauthausen nicht durch ost-europäische Länder monopolisieren lassen sollte' ('The Department of State declared at this juncture that one should not let Eastern European countries have a monopoly of the commemorative plaques erected at Mauthausen').[7] During preparations for the 1949 *Befreiungsfeier* (the annual anniversary celebration of the liberation) the Ministry received instructions from the Bundeskanzleramt (Federal Chancellery) to prevent the hoisting of flags by certain countries: the newly founded Israel, on the grounds that it had not existed when the Jewish prisoners were interned; Franco's Spain, for unstated but obvious reasons (Franco having agreed to Hitler's internment of the Spanish Republican prisoners); and Germany, because Germany was considered not to have a flag.[8] Nor was diplomacy always an international affair: in 1970 a Lutheran dean, asked to provide a pastor for that year's liberation commemorations, complained that the organizers were not asking for a bishop, to match the Catholic celebrant, and pleaded that in future they take care 'einigermaßen das protokollarische Gleichgewicht zu beachten' ('to observe, as far as possible, the balance required by protocol').[9]

Even without access to these files at the Mauthausen Archive, one could read a political and social history from the memorials (erected for the most part in a memorial garden between the camp and the quarry) and from the commemorative plaques (most of which are hung along the *Klagemauer* or Wailing Wall). In particular, the order in which they were erected and the groups responsible for them tell stories about changing memorial values, both in Austria and in the inmates' states of origin. As the only national group whose state disowned them, for instance, the Spanish Republicans were honoured by the French survivors' association to which many belonged and by a private plaque on the *Klagemauer*. Spain finally honoured its victims in 1978, three years after Franco's death, but, unlike the other two memorials, this modest plaque does not name them as Republicans, only as Spain's 'fallen sons', a rhetoric of national unity typical of post-dictatorial eras. In the last ten years, some of the new post-communist states have expressed their independent statehood by honouring 'their' dead separately from the federations under which they were previously subsumed, either at the *Klagemauer* (Croatia, Azerbaijan, and Belarus) or in the memorial garden (Ukraine and Slovenia).[10]

---

[7] MA V/1/102/9.   [8] MA V1/1/76.   [9] MA V/1/78.

[10] Archive files show that several Eastern European states that retained their national borders after the fall of communism applied to alter the inscriptions on their plaques or memorials to expunge communist epithets and sentiments.

A central concern of Museum Studies is the way in which museum displays, by telling the story of the dominant culture, may exclude socially marginal groups and perpetuate social inequality.[11] In one sense memorial sites to the victims of the Third Reich would seem to be exempt a priori from this accusation, since they embody the shame of a dominant culture for an earlier, unprecedented act of social exclusion. However, studies of memorial sites show that they can indeed be used to tell the story that the dominant culture would like to tell about itself and that they can, in the process, exclude those who are not valued by the state or by the social majority. The relative lack of remembrance, before 1990, of the murdered Sinti and Roma, and of homosexuals, was a function, at least in part, of the continuing marginalization of these groups in contemporary German and Austrian society, but the Mauthausen memorials now testify to the greater inclusiveness and particularization that Niven dates from the beginning of the 1990s: homosexuals, Roma and Sinti, Jehovah's Witnesses, Wehrmacht deserters, and conscientious objectors have all been honoured at the *Klagemauer* since 1990 and a second memorial to the Roma and Sinti prisoners, erected in the memorial garden in 1998, accords this supranational group the same status as the nationalities commemorated elsewhere in the garden. Child victims of the camp, once subsumed under the majority adult population, are now also honoured separately in the memorial garden.

While governments are responsible for most of the monuments in the memorial garden, the commemorative plaques are more diverse in origin. Many have been put up by 'successor groups' to honour inmates who belonged to their organization or supported its aims. Without questioning what are undoubtedly sincere acts of commemoration, one can interpret these as a means of shaping and strengthening the identity of the association at the time of the plaque's dedication and at successive *Befreiungsfeier*. Thus, the numerous left-wing and Catholic organizations that honour their fellows strengthen their group identity and sense of purpose in the present by identifying themselves, through a symbolic rite, with men and women who were imprisoned and killed for holding comparable beliefs.

In other cases a more oblique connection with Nazi persecution makes the role of the present in the act of commemoration all the clearer. On the back of the punishment block the Niederösterreichischer Bauernbund (Lower Austrian Farmers' Association) honours the late *Bundeskanzler* Leopold Figl, head of the Bauernbund at the time of his

---

[11] See e.g. Richard Sandell (ed.), *Museums, Society, Inequality* (London: Routledge, 2002).

arrest but not imprisoned for that reason. The plaque is therefore an act of self-definition by the modern-day Bauernbund, which identifies itself with the democratic values of the Second Republic by honouring a *Bundeskanzler*, and aligns itself with the post-Waldheim culture of memory by honouring him at Mauthausen, but also proclaims its conservative values by identifying Figl's faith in God as the key to his survival. Another case in point are the organizations representing Austria's Kurdish minority, who attend the *Befreiungsfeier* not because they were persecuted under National Socialism, but to draw attention to discrimination against Kurds in the present.[12]

In a further instance of the particularization of memory, the Cuban members of the International Brigade are honoured separately from their fellow Republicans by the Österreichisch-Kubanische Gesellschaft (Austro-Cuban Society). Cross-cultural friendly societies have played a significant part in Austrian and German memorial culture, but while many were set up by survivors of Nazi persecution, this one has no connection with the events of the Third Reich. Instead, by acknowledging within the walls of Austria's state memorial the sufferings of a group of Cubans, the Society challenges Cuba's present-day pariah status.

Finally, the French, German, and Austrian scout movements honour the now sainted Marcel Callo, a one-time scout who was imprisoned by the Nazis for his Christian opposition to Nazism (and not for his scouting). While some youth-group leaders, including scout and Sokol leaders, were indeed imprisoned by the National Socialists because their organizations were considered subversive, the prevalence of youth organizations among the successor groups who have erected plaques needs to be understood in relation to the practices of these groups more generally. Youth groups who already have a tradition of ceremonial in their practices—hoisting or carrying flags, playing or singing music, wearing uniforms, and processing—are likely to find the unveiling of a plaque at Mauthausen, where such ceremonial is the norm, more meaningful than youth groups that operate without such practices. This element of memorial sites would benefit from further sociological study.

Possibly the last victim groups yet to benefit from the new inclusiveness, at Mauthausen as elsewhere, are those prisoners categorized as 'Asoziale' ('Asocials') and 'Kriminelle' ('Criminals'). The former were an extraordinarily heterogeneous group of people who had in one way or another fallen foul of normative precepts about community life; the

---

[12] Gerhard Botz and Alexander Prenninger (eds.), *Zur Geschichte der Befreiungsfeiern in der KZ-Gedenkstätte Mauthausen*, LBIHS-Arbeitspapiere, 19 (Salzburg: Ludwig Boltzmann-Institut für Historische Sozialwissenschaft, 2002), 10.

latter were either serving prisoners transferred to the camp from a regular jail or free men rearrested because of previous convictions. Both groups were the victims of injustice, since even the convicted murderers among the 'Criminals' had the right to serve the sentence passed down to them by a judge and not to be reassigned, without due judicial process, to an unlimited sentence of potentially fatal hard labour under a penitential regime that operated outside the rule of law. Hans Maršálek, for many years curator of the site, notes in interview that small numbers of the 'Criminals' attend the *Befreiungsfeier*, but march with their compatriots rather than as a group. By characterizing the 'Criminals' who attend the ceremonies as 'wer irgendwie sich anständig benommen hat im Lager' ('anybody who behaved more or less decently in the camp'),[13] Maršálek hints at one reason for the absence of a memorial to the sufferings of this group: a minority of 'Criminals' abused the powers invested in them by the SS, in a cynical attempt to divide and rule, so that honouring them would offend other survivors.

It follows from my analysis above, however, that the commemorative neglect both of the 'Criminals' and of the 'Asocials' must also have to do with the nature of their successor groups. In the case of the 'Asocials', the designation was so diffuse in the first place, and felt to be so shaming even after 1945, that this group has never formed into an organization. The current homeless population represent a potential successor group, and a recent series on the subject of 'Asocials' in the Viennese magazine *Augustin*, produced by and for the homeless, while not initiated by a homeless person, suggests that the homeless could, in theory, strengthen their current identity and fight for recognition through the commemoration of this victim group. It is less easy to see who might take up the commemorative cause of the 'Criminals', but growing interest in the National Socialist justice system, which has produced a number of new memorials and exhibitions, may lead to greater public awareness of their experience.

Studies of memorial sites usually include an element of aesthetic analysis, though Young cautions against applying art-historical methods too literally. Since art history, much like literary history, has traditionally evaluated works of art against criteria such as originality, innovation, and complexity, it tends, so Young's argument runs, to belittle or, at best, marginalize memorial art, which it views as conventional and lowbrow. Yet such criteria make little sense for memorial art, because unlike art in the free market it has obligations to its public and to communities

---

[13] Ibid. 55.

of survivors: 'public art like this demands additional critical criteria if the lives and meanings of such works are to be sustained—and not oppressed—by art historical discourse.'[14] While Mauthausen contains very little of the kind of crudely figurative 'testimonial realism' that Young considers most vulnerable to academic oppression, it is true that there is also little that is original or intellectually challenging in its memorial aesthetics, whose principal frame of reference is the tradition of the public memorial.

Nevertheless, Mauthausen testifies to the fact that memorial art has, over the last twenty years, become more open to trends in mainstream (non-public) art, largely, no doubt, as a result of the increasing use, at least in Germany and Austria, of open competitions to generate memorials. This is apparent in Fritz König's memorial for the Federal Republic of Germany, chosen by competition and unveiled in 1983, which casts geometric shapes in rusting iron; in the children's memorial, erected in 2001, which is a loose assemblage of forms in a variety of media; and in Marcus Pillhofer's memorial to the Roma and Sinti, another competition winner, unveiled in 1998. Where the majority of memorials use no more than two media and have either a central focus or, at the very least, a sense of ordered composition, Pillhofer's memorial is deliberately fragmented and difficult of access, physically and intellectually. A single railway track, clearly evoking transportation to the camps but mysteriously missing its partner, leads at an oblique angle towards a square platform. To the left, two stone plaques are inscribed in German and Romany, in the conventional fashion. It is necessary, however, to walk into the memorial to read them: they do not form a visible centrepiece as elsewhere. A niche houses an expressionist sculpture of a distorted and maimed human form, something of a cliché in post-Holocaust memorial art, but here, again, demanding to be discovered by the viewer. To the right of the platform, metal sheets, bolted together, sink into the ground, perhaps evoking the combination of industrial order and death at the heart of camp life. In front of them metal stakes, reminiscent of rudimentary grave markers, bear the names of other camps at which Roma and Sinti were killed. Finally, at the back of the square platform a sheet of glass affords a view of the valley. Other sculptures positioned at the edge of the drop into the valley likewise frame the outside world as visible and yet barred. That this evokes the experience of the prisoners is clearest in the GDR monument, which allows glimpses of the valley through sculpted barbed wire. The semi-transparency also reminds us that the camp was clearly visible to the farms in the middle distance.

[14] Young, *Texture of Memory*, 12.

Though the predominance of stone in all but the most avant-garde memorials is less than surprising given its central role in Western memorial and funerary traditions, none of the stone memorials reflects openly on the fact that it uses stone blocks to commemorate those who suffered or died working in the quarry below or carrying stone blocks up the *Todesstiege* ('Stairway of Death') in what was a deliberately punitive exercise since the stone could have been lifted mechanically. The carefully shaped and dressed stone of the memorials makes no reference to the roughly hewn blocks shouldered by the inmates. Archived correspondence suggests that, in its original conception, the British monument was intended to work in this way ('The overall roughness of the monument is meant to depict exactly how the British prisoners died, and in this conception it will succeed for they died carrying such granite from the quarry'),[15] but the monument that was built is of smooth stone. Moreover, the architecture of the more monumental, mostly communist, stone structures is in essence no different from that favoured by Hitler and for which the stone in the quarry was intended. To feel the absence of such self-reflection is arguably to apply the kind of art-historical criteria that Young believes 'oppresses' memorials. However, as we shall see, self-reflection is now very much the order of the day at Mauthausen and when blocks quarried by inmates were uncovered on the site of the new Visitors' Centre the architects decided to display them, haphazardly and in their rough-hewn state, as a memorial art installation, rather than choosing one to function literally as an exhibit.

Despite their obvious aesthetic limitations, the communist memorials provide material for an analysis of Cold War rhetoric and iconography. A typical feature is their use of a visual and verbal rhetoric of fighting. This honours the dead and the survivors by stylizing their enforced passivity in the camp as a form of active combat; at the same time it recruits them to the cause of communism by eliding their suffering with attempts to establish a communist society, also frequently stylized as a 'Kampf' ('fight' or 'struggle'). For instance, in a rhetorical address to the sculpture of a woman—identified, by means of a second inscription, as Brecht's embodiment of 'Deutschland'—the East German memorial states: 'Deine Söhne, die hier kämpften und starben, trugen den Glauben an das wahre Deutschland in die Zukunft' ('Your sons, who fought and died here, carried their faith in the true Germany into the future'). The suggestion that the GDR is the 'true Germany', the one that is carrying on the tradition of resistance to fascism, is typical of the GDR's rhetoric

---

[15] Letter from Evelyn B. Franks to the Ministry of the Interior, no date (almost certainly late 1960s), MA V/1/102/11.

of self-legitimation, which here takes precedence over the mourning of the dead (reduced syntactically to a relative clause within the main-clause statement about the meaning of the past for the present). A plaque honouring General Karbischew, dedicated in 1948 by the Soviets, describes Karbischew as a 'feuriger Kämpfer' ('a passionate fighter') even at the moment of his 'Heldentod' ('hero's death'), despite the fact that the manner of his death rendered him helpless and immobile. In accordance with the communist cult of the exceptional individual, expressed at the unveiling ceremony by the juxtaposition of a large picture of Karbischew with a large picture of Lenin, the inscription also edits out the other 200 men who died in this particular execution.

Two of the communist memorials attempt, not entirely successfully, to distinguish between the 'fight' for a better society on the one hand and war on the other, reflecting the fact that, despite a massive build-up of arms, the countries of the Eastern Bloc defined themselves as peace-loving nations in opposition to the warmongering imperialist states of the West. The Bulgarian memorial, for instance (Fig. 7), combines a sculpture of a man in militant pose, unarmed but heroically muscular, his fist raised defiantly, with an inscription proclaiming that the fight against fascism must include the fight against war. The Albanian memorial, which describes the inmates as 'heldenmütig kämpfend' ('fighting heroically'), includes a sculpture of what is presumably an Albanian partisan subduing a cowering German soldier. Once again, communism is associated with the overpowering of an enemy, but the partisan is distanced from the naked aggression of war because he is subduing the soldier with the butt of his rifle, not its muzzle, a sign that he is taking him prisoner rather than killing him.

The obvious limitation of an aesthetic reading of memorial sites is that it reduces memorials to static objects. This can be exacerbated by a purely illustrative use of photographic plates that frame a memorial front-on—all but the most avant-garde have a 'front'—and in its entirety, leaving space around its contours and keeping people out of the frame. My illustration of the Bulgarian memorial exemplifies this practice: even the side view, with its silhouette of the figure's musculature, serves to make a point about communism's heroic symbolization of the human form. While certainly not precluding critical analysis, this method of deploying photographs presents memorials as their maker intended them to be presented and invites the reader to view them in that way.

One way of avoiding this objectifying approach is to photograph memorials as the scene of social processes, capturing the ceremonies enacted in front of them and the behaviour of visitors to them. Rudy Koshar, for instance, reproduces photographs of GDR school classes

Fig. 7. The Bulgarian memorial at the former concentration camp of Mauthausen in Upper Austria, from the front and in profile

visiting memorials, to demonstrate the role played by Third Reich remembrance in GDR education.[16] However, just as memorials tend to be photographed in sympathy with their artists' intentions, so most ceremonies are photographed in accordance with their own choreography: they too have a 'front', and suggest a frame and a focal length to the photographer by arranging the main protagonists and the props (banners, wreaths, and so on) into clear tableaux. The work of Stephan Matyus, the photographer at the Mauthausen Archive, shows that it is possible to counter this effect: charged with recording the yearly liberation ceremonies, Matyus attempts to take at least some shots that resist the self-framing of the ceremonial act. For instance, conventional tableau shots of the remembrance ceremony at the French memorial are supplemented by a behind-the-scenes shot of a saluting French soldier, his

[16] Rudy Koshar, *From Monuments to Traces. Artifacts of German Memory, 1870–1990* (Berkeley and Los Angeles: University of California Press, 2000), 196, 215.

Fig. 8. A money-box forming part of the children's memorial at Mauthausen became a repository for sweet wrappers and other litter

free hand holding a ghetto-blaster (presumably playing the Marseillaise). I reproduce here another of Matyus's photographs (Fig. 8) that shows part of the children's memorial. The intention of this perspex money-box was to encourage a small commemorative ritual that could be enacted by even young children. In the event, as Matyus's photograph records, children deposited sweet wrappers, chewing gum, and all manner of other small objects and the box had to be closed. Though he does not always analyse his photographs, Young takes a comparable approach: several photographs in his works show how people integrate memorials into their normal behaviour rather than adapting their behaviour to the demands of the memorial.[17]

Analogous questions of method apply to museum exhibitions at memorial sites: if one treats them as static objects one can read them as a testament to particular stages in the evolution of cultural memory and museum practice. I begin by demonstrating this approach, then consider its limitations. At the time of writing, the Mauthausen Memorial is home to three permanent exhibitions: one on the history of the main camp

---

[17] Young, *Texture of Memory*, 94, 109; James E. Young, *At Memory's Edge: After-Images of the Holocaust in Contemporary Art and Architecture* (New Haven and London: Yale University Press, 2000), 132–3.

and its satellites (opened in 1970), one on the fate of Austrian citizens in German concentration camps (opened in 1982), and one on memory and historiography (opened in the new Visitors' Centre in 2003). The 1970 exhibition centres on documentary and other material proof, reflecting a need to put beyond doubt the truth of what happened at Mauthausen. A minimum of narrative is interposed between the visual and textual traces of the camp. The extensive use of documents, which feature on more than half of the exhibition boards, was no doubt influenced by the role of Maršálek, a former camp clerk, in setting up the exhibition, but developments in copying and print technology may also have facilitated this approach. That visitors must have struggled to interpret the profusion of statistics is clear from the rudimentary explanations pasted over some of the columns of numbers, such as: 'Immer mehr Häftlinge... immer mehr Sklaven für die Rüstung' ('more and more inmates... more and more slaves for armaments production'). Photographs, blown up to ten or twenty times the conventional size, are used to shock and accuse by showing the violence done to the prisoners' bodies.

The 1982 exhibition uses photographs less dramatically, and statistics and documents more sparingly, no doubt partly because this time the Memorial was not exploiting its own archives, but almost certainly also because of a changing understanding of how museum visitors process material. Whereas the first exhibition distinguishes spatially between general narrative (in the upper rooms) and (in the lower rooms) sub-narratives such as the fate of different groups of inmates and of everyday life in the camp, the 1982 exhibition interweaves the impersonal macro-narrative with personal micro-narratives, using a magazine format of the kind still widely used in museums today, with pieces of general background narrative supplemented by personal stories and descriptive cameos. Moreover, where the 1970 exhibition arguably privileges the agency of the camp authorities—showing how they categorized, inventorized, exploited, degraded, and murdered the prisoners—the 1982 exhibition gives rather more space to the ways in which prisoners experienced and represented their own suffering (though still much less space than in the contemporary documentary films outlined in Chapter 3). This change of approach necessitates a new aesthetics of display. Whereas boards in the 1970 exhibition have the geometrical character of a Mondrian painting, arranging information in contiguous rectangles of varying dimensions, often with four, six, or eight pieces of typescript aligned squarely edge to edge, in the 1982 exhibition the emphasis is on layering and overlapping, on the juxtaposition of shapes and textures. This corresponds to the non-linear, associative structure of the information.

The building of a Visitors' Centre has allowed the Memorial to free camp buildings of occupation, a move towards restoring authenticity that Niven notes at other sites. It has also allowed the Memorial to bring its exhibition practice into the twenty-first century. While the two earlier exhibitions were acts of memory, they performed their role unselfconsciously, without reference to the term 'Erinnerung', and neither problematized the status of its historical sources. The new exhibition is devoted entirely to the question of how the past is remembered, foregrounding the roles of memorial technologies, memorial aesthetics, memorial politics, and historiographical methods. In a clear sign that a straightforward narrative approach has been abandoned, the 'exhibition' is actually four separate installations (or 'modules' as the Memorial styles them) that do not suggest an itinerary to the visitor. A video installation presents a selection of interviews from an oral history project; a computer installation disperses memory outwards from the Memorial by mapping reconnaissance photographs of the camp and its outlying structures onto aerial photographs of the landscape today; the history of the memorial site is presented in the third module, not, the Memorial insists, in the form of a self-congratulatory narrative but with a degree of self-criticism; and the fourth module ('Objekte erzählen Geschichte', 'Objects tell history') considers what it is possible to deduce from archaeological finds. Niven notes that memorial sites tend to document everything but their own history as memorials; Mauthausen is one of the first to do this. It is also the first, to my knowledge, to take this open and critical approach to its role as historiographer.

Apart from the introduction of new media, the main change in the aesthetics of display is that whereas the collage style of the 1982 exhibition created an effect of layering, but used flat boards, the third and fourth modules of the 2003 exhibition use the pane of glass in front of (or above) the exhibits to display the interpretative texts. This has become common museum practice because it makes visible the gap between historical evidence and its interpretation by the museum (precisely the gap that is the subject of the module 'Objekte erzählen Geschichte'). Thus, an exhibition opened in 2001 at the Zeitgeschichte-Museum Ebensee uses similar methods (though the museum employed a different design company): on an opaque back board are narrative texts and captions sourcing the documents and photographs that are distributed around a perspex front board. Here, the layering allows for a second distinction: the white text on the red back board (in Austria's national colours) gives an overview of the national situation, while the evidence on the front board is, as far as possible, taken from the local sphere. The visitor is thus invited to understand National Socialism as something that, while conceived and led elsewhere, was lived out in the local community. By contrast, the 1970 Mauthausen exhibition uses the colour red to create a visual 'roter Faden' (a 'red thread' or running theme) linking together instances of resistance. In this narrative construction—which culminates in a red board headed 'Die Österreicher grüßen die befreite Heimat' ('Austrians greet the liberation of their country')—post-war Austria was founded on resistance to Nazism and Austrian visitors are invited to align themselves retrospectively with that resistance. Such an optimistic and conciliatory narrative, though understandable as the self-expression of survivors, would seem rather unlikely today.

What I said of the study of memorials also applies here: that however fruitful this 'static' approach, it excludes the element of social practice. While such research is beyond my competence, visitor research at Sachsenhausen suggests that an equivalent study of Mauthausen would relativize my reading, exposing the fact that the academic researcher tends to adopt the role of an ideal visitor who, in reality, exists only in statistically negligible numbers. While it comes naturally to an academic to celebrate the high-quality information provided by the exhibitions at Mauthausen and Ebensee, and particularly the intellectual sea change represented by the new Mauthausen exhibition, research shows that very few visitors go to a museum (any kind of museum) with the intention of learning anything in any detail, and 'only a very small share of exhibits and contents, visitor research claims no more than five per cent, is [examined] at all'.[18] Moreover, whereas the small proportion of visitors who return regularly to museums other than concentration-camp memorial sites tend to deepen their knowledge of the exhibited subject on successive visits, the proportion of regular visitors to concentration-camp memorial sites is not only markedly smaller (6 per cent of the total number of visitors, compared to 25 per cent at some other types of museum) but also less concerned with knowledge on return visits: 'They return [...] primarily to have a close look at what has changed meanwhile at the memorial in terms of concept, creative and architectural design.'[19] In that sense, at least, the academic visitor has much in common with the ordinary visitor, but there is nevertheless clearly a wide gap between the vision of museum pedagogues and actual visitor behaviour.

---

[18] Günter Morsch, 'Authentic Places of KZ-Crimes: Chances and Risks from the View of Visitor Research', trans. Stefan Menhofer, *Beiträge zur historischen Sozialkunde*, Special Issue 2001, 19–22 (19). The translation is rather poor and I have been unable to locate the original. Where I have 'examined', the translator has 'received', presumably a translation of 'rezipiert'.

[19] Ibid. 21.

Ideally, a visitor-research approach would include the behaviour of those who work at memorial sites. Schloss Hartheim in Upper Austria, a fine example of the new inclusiveness, houses both a memorial to 'euthanasia' victims murdered there during the Third Reich and, since 2003, a museum of disability. When I visited, a young volunteer in the bookshop recommended a biography to me, explaining that it told the story of a woman who was a bit—and here she raised her hand to her head and twisted it, in the internationally recognized sign for 'not right in the head'—but who nevertheless led a courageous life. In the museum itself, a guide repeatedly used the term 'wahnsinnig' ('mad') to speak of the pre-twentieth-century mentally ill, even as the exhibits she was presenting detailed the marginalizing effects of the social construction of 'madness'. I make no apology for the anecdotal nature of this evidence, which serves only to make the point that if we study museums as static objects we are more likely to read them as they would want to be read; introducing the human dimension of museum visitors and staff is likely to highlight discrepancies between a museum's script and its performance.

Ebensee and Local Memory

The opposition between national and local memory is often an opposition between urban and rural memory: as a nation, Germany commemorates the inner-German border in Berlin, for instance, not along the hundreds of kilometres of the GDR's rural western border. In the case of Mauthausen and Ebensee, national and local memory are both enacted at rural sites, yet this has not weakened the opposition: for decades the centralized model of commemoration chosen by Austria after 1945 diverted state funds and public attention away from Mauthausen's many satellite camps. Although the Ministry of the Interior corresponded with survivors' groups and diplomatic missions about the sub-camps, it delegated their upkeep to the federal states. This is changing, thanks in part to a recent 'reform initiative' for the Mauthausen Memorial, and the Ministry has part-funded a visitors' centre at Gusen, a sub-camp which, despite being situated only a few miles from Mauthausen and surpassing all others in brutality, was for decades abandoned to the often competing claims of survivor memory and local memory.

Unable to rely on the State to do their memory-work for them, Austrian towns and villages other than Mauthausen have had to negotiate their relationship with the past for themselves. While in the early post-war years survivors and their families were able to exert some influence, in the decades that followed local communities did little or nothing to remember, and most reused camp land. Since the middle of the 1980s local initiatives have attempted to reintegrate the history of the sub-camps into local memory. This is the case at Ebensee, whose camp was left to disintegrate and then bulldozed, though survivors managed to secure the preservation of a single archway. Since 1988 a local history society has overseen several memorial projects: information boards have been erected at the site of mass graves; in 1996 an exhibition was set up in a *Stollen* (underground gallery), explaining how it was carved out of the rock by prisoners to form a factory floor in which they were forced to work; and in 2001 a museum of contemporary history was opened that sets National Socialism within the broader context of twentieth-century Austrian politics. At the time of writing the society was still unable to secure long-term government funding and administrative support.

Although Ebensee is a more modest site than Mauthausen, it would in theory be possible to carry out an equivalent study of its history, its memorial art, its ceremonies, and so on. Rather than go over that ground again I have picked out one element of Ebensee's history that has to do with place and with the dispersal and centralization of memory: the burial of the dead. At Ebensee, memory of the camp was initially not so much dispersed as displaced, as American forces oversaw the creation, two kilometres away, of a burial ground for the recent dead. This made sense in the context of liberation, when the prevention of disease was paramount and the camps were unsuitable places for a dignified burial, but the ahistorical isolation of this semi-rural resting place severed the connection between the deaths and the camp system. In 1946, a stone monument inscribed with the words 'Zur ewigen Schmach des deutschen Volkes' ('To the eternal shame of the German people') was erected at the cemetery. Although explicable in the context of the Allies' recent victory over the German Reich, the word 'deutsch' obscured Austrian co-responsibility for the events at Ebensee. Now cut loose from Germany, Austrians were not enjoined to understand the 'Schmach' as their own. Local administrative correspondence from 1952–3 notes with alarm the threat that the monument poses to tourism, as more and more German tourists voice their outrage at the inscription, implying that for locals it went without saying that the message was directed at Germany.[20]

That the bodies were exhumed only six years later and returned to the site of the former concentration camp is indicative of the way in which places take on new meanings even over a fairly short period of

[20] Wolfgang Quatember, 'Die Geschichte der KZ-Gedenkstätte Ebensee', *Betrifft Widerstand* (1996), no. 33, 4–10.

time and also typical of this stage in the history of the former camps. In the chaotic conditions of 1945 victims tended to be buried where they died (typically on farmland or in woods, if they were shot during a forced march, or in a local cemetery, if they survived liberation and were treated in a hospital), but successive programmes of exhumation, one lasting from the late 1940s to the early 1950s and a further one in 1968, aimed to retrieve bodies from resting places outside the camps. In this way 525 bodies were moved to the camp at Ebensee. Though the concern was to provide an appropriate context for mourning, the effect has arguably been to centralize evidence of Nazi crimes in a few camps and town cemeteries, obscuring the fact that crimes were committed throughout the local countryside and effacing memories of 1945, when the boundaries between the camps and the outside world broke down. Of some 67 dissolved graves listed in a catalogue of memorial sites in Upper Austria, only 4 are recorded as being marked by memorials.[21]

Plans for an ossuary at Mauthausen, drawn up on behalf of French survivors in 1951 but never realized (Fig. 9), would have led to a secondary form of centralization, assembling the remains from all the mass graves at Mauthausen in a single building. This project, which drew on the tradition of French First World War cemeteries, would arguably have imposed a culturally specific treatment of mortal remains on national and other groups with quite different funerary conventions. Centralization through exhumation is still occurring, though in a quite different context: since the end of communism the Volksbund Deutsche Kriegsgräberfürsorge (German War Graves Commission) has dissolved the scattered graves of thousands of *Wehrmacht* soldiers in the former states of the Soviet Union, removing the remains to large cemeteries.

One final point about memory and place can be made with reference to Ebensee. The former camp was divided into building plots as early as 1949 and local government documents suggest that at least some Ebensee officials advanced openly racist arguments for this practice, seeing it as a means of driving out the remaining Displaced Persons.[22] Niven criticizes a similar housing initiative on the site of Flossenbürg concentration camp, as well as the reuse of sites elsewhere for commercial or local administrative purposes, taking the view that the original traces of camps and their buildings ought, where practicable, to be preserved, and that to reuse a site is to overwrite, and so suppress, its history. Matyus, the official Mauthausen photographer mentioned earlier, holds similar

---

[21] Siegfried Haider and Gerhart Marckhgott, *Oberösterreichische Gedenkstätten für KZ-Opfer. Eine Dokumentation* (Linz: Oberösterreichisches Landesarchiv, 2001).

[22] Quatember, 'Ebensee', 6.

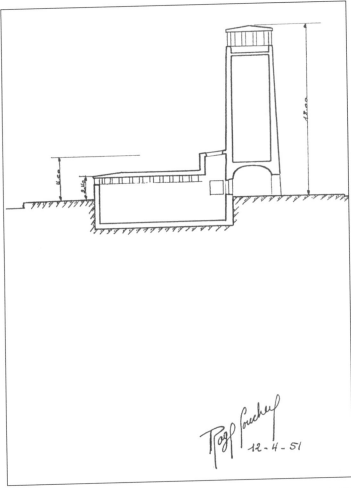

Fig. 9. A cross-section of a plan for an ossuary at Mauthausen, drawn up in 1951 but never realized. The signature is that of the architect, Roger Souchère

views: one of his photographs shows cows grazing within clear sight of the remaining camp buildings and is intended to record the disrespect shown in allowing the reuse for agricultural purposes of parts of the site. Yet to anyone who does not hold his views it will simply show cows grazing near the Mauthausen Memorial. For one could argue that provided that certain conditions are met (that the sites of National Socialist crimes are marked;

that a space is provided for survivors and bereaved families to mourn; that graves are given a respectful environment; and that historians are afforded adequate opportunity to assess the historical evidence), there is no necessity for the entire domain of every camp to be for ever excluded from reuse. No magic attaches to places and, on its own, the reuse of a former site of Nazi terror, for whatever purpose, makes it no more or less likely that Nazism or even lesser forms of xenophobic and racist power will return. The fact that the former crematorium at Gusen is closely encircled by houses might be viewed as a shameful covering of traces, but it does also mean that the locals in the houses must live permanently with this reminder of Nazi murder. This is, however, very much a matter for debate.

Ransmayr's *Morbus Kitahara*

A good starting point for an analysis of Ransmayr's *Morbus Kitahara* is its core technique: defamiliarization. Using a method that, as Ian Foster has shown, has wide currency in science-fiction writing, Ransmayr takes known historical realities (here the history of post-war Austria) and, by a careful process of omission, distortion, concentration, and substitution, creates an alternative historical realm that appears all the stranger for having a superficial familiarity.[23] The former prison camp at the centre of the novel has elements both of Mauthausen (a stone stairway linking quarry and camp) and Ebensee (underground galleries and a lakeside setting), but bears the name of the fictional town of Moor. On its own this elision would represent a conventional enough fictionalization of reality, but Ransmayr combines it with a studied avoidance of historical terms such as SS, Nazi, concentration camp, Wehrmacht, and Hitler. Also conspicuous by its absence is the word Austria, though Vienna is mentioned and the novel has an Alpine setting. The Allies who have defeated an unnamed dictatorship number six rather than the historical four and seal a fictional Peace of Oranienburg.[24]

These details form the backdrop to a more fundamental distortion: instead of restoring the defeated country to democratic prosperity, the Americans, under the fictional leader Stellamour, impede its regrowth

[23] Ian Foster, 'Alternative History and Christoph Ransmayr's *Morbus Kitahara*', *Modern Austrian Literature*, 32 (1999), 111–25.

[24] Kurt Bartsch argues that, since Oranienburg was the site of Sachsenhausen concentration camp, the name stands for a peace based on revenge for the Holocaust. Kurt Bartsch, '"Spielen mit den Möglichkeiten der Wirklichkeit". Zu Christoph Ransmayrs Roman *Morbus Kitahara*', *Jahrbuch der Österreich-Bibliothek in St. Petersburg*, 3 (1997/8), 95–108 (99).

through drastic de-industrialization, and subject it, over more than two decades, to a punitive regime that favours a few collaborators and disadvantages the great mass of citizens. The injustice is compounded by the fact that the policies are unevenly enforced, with large garrison towns allowed access to American technology and a measure of affluence, while smaller towns and villages such as Moor are left to revert to a pre-industrial state, without electricity, petrol, and transport.

As reviewers were quick to note, Ransmayr has taken inspiration from the so-called Morgenthau Plan, formulated by one of Roosevelt's advisers but never implemented. As one component in a raft of measures that would have limited post-war Germany's strength, the Plan envisaged systematic de-industrialization. However, rather than offering a realistic guess at what would have happened had the Plan been executed in Austria, Ransmayr elaborates a wildly dystopian vision of social antagonism and disintegration. The townspeople of Moor, who comment on events, chorus-like, from their collective point of view, embody all the worst aspects of provincial tribalism: nosiness, envy, spite, rumour-mongering, and mob violence. In their undifferentiated mass they act as a foil to three equally ill-starred main characters. Ambras, a concentration-camp survivor, presides autocratically over the quarry in which he once laboured; Lily is the daughter of an officer whose involvement in the atrocities of the former regime is unproven but who becomes the victim first of a lynch mob and then of the Allies; and the blacksmith Bering escapes his imperious war-veteran father and his crazed Mariolatrist mother by agreeing to work for Ambras, only to fall unhappily in love with Lily. When Moor is evacuated to make way for a US military training ground, the three characters depart for Brazil, but hopes of a new beginning are dashed by the deaths of Bering and Ambras.

Ransmayr has suggested in interview that the motor of his writing was anger: at those who would draw a line under the Nazi past while survivors of Nazi torture are compelled to relive it daily and at Austrian communities that pride themselves on their imperial past while forgetting the events of 1938–45. Speaking of the Salzkammergut region, and specifically of Ebensee and Mauthausen, he described the construction of a selective historical geography: 'auf Gedenktafeln wird zwar an die Kaiserzeit und die Kaiservilla und die Kaisersommerfrische erinnert, nicht aber an die Ermordeten' ('commemorative plaques recall the imperial age and the Kaiser's villa and the Kaiser's summer retreat, but not those who were murdered').[25] This statement ought not to be

---

[25] Christoph Ransmayr in conversation with Sigrid Löffler, 'Das Thema hat mich bedroht', *Falter*, 22–8 Sept. 1995.

taken too literally since the former camps at Mauthausen and Ebensee have always been marked by memorials, and since the notoriety of the Mauthausen camp makes it unthinkable that the town of Mauthausen could hide this heritage behind a more favourable one. However, two journalistic pieces by Ransmayr set out his views on Austrian memory in more sophisticated terms than is possible in interview. In 'Kaprun oder die Errichtung einer Mauer' (1985), he analyses local and national memory of the construction of the Kaprun dams, which, though built partly with forced labour under National Socialism, became a symbol of Austria's post-war Second Republic. Ransmayr contrasts the locals' concern to promote tourism with their distaste for a memorial to Soviet forced labourers and mimics their self-exculpatory rhetoric ('das war schließlich eine großdeutsche Zeit und keine österreichische', 'after all, that was the time of Greater Germany, not Austria'),[26] which echoes the responses of officials in Ebensee to the troublesome cemetery memorial. In the other essay, 'Die vergorene Heimat. Ein Stück Österreich' (1989), Ransmayr discusses the efforts made by locals in the Mostviertel district to preserve the remains of their rural heritage. Although he makes a studied effort to enter into their concerns and carefully contextualizes their actions within the broader economic situation, Ransmayr is also critical of what he sees as a tendency to gloss over the past:

> Die vielen Hakenkreuze, Eichenlaubkränze und Hitlergesichter, die das Mostviertel wie das ganze Land ein tausendjähriges Reich lang schmückten, haben in den heimatkundlichen Sammlungen [. . .] keinen Platz gefunden. In der Heimat war es immer schön: es wurden dort Brautbäume und Maibäume errichtet, aber keine Galgen. Und auf den Höfen wurden Senkgruben und Mostkeller ausgehoben, aber keine Massengräber.[27]

While some locals will admit to having feared the Mauthausen camp, the populace as a whole recalls only the local man who was sent to the camp for dealing illegally in meat, not the sufferings of the great mass of prisoners interned for ideological reasons.

Taking one's cue from Ransmayr's extra-textual comments about the Nazi past, one can extract from *Morbus Kitahara* a conventional liberal message about the need for a belated confrontation with a murderous

---

[26] Christoph Ransmayr, *Der Weg nach Surabaya. Reportagen und kleine Prosa* (Frankfurt/Main: Fischer, 1997), 79.

[27] 'The many swastikas, oak-leaf wreaths, and portraits of Hitler that decorated the Mostviertel region, as they did the whole country, for the duration of a thousand-year Reich, have found no place in local history collections. The *Heimat* was always beautiful: wedding trees were planted and maypoles set up, but not gallows. Cesspits and cider cellars were dug out but not mass graves.' Ibid. 58.

past that has been too readily forgotten. A series of passages confront the reader with the horrors of the Third Reich (which, unlike the grotesquely drawn post-war period, is only lightly defamiliarized). These include memories of cattle wagons full of people arriving at Moor station (p. 23 (pp. 15–16)); the testimony of a man shot by a guard as he tried to beg water for his dying wife (pp. 116–17 (p. 92)); and, most importantly, Ambras's recollections: of his brutal arrest and forced separation from his Jewish girlfriend (pp. 214–16 (pp. 173–4)), of the dehumanizing effects of the camp (pp. 206–8 (p. 167)), of the tortures inflicted on him (pp. 174–5 (pp. 140–1)), and of liberation, when he is taken for dead and thrown on a cartful of corpses (p. 74 (p. 58)). Alongside this testimony, Ransmayr offers, in the people of Moor, a negative model of forgetfulness and the absence of contrition. Having hastily disposed of the evidence of their collaboration with the former regime (p. 14 (p. 9)), they deny knowledge of its crimes (p. 47 (p. 36)), and later fantasize about having resisted it (p. 62 (p. 49)). Their lack of remorse expresses itself in their language, as mimicked by the narrator. Here, the locals attempt to justify forgetting as the natural way of things, by implication condemning remembrance as unnatural: 'Anstatt den Dingen ihren Lauf und die Schrecken der Kriegsjahre allmählich blaß und undeutlich werden zu lassen, erfand Elliot [...] immer neue Rituale der Erinnerung' ('Instead of letting things take their course, letting the horrors of the war years gradually grow pale and indistinct, Elliot constantly invented new rituals of remembrance'; p. 44 (p. 34)). They call Ambras 'dieser entlaufene Sträfling' ('that escaped convict'; p. 235 (p. 190)), suggesting that he has made an illegal escape from a prison in which he still rightly belongs (rather than having been freed from a camp in which he was wrongly imprisoned). Yet despite the pervasive desire for oblivion, Ransmayr creates the impression of a society that is dominated by the past, an effect achieved partly through physical description (of ruins, for instance, or of acts of remembrance), partly through the psychology of the main characters, each of whom is in some way traumatized, and partly through the narrative structure, in which flashbacks play a major role.

What I have described so far are the ingredients of countless critical representations of the Nazi past and its aftermath: atrocities, an intransigent populace that refuses to acknowledge them, and a past that refuses, with equal stubbornness, to go away. Even the title of the novel, the name of an illness causing temporary partial blindness, can be pressed into the service of this conventional reading, as a symbol of society's blindness to the horrors of the past. Yet this reading does little justice to a complex text.

Much of the complexity lies in the defamiliarization of acts of public remembrance and contrition. As with other aspects of the text, Ransmayr builds on historical foundations, notably the American programme of *Umerziehung* (Re-education), which aimed to instil in ordinary Germans and Austrians a sense of responsibility for the crimes committed in the concentration camps by means both of direct confrontation (forcing local people to visit the camps or assist with the clearance of corpses) and of mediated appeals to conscience (in the form of films, photographs, posters, and leaflets). The American occupiers in Ransmayr's Moor, under Major Elliot, subject the locals to just such a regime, except that they do not stop at films, documents, and photographs: Elliot stages mass re-enactments of scenes captured in photographs of the camp, with the local people playing the parts of the camp inmates. He also has local stonemasons carve huge letters and erect them along disused terraces in the quarry, spelling out the message: 'Hier liegen elftausendneunhundertdreiundsiebzig Tote, erschlagen von den Eingeborenen dieses Landes. Willkommen in Moor' ('Here eleven thousand nine hundred seventy-three people lie dead, slain by the inhabitants of this land. Welcome to Moor'; p. 33 (p. 24)). Foster identifies the source of this message as the inscription on a Soviet memorial that Ransmayr cites in his essay on Kaprun: 'Hier liegen 87 Sowjetbürger von deutsch faschistischen Eroberern ins Elend getrieben und fern von der Heimat ums Leben gekommen' ('Here lie 87 Soviet citizens who died far from home having been driven to a desperate state by German fascist conquerors'), but Ransmayr may also have had in mind the inscription at the first Ebensee cemetery, mentioned above. Either can serve to gauge his fictional exaggeration: whereas both of the real inscriptions lay the blame on a German nation to which the local population no longer belongs, and whereas neither states that the dead were murdered, Ransmayr's fictional inscription calls a murder a murder and states explicitly that the crimes were carried out, if not directly by the people of Moor, then by their compatriots. Moreover, where the real Soviets who erected the memorial at Kaprun were (perhaps unintentionally) diplomatic, and the real survivors who erected the memorial at Ebensee righteously angry, the fictional Americans are disagreeably vindictive, adding a sarcastic final line, 'Willkommen in Moor', that feigns to welcome tourists even as the rest of the inscription repels them.

One possible reading of the text is as a critique, sharpened by means of surreal exaggeration, of the American Re-education campaign. If this is so, then Ransmayr is in line with other recent re-evaluations of the effectiveness of the campaign, notably by Aleida Assmann, who argues that the Re-education campaign evoked feelings of shame (a sense of having done wrong in the eyes of others) rather than guilt (a sense of having done wrong according to one's own conscience).[28] Ransmayr's objections are slightly different. In an unusually 'straight' passage in *Morbus Kitahara* (pp. 175–7 (pp. 141–2)) he argues that the shock tactics employed by the Americans in their film and photograph campaigns are counter-productive: children grow up thinking that the victims of the concentration camp have no voices (because they are silent in the documentary reels) and that, having died in the concentration camps, they are not part of the post-war world. By placing this passage immediately after Ambras's revelations about his past, Ransmayr implies what he states more explicitly in interview, that survivors can better educate young people about the Holocaust than can museum visits.[29]

There is, however, something questionable about ascribing to the Americans a vindictiveness and high-handedness that far surpasses in intensity, systematization, and longevity anything witnessed under the short-lived Re-education campaign of historical reality. To put it another way, one might ask what purpose it can serve to give a fictional community more cause for anger, hatred, and resentment than the real historical circumstances of 1945, however grim, can ever have afforded. A more conservative reader might feel aggrieved at Austria's harsh treatment at the hands of the fictional Americans and project this sense of injustice retrospectively onto historical fact, concluding that Austria's unmerited humiliation after 1945 justifies the desire to forget the Third Reich or even cancels out some of its crimes. Given that for far-right revisionist groups it is an article of faith that the Allied occupation was unjustifiably brutal and vindictive, there is an odd discrepancy between Ransmayr's stated, straightforwardly moral intentions and the fictional scenario with which he expresses them.

However, the same scenario might equally be read as a fictional punishment meted out by Ransmayr to an intransigently amnesiac Austria, a punishment that, however excessive, is nevertheless more appropriate to Austria's crimes than the velvet-glove treatment accorded it in reality. If read in this way, the novel can be compared to other mischievous authorial fantasies such as Josef Haslinger's *Opernball* (in which Haslinger subjects the Viennese haute bourgeoisie to a terror attack in its defining locale, the ballroom), and Grass's *Unkenrufe* (in which

[28] Aleida Assmann and Ute Frevert, *Geschichtsvergessenheit, Geschichtsversessenheit. Vom Umgang mit deutschen Vergangenheiten nach 1945* (Stuttgart: Deutsche Verlags-Anstalt, 1999).

[29] 'Einsicht, Reue, Aufklärung ist etwas Individuelles, Bewußtsein kann nur im einzelnen Kopf stattfinden' ('Insight, remorse, enlightenment is something individual, conscience can only take place inside individual minds'): Christoph Ransmayr in conversation with Roland Mischke, 'Die Verwilderung der Gesellschaft geht weiter', *Badische Zeitung*, 2 Jan. 1996.

Grass takes pleasure in visiting on Germany and Poland an Asian-dominated future that he knows his readers will find alarming). Yet even on this reading, as authorial punishment fantasy, multiple reader responses are possible. The reader closest to Ransmayr's stated intentions would be one who felt contrition at Austria's evasion of proper atonement for its crimes, but a reader might equally feel self-pity at the thought of Austria victimized, if only by the author, while yet another kind of reader might derive a value-free thrill from experiencing a nightmarish national humiliation at the safe distance afforded by literature.

The fictional Americans could also be read as tools in the service of Ransmayr's programme of defamiliarization. On this reading, the US substitutes for the communist countries, the better to make strange the over-familiar characteristics of communist rule. The American leader Stellamour, for instance, is the subject of a cult, his image displayed on colossal banners, his form immortalized on town squares, his sayings quoted, and his greatness celebrated in song. The locals' reluctant attendance at mass gatherings for fear that absence will be punished (p. 39 (p. 30)) and their fear of ubiquitous surveillance (p. 86 (pp. 67–8)) both recall social experience under communist rule. Finally, the contradictory attitudes towards war that I noted in the context of the communist memorials at Mauthausen find expression in the paradoxical formulation 'der Friedensbringer und seine Generäle' ('the peace-bringer and his generals'; p. 375 (p. 302); see also p. 340 (p. 273)). Perhaps, then, Ransmayr presents us with a vision of what might have happened had the most punitive of the US Re-education practices been combined with the worst aspects of communist state control (and then exaggerated). But the elision of the US and the communist countries may also have the effect of highlighting real similarities. In the year 2000, George W. Bush declared that while the US's allies could usefully fulfil the role of 'peacekeepers', he reserved for the US the special role of 'peacemaker'. Though his words post-date Ransmayr's novel by some years, the use of a rhetoric of peace to justify military activity does not.[30]

Ritual remembrance in *Morbus Kitahara* is not restricted to ceremonies imposed by the army of occupation. Groups of local people voluntarily form *Büßergemeinschaften* or Penitents' Societies, to atone for the atrocities of the previous regime. Their activities are a mixture of archaic religious practices and rituals of Ransmayr's own contriving.

---

[30] I am indebted to Gar Yates for pointing out that Austria has its own history of a misuse of the rhetoric of peace. In his proclamation of war in 1914, Franz Josef I declared: 'So muß Ich denn daran schreiten, mit Waffengewalt die unerläßlichen Bürgschaften zu schaffen, die Meinen Staaten die Ruhe im Innern und den dauernden Frieden nach außen sichern sollen.'

As with Ransmayr's American army, the fantastic nature of the *Büßerge-meinschaften* makes their meaning peculiarly elastic. A group of penitents from the village of Eisenau makes a yearly pilgrimage to the stone script in the quarry, in memory of the day when the commandant of the concentration camp, a native of Eisenau, blew up an underground gallery containing ninety camp inmates (p. 246 (p. 198)). On the one hand this throws into relief the behaviour of real communities of post-war Austrians, who, with few exceptions, did not acknowledge (let alone publicly atone for) the crimes committed by the sons and daughters of their locality. As such, it contributes to Ransmayr's critique of Austrian repression of the past. On the other hand, the *Büßergemeinschaft* is hardly held up as a model. By performing an annual pilgrimage on a saint's day dressed in the striped ticking uniform of concentration camp inmates, carrying flags and banners emblazoned with the sayings of Stellamour, and laying wreaths and lighting torches in the quarry, the Eisenau Penitents' Society demonstrates all that is worst about ritual remembrance: a facile identification with the victims, repetitious and carefully choreographed actions that leave no room for individual conscience, an unthinking adoption of religious habits in secular ceremonial, and a susceptibility to political instrumentalization.

The text's critique of commemorative culture culminates in an angry outburst when Bering discovers that the town of Brand, far from atoning for the past through economic privation, is enjoying the benefits of technological advance and urban renewal. Bering feels 'daß dieses ganze Scheißgerede von Sühne, von Besinnung und Erinnerung ein riesiger Schwindel war' ('that all the bullshit about penitence, about reflecting and remembering, was a giant hoax', p. 332 (p. 267)). Though the situation in which Bering finds himself has no historical equivalent (and is therefore arguably a distraction from the real problems of commemorative culture), his suspicion of the political rhetoric of contrition is certainly of a piece with the more general suspicion of commemorative ritual expressed elsewhere. This corresponds both to Ransmayr's stated preference for personal conscience over organized remembrance,[31] and to the views put forward by Martin Walser, three years later, in his controversial Paulskirche speech. One can raise similar objections to both: that leaving remembrance up to the individual is, potentially, the first step to widespread erasure of the past, since a free conscience can easily mean no conscience; and that the condemnation of organized remembrance ignores the legitimate needs of nations to express their

---

[31] Ransmayr in conversation with Löffler.

attitudes towards the past through public ceremonial. Aleida Assmann argues, in her analysis of Walser's speech, that memory can only be stabilized, and therefore passed on to future generations, through public symbolization.[32] Whether Ransmayr's novel does a public service by opening up the question of how to give appropriate form to public remembrance, or whether it simply brings commemorative culture into disrepute by associating it with fantastical excesses and rank injustice is a moot point.

Ransmayr's portrayal of the townspeople is also complex, for while they might try to justify forgetting as the natural way of things, they do have a point when they say that Major Elliot's obsession with the past is unhealthy; and while they might cast scurrilous aspersions on Ambras's innocence, they do so only after his acceptance of privileges from the Americans and his uncaring attitude towards his workers have given them cause for resentment. Ransmayr's description of the privations suffered by the locals not just in the chaotic (and historically realistic) war years—bombings, extreme hunger, lack of proper medical care, loss of property, and so on—but also in the long, lean, oppressive (and largely fantastical) decades that follow, invites understanding, if not exactly sympathy, from the reader.

Moreover, Ransmayr sets up an interesting parallel between Ambras and Bering's war-veteran father: both have physical scars that symbolize ineradicable traces of trauma; both have difficulties communicating their experience, not least because of a lack of willing listeners; and both end their days under the deluded impression that they have returned to the theatre of their sufferings, Bering's father to the battlefield and Ambras to the concentration camp. Despite the parallels, Ransmayr is careful not to equate the sufferings of the two, subjecting Bering's father to a series of narrative humiliations not visited on Ambras: Bering senior's senile war games make him a figure of fun, he is described as incontinent, and is discarded as a character three-quarters of the way through the novel without the narrator even paying him the compliment of following him to the point of death. Ambras, on the other hand, for all his unappealing hardness, is treated with respect by the narrative, allowed to articulate his experiences at length, and dignified by being made the focus of the novel's ending, which relates the traumatic flashbacks that result in his fatal plunge from a cliff-face. In this way, while Ransmayr acknowledges the dual origins of Bering senior's sufferings, in his military service in the Wehrmacht, or its unnamed fictional equivalent, and in his experience

---

[32] Assmann and Frevert, *Geschichtsvergessenheit*, 79 ff.

of marginalization in the post-war years, he also makes clear that he considers the suffering of victims of Nazi terror to be of a different order and deserving of more respectful attention than the sufferings of the passively acquiescent foot soldiers of the Nazi regime.

Ransmayr's novel, then, opens the messy, complex wounds of 1945, whose pain consists not just in different sources of suffering, but in their sheer irreconcilability.[33] By extending the atmosphere of 1945 over several decades and by stretching to breaking-point the tensions between the occupiers and the locals, between survivors and the majority culture, and between different groups within the majority culture, Ransmayr magnifies the real historical trauma of 1945 to fantastical proportions. Foster has argued that the detailed descriptions of violence in the text that some critics find indulgent could be read as a form of homeopathic remedy, a way of immunizing readers against violence by exposing them to a controlled amount. Similarly, one could read the re-enactment, in grotesquely magnified form, of the sufferings and tensions of 1945 as a way of working through that pain by inviting the reader to experience it in an exaggeratedly intense dose, but from the safe distance afforded by aesthetic form. If so, then this is a risky strategy, since there is little to stop readers confusing the exaggerated fictional vision of Austrian suffering with its less drastic historical counterpart.

With the artistic freedom denied to the creators of state memorial art, Ransmayr is able to explore the multiple meanings of stone and to suggest that it is not, as most memorial art would appear to assume, an innocent artistic medium. He forges a direct link between the stone in the camp quarry and the ritual practice of memorial art by determining that the stone be used in mausoleums and for memorial plaques. In fact, the narrator cites two apparently complementary uses for the stone: 'Quader, aus denen Mahnmäler—und immer wieder die Gestalten des Friedensbringers und seiner Generäle geschlagen werden konnten' ('ashlars from which to hew monuments and ever more statues of the Bringer of Peace and his generals'; p. 269 (p. 216)). This implies that the practice of erecting memorials to the victims of dictatorship cannot be separated from a wider culture of public monumentalization that may be used in the service of a dictatorship. Ransmayr also describes the stone blocks abandoned on the quarry floor as 'Denkmäler ausgestandener Todesqualen' ('monuments to the agonies of death endured there'; p. 47 (p. 36)), while contriving that the stone out of which the incriminating lettering is carved be recycled from the foundations of the watchtowers

---

[33] See Schmitz, *Legacy*, 8–9, on the irreconcilability of victim and perpetrator experiences.

and bunkers of the former concentration camp. For Ransmayr, then, stone is laden with historical significance, not de-contextualized as in most real memorial art.

Ransmayr's stress on the vast age of the mountains that outlive the demise of Moor connects stone to broader themes, which I consider briefly here as a conscious corrective to the tendency of studies like this to fillet novels for their Nazi-related content. Like other writers concerned with environmental issues, Ransmayr believes that geological time puts human history into perspective.[34] Although Ransmayr only hints at this in *Morbus Kitahara* (having a minor character remark that nature thrives once human beings disappear (pp. 399–400 (p. 322))) and allowing the jungle to swallow up the bodies of Bering and Ambras), he pursues rather more determinedly a related Green strategy: the relativization of Western society. For, in at least one sense, the novel depicts not so much an alternative past as a real present transplanted into Europe from other parts of the globe. In interview Ransmayr has taken issue with those reviewers who see in Bering a descendant of mythological blacksmiths; on the contrary, says Ransmayr, Bering arose out of a modern experience, for in places like Ukraine, Poland, and India, people who can make machines out of scrap metal are highly valued.[35] The novel, in other words, confronts the reader not just with the European past but also with the present-day experiences of people in the Third World and the post-communist countries, living amongst the ruins of a more prosperous (colonial or communist) past whose remnants they must endlessly recycle and cobble together, and given tantalizing glimpses of the wealth of other regions of the world without being allowed to share in it. Like post-colonial Asia, the Europe of the novel is a place to which tourists from richer continents travel in search of the adventure of the primitive, and its cultural heritage, like that of post-colonial Asia, is plundered by antiques dealers who prey on the destitute (p. 407 (p. 328)). Once again, Grass's *Unkenrufe*, which likewise strives to counter the reader's Eurocentric perspective, makes a useful point of comparison.

It would, however, be arrogant to assume that all the more primitive aspects of Moor are a reference to underdeveloped countries. In his reportages, Ransmayr explores the archaic and pre-technological traditions that linger on in rural Europe, and particularly Austria. The practice of painting the skulls of exhumed bodies, for instance, still carried out

---

[34] Christoph Ransmayr in conversation with Hans-Dieter Schütt, 'Vom Verschwinden. In die Welt hinein', *Neues Deutschland*, 25–6 Mar. 2000.

[35] Christoph Ransmayr in conversation with Piet de Moor, 'Dat de tijd geneest, geldt niet voor alle mensen', *De Republik der Letteren*, 23 Dec. 1995.

in the Austrian town of Hallstadt when Ransmayr visited in 1988,[36] is as archaic as any of the strange rituals in *Morbus Kitahara*, while Bering's fantastical mechanical creation, a customized Studebaker, owes as much to a fanciful 'Weltmaschine' built, with the help of the local blacksmith, by an Austrian smallholder (and described in a reportage by Ransmayr), as it does to the inventiveness of Third World mechanics.[37]

Foster has identified a discrepancy between Ransmayr's cultivated public image as a rootless, international writer and the profoundly Austrian concerns of his journalistic work from the 1980s.[38] Unlike, say, Elfriede Jelinek, whose frequent interviews almost without exception touch on Austrian politics and national identity, and who is called upon by newspapers to act as a commentator on key events in Austrian public life, Ransmayr rarely speaks publicly about Austria; nor do his interviewers ask him to. Moreover, Ransmayr arguably makes a calculated effort to open out *Morbus Kitahara*, his first novel to have a recognizably Austrian setting, to a wider German-speaking readership, by keeping the geographical location vague, by effacing the German/Austrian divide, and by omitting all mention of Austrian politics. Yet I agree with Foster that the novel makes no sense without its Austrian context. For W. G. Sebald, one of the characteristics of twentieth-century Austrian literature was a concern with the dialectic *Heimat* and *Fremde*.[39] This may seem odd, given that the very same themes occur in German culture;[40] however, it is fair to say that Austria has especially strong, mainstream traditions both of positive, or nostalgic, *Heimat* culture and of critical *Heimat* culture, the big names in post-war Austrian literature—Bernhard, Handke, Jelinek—all having written virulent attacks on the country's conservative rural communities. One factor in the development of Austria's post-war *Heimat* culture that is not mentioned by Sebald but is of relevance to *Morbus Kitahara* is tourism: in a land that relies heavily on the tourist industry (which accounts for nearly 10 per cent of the gross domestic product), there are strong reasons for investing in positive myths of the native countryside.

[36] Ransmayr, *Weg nach Surabaya*, 63–74.

[37] Martin Pollack and Christoph Ransmayr, 'Nach dem Ebenbild der Welt. Eine Schöpfungsgeschichte', in Uwe Wittstock (ed.), *Die Erfindung der Welt. Zum Werk von Christoph Ransmayr* (Frankfurt/Main: Fischer, 1997), 139–47 (originally published in *TransAtlantik*, 1985).

[38] Ian Foster, 'The Limits of Memory: Christoph Ransmayr's journalistic writings', in Ian Foster and Juliet Wigmore (eds.), *Neighbours and Strangers: Literary and Cultural Relations in Germany, Austria and Central Europe since 1989*, German Monitor, 59 (Amsterdam: Rodopi, 2004), 159–71.

[39] W. G. Sebald, *Unheimliche Heimat. Essays zur österreichischen Literatur* (Salzburg and Vienna: Residenz, 1991).

[40] See Boa and Palfreyman, *Heimat*.

Morbus Kitahara, with its vision of an isolated, backward-looking town, characterized by pre-enlightened religious practices, patriarchal family values, and a suspicion of outsiders, undoubtedly owes much to the Austrian tradition of critical *Heimat* literature. Moreover, in the fictional world of *Morbus Kitahara*, Ransmayr reverses the post-war tourist boom by consigning all tourist activity to the past, rubbing salt in the wound by making the locals live among the ruins of their hotels and bathing places. He destroys any chance that Moor might have of reviving tourism by ripping up the railway tracks and by erecting the sign in the quarry, which 'welcomes' visitors with the information that the locals are murderers. By means of this fantastic scenario, Ransmayr draws attention to the opposite development in the real, non-fictional Austria, whose tourist industry was able (as his journalism testifies) to regain and then surpass its pre-war position of strength, partly by hiding traces of the Third Reich behind a picture-postcard façade.

However, one might question the implication that tourism and remembrance of past crimes are necessarily inimical. In the real world, as opposed to Ransmayr's seething text, tourism and commemoration of the Third Reich must and do interact, not least because a large proportion of visitors to memorial sites are also, at the time of their visit, tourists. Leaving Mauthausen memorial site, one is greeted by a sign reading 'Die Gaststätten von Mauthausen laden ein' ('Mauthausen's inns welcome you'), followed by a list of local restaurants. It would make no sense to read this as the cynical exploitation of the memorial site for local profit: visitors to the site do not suspend normal behaviour because they are attending a place of mourning; nor can local tourist offices be expected to neglect the legitimate needs of visitors to their town.

Near the quay in Ebensee a board erected in 1998 as part of a regional tourist initiative invites tourists to take a two-hour stroll around the town's industrial heritage. After passing the site of early workshops, the walk takes in a chemical works, the former concentration camp, and an old textile mill. The guest is then brought back to the quayside: 'und damit zu den Ursprüngen des Fremdenverkehrs und der gepflegten Gastlichkeit von Ebensee' ('and so to the origins of tourism and the warm hospitality of Ebensee'). One could criticize the writer of the itinerary for constructing a redemptive narrative that, while acknowledging the negative significance of the former concentration camp, nevertheless neutralizes it by subsuming its brief history into the considerably more venerable tradition of local hospitality. On the other hand, both the topography of the town and the needs of visitors mean that the only sensible route is one that gives hospitality the last word. Besides, one could argue that the tourist office has found a clever way of pointing visitors towards the concentration camp without abdicating its responsibilities as curator of the town's welcoming image.[41]

Conclusion

Much of what has been said in this chapter about memory and place (the increasing tendency to dispersal, the role of the Cold War powers in shaping memory spaces, and so on) could be applied equally to German memorial sites and to the fictional landscapes of German novels. Nevertheless, my analysis suggests that, for Austria, memory and place stand in a particular relationship to one another, marked by tensions between the urban state centre and the rural periphery and by tensions between landscape as national myth and as burial ground.

A memorial site is a multi-authored, multi-media space that is subject to recurrent social and political interventions; even allowing for their inherent intertextuality and the process of their reception, literary texts are, in comparison, homogeneous, stable and clearly bounded entities. There is therefore a sense in which this chapter has compared apples with pears, as the German has it. I hope nevertheless to have shown that such a juxtaposition can be made productive. The surprisingly tenacious disciplinary practices that isolate the analysis, in print, of literature and/or film about the Nazi era from the analysis of other forms of memory are likely to persist for some time to come, if only because there will always be enough high-quality literature, and enough interesting cinema of more mixed quality, to fill whole academic studies. In the meantime, my Conclusion exhorts students and scholars of literature to venture an occasional glance beyond the walls of this curiously self-defining subject.

---

[41] Like other tourist towns in the Salzkammergut, Ebensee has a Janus-like identity, even without its association with Nazi crimes. The spectacular mountain scenery that is the principal draw for tourists is also important to industry, and Ebensee is not the only town to have quarries and factories within a short distance of a picturesque town centre. It would therefore be simplistic to assume that all Austrian tourist offices have a vested interest in obliterating traces of the Nazi past as blots on an otherwise perfect landscape. Reinterpreting old industrial sites as a heritage attraction is one way for tourist offices to address this ambiguity, and Ebensee seems to be counting on this strategy.

Conclusion

Literature is just one, and not necessarily the most prominent, of a wide range of forms in which the Third Reich and its crimes are remembered in Germany and Austria. Schlink's *Der Vorleser* may have sold millions of copies and become compulsory reading for a generation of schoolchildren but in their everyday lives Germans and Austrians are still more likely to encounter traces of the Third Reich and the Holocaust in other media and through other social processes. Literature has been set alongside some of those non-literary memorial media in this study: in particular film, but also museum exhibitions, photography, memorial art, and sites of memory. A rather different way of decentring German-language literature on the subject of the Third Reich is to acknowledge that the overwhelming majority of fictional texts written in German today do not engage with the Nazi past. A writer such as Patrick Süskind, to name one prominent example, owes his considerable success to texts that have nothing to do with the Third Reich. Other best-selling authors like Sten Nadolny and Jens Sparschuh *have* written about the Third Reich (Nadolny in his *Ullsteinroman* and Sparschuh in *Der Schneemensch*), but these novels are untypical of their output, and the work for which they are known deals either with contemporary issues or with the more distant past. In other words, any German-speaking writer with an interest in the relationship between past and present is likely to be drawn at some time to the Third Reich, but there are nevertheless comparatively few non-Jewish German and Austrian writers whose major preoccupation is the Nazi past.

While it would be absurd to continue listing the many hundreds of writers writing in German today for whom the Third Reich is of little interest, one identifiable group whose programmatic indifference to the past is worth pausing over is the latest generation of 'pop' writers,[1] whose themes include fashion, consumer products, the music industry, the club and drug culture, and cyberspace, and whose interest in ephemera has earned them the label 'die neuen Archivisten' ('the new archivists').[2] A

---

[1] I use the term 'pop' here as a literal translation for the German labels *Popliteratur* and *Popliterat*, though it is not commonly used for the equivalent trend in British and American writing.

[2] Moritz Baßler, *Der deutsche Pop-Roman. Die neuen Archivisten* (Munich: Beck, 2002).

brief and rather frivolous mention early in Norman Ohler's novel *Mitte* (*Berlin Central*) reinforces the peripheral status of the Third Reich in a novel whose clear focus is the present.[3] During the Weimar Republic, the basement of the narrator's apartment block contained a notorious drink and drugs den that supplied its clientele with mescaline, cocaine, MDMA, and heroin. After 1933, those who had nothing to gain from the world on the surface stayed underground and pursued their drug-taking until the battle for Berlin, when a Soviet missile immured them. Ohler thus situates contemporary drug-taking within a tradition that stretches back well beyond the hippy era, the conventional point of origin in foundational myths of drug culture, while the explosion of the Soviet missile is perhaps intended to represent a caesura in that culture that lasted until drug-taking gained ground again in the 1960s. Whatever the exact implications, the Third Reich, which in most other situations enjoys the status of dominant narrative, is here subordinated to another, minority narrative: the history of recreational drug-taking. Within that narrative scheme the Nazi years are little more than a disruption to normal service for the drug-using community.

The novel's central locale is a semi-derelict apartment block in East Berlin that is scheduled for redevelopment. In a more conventional novel the hero's exploration of the labyrinthine building might easily serve as a pretext for the revelation of carefully manufactured secrets from the dark days of the Third Reich. Even Brigitte Burmeister, whose *Unter dem Namen Norma* (*Codename Norma*) one would hesitate to call conventional in other respects, populates a similar Berlin apartment block with two elderly sisters whose flat is 'ein Museum für Kriegsnarben' ('a museum of war scars') and who achieve the symbolic, if not literal, status of ghosts by continuing to preoccupy the narrator after their death.[4] The ghost that haunts Klinger in Ohler's apartment block has likewise been dead only a matter of months but, in contrast to Burmeister's 'ghosts' and in keeping with pop fiction's short memory, was, in life, a young drug-user and DJ.

The subtitle of Joachim Lottmann's *Deutsche Einheit. Ein historischer Roman aus dem Jahr 1995* (*Germany Unity: A Historical Novel from the Year 1995*) suggests a similarly telescoped memory: in contrast to the epic pasts of an older generation of writers, the historical past here stretches back no more than four years (though it must be said that Lottmann, born in 1956, is rather older than most 'pop' writers). In the novel itself, Lottmann attacks writers who wallow in the past, holding up

3 Norman Ohler, *Mitte* (Berlin: Rowohlt, 2001), 21.
4 Brigitte Burmeister, *Unter dem Namen Norma* (Stuttgart: Klett-Cotta, 1994), 28.

Christian Kracht's pop novel *Faserland* as a solitary example of present-oriented fiction: 'Ich dozierte, von tausend Neuerscheinungen würden mindestens neunhundertneunundneunzig den Blick zurück pflegen, und eine einzige, nämlich Christian Kracht, nicht. Das sei zu wenig' ('I got on my soap box and said that of the thousand most recently published books at least nine hundred and ninety-nine adopted a backward-looking attitude and only one, namely Christian Kracht, didn't. That was too few, I said').[5] He reserves particular scorn for those of his colleagues who earn accolades by writing in socially acceptable ways about the Nazi past: 'Und jetzt, *her mit dem Preis!*' ('And now *hand over the prize!*'), he demands, after composing a right-minded and affecting description of the Battle of Kursk.[6]

The relationship of Kracht and his self-styled disciple Lottmann to liberal writing about the Third Reich is ambivalent: both *Faserland* and *Deutsche Einheit* contain surprisingly pious sentiments about the centrality of the Holocaust to German national identity,[7] but these are deliberately outnumbered by frequent and provocatively flippant allusions to the Nazi past. While an earlier generation of pop writers defined itself in opposition to an authoritarian, 'fascist' generation that had lived through the Third Reich, the new pop writers (or at least their narrators) define themselves in opposition to anybody who does not share their personal tastes. Consequently, as Frank Finlay and Stuart Taberner have shown, the insult 'Nazi' is emptied of all political meaning and directed against the chronically unfashionable,[8] especially old people, whose nylon blouson jackets and beige stay-pressed trousers repulse Kracht's narrator, eliciting the fatuous observation that old men looked much less like Nazis in their Nazi youth than they do now. Lottmann's narrator, meanwhile, uses the label 'Nazi' to bemoan the nuisance of sexually unattractive women and makes fun of women who are attracted to Jewish Germans solely because of their victim heritage. The Jewish writer Rafael Seligmann is invoked admiringly, not for the sensitivity of his writings on German–Jewish relations, but for his success in picking up women in bars despite the handicap of his less-than-perfect looks.

---

[5] Joachim Lottmann, *Deutsche Einheit. Ein historischer Roman aus dem Jahr 1995* (Zurich: Haffmanns, 1999), 149; Christian Kracht, *Faserland* (Munich: Goldmann, 1997; first publ. 1995).

[6] Lottmann, *Deutsche Einheit*, 214.   [7] Esp. ibid. 5, 108; Kracht, *Faserland*, 149.

[8] Frank Finlay, ' "Dann wäre Deutschland wie das Wort Neckarrauen [*sic*]": Surface, Superficiality and Globalisation in Christian Kracht's *Faserland*', in Stuart Taberner (ed.), *German Literature in the Age of Globalisation* (Birmingham: University of Birmingham Press, 2004), 189–207; Stuart Taberner, *German Literature of the 1990s and Beyond: Normalization and the Berlin Republic* (Rochester, NY: Camden House, 2005), 88–91.

All this is more than empty provocation. Politically incorrect they may be, but Kracht and Lottmann tell us more about the lack of reverence accorded to the Nazi past in the popular German consciousness than do the more earnest works of their near contemporary, Beyer. Lottmann describes a rock concert at which Courtney Love, lead singer of US band Hole, fails in her bid to rile her German audience by calling them Nazis, partly because the crowd considers insults her stock-in-trade and partly because they do not follow her English. This suggests that pop writers are not faced with a straight choice between writing about global popular culture and writing about the German past, since the two are interconnected in complex ways, with popular US sentiments about the Third Reich losing something in translation as they pass into the German-speaking sphere, rather as the word *Vaterland*, once translated into English and pronounced with a German accent, as it is in Hollywood movies, returns in distorted form as *Faserland*.

Kracht demonstrates the continuing power of the Third Reich as a point of reference for young people even as he demonstrates his generation's lack of any affective connection with it. For instance, he shows his narrator to be incapable of reaching out across generational boundaries to satisfy his instinctive curiosity about the sufferings of the German population during the Third Reich:

> **Hamburg wacht auf, denke ich, und dann muß ich plötzlich an die Bombennächte im Zweiten Weltkrieg denken und an den Hamburger Feuersturm und wie das wohl war, als alles ausgelöscht wurde, und ich würde gerne mit dem Taxifahrer darüber reden, aber er hat Mundgeruch, und außerdem riecht er alt und verwest, so wie ein Buch, das zu lange im Regen auf dem Balkon lag und jetzt schimmelt.**[9]

This passage offers an interesting counterbalance (if only a fictional one) to the well-documented dialogue between the generations that was prompted by the *Wehrmachtsausstellung* (another of 1995's cultural landmarks), and that is cited in optimistic narratives of Germany's increasingly open attitudes towards the past.[10]

By convention, studies like this one end by considering what the future holds for the artistic representation of the Third Reich and its painful

---

[9] 'Hamburg is waking up, I think, and that gets me thinking about the bombing raids in the Second World War and the Hamburg fire storm and what it must have been like when the fire was finally put out, and I'd like to ask the taxi driver about it but he has bad breath and besides he smells old and decayed, like a book that's been out in the rain on the balcony for too long and has gone mouldy.' Kracht, *Faserland*, 43.

[10] Niven, *Facing the Nazi Past*, 154–5, and Schmitz, who quotes this passage of Niven's study, *Legacy*, 225.

legacy. Logic dictates that this study should end instead by considering what the future holds for the academic study of the artistic representation of the Third Reich and its legacy. German *Popliteratur* of the 1990s (it is mostly German rather than Austrian) is uneven in quality and, at least in its present form, indifferent to the task of finding appropriate ways to mourn the victims of Nazism. Future studies are therefore likely to continue to focus on how each new generation of more mainstream liberal writers and film-makers engages critically with each successive wave of commemorative activity and on the ways in which new films and novels give voice to the sufferings of previously neglected victims. It is nevertheless to be hoped that such studies will keep a weather eye on how other writers and film-makers variously marginalize, ignore, assimilate, or reinvent the Nazi past.

Further Reading and Viewing

Introduction

A number of related studies appeared in print or came to my notice just as this book was completed. Written by academics in South Africa, Great Britain, the USA, and Italy, they support my contention that Germanists working outside Germany and Austria are driving research in the field; like much previous work they treat literature in isolation from other media and German literature in isolation from Austrian. Notwithstanding certain differences in emphasis, three of these studies suggest that a further phase in scholarship might be added to those proposed in my Introduction, since all three analyse the construction of post-*Wende* identities in fictional narratives about Germany's three 'recent pasts' (the Nazi era, the GDR, and the old Federal Republic). See Friederike Eigler, *Gedächtnis und Geschichte in Generationenromanen seit der Wende* (Berlin: Schmidt, 2005); Stuart Taberner, *German Literature of the 1990s and Beyond: Normalization and the Berlin Republic* (Rochester, NY: Camden House, 2005), which, like my Conclusion, also considers the range of fictional topics beyond the historical; and Joachim Garbe, *Deutsche Geschichte in deutschen Geschichten der neunziger Jahre* (Würzburg: Königshausen & Neumann, 2002), which is useful principally for its overview of a large number of literary texts. 'The past' is defined more narrowly as the Nazi past in Elena Agazzi, *Erinnerte und rekonstruierte Geschichte. Drei Generationen deutscher Schriftsteller und die Fragen der Vergangenheit* (Göttingen: Vandenhoeck & Ruprecht, 2005): like other monographs discussed in my Introduction, it gives its very last word to Sebald.

Of these scholars, Eigler in particular asks questions not just of her chosen texts but also of the field, challenging, amongst other things, the exclusion of German-Turkish and other non-Jewish minority voices from memory discourses and attendant scholarship, including, rather to my regret, my own. Zafer Şenocak's novel *Gefährliche Verwandtschaft*, to which Eigler devotes a chapter, is currently the only work that offers itself readily for analysis under this heading—not surprisingly, given that the communities in question began to form some time after 1945. Nevertheless, the ways in which new generations of ethnic minorities deal with a historical past that, while not the history of their grandparents, is a part of their identity as German or Austrian citizens, is likely to become an increasingly important subject of study.

The following volumes of essays are particularly valuable: Anne Fuchs, Mary Cosgrove, and Georg Grote (eds.), *German Memory Contests: The Quest for Identity in Literature, Film, and Discourse since 1990* (Rochester, NY: Camden House, 2006); Stephan Braese (ed.), *In der Sprache der Täter. Neue Lektüren deutschsprachiger Nachkriegs- und Gegenwartsliteratur* (Opladen: Westdeutscher Verlag, 1998);

Stephan Braese et al. (eds.), *Deutsche Nachkriegsliteratur und der Holocaust* (Frankfurt/M. and New York: Campus, 1998); and Helmut Schmitz (ed.), *German Culture and the Uncomfortable Past. Representations of National Socialism in Contemporary Germanic Literature.* (Aldershot: Ashgate, 2001). Studies of writing by German-Jewish and Austrian-Jewish writers include Stephan Braese, *Die andere Erinnerung. Jüdische Autoren in der westdeutschen Nachkriegsliteratur* (Berlin: Philo, 2001) and Pól O'Dochertaigh (ed.), *Jews in German Literature since 1945: German-Jewish Literature?* (Amsterdam and Atlanta, GA: Rodopi, 2000). For an introduction to recent memory debates in Austria, see *Austrian Studies*, 11 (2003), themed issue: ' "Hitler's First Victim"? Memory and Representation in Post-War Austria'.

　　Studies of the National Socialist past in film are mostly international in their scope and concerned principally with representation of the Holocaust (as distinct from other aspects of German experience of the years 1933–45). Annette Innsdorf's *Indelible Shadows: Film and the Holocaust,* for many years a standard work in the field, has recently been updated: 3rd edn (Cambridge: Cambridge University Press, 2002). Other recent work includes: Lawrence Baron, *Projecting the Holocaust into the Present: The Changing Focus of Contemporary Holocaust Cinema* (Lanham, MD: Rowman & Littlefield, 2005); Toby Haggith and Joanna Newman (eds.), *Holocaust and the Moving Image: Representations in Film and Television Since 1933* (London: Wallflower, 2005); and Joshua Hirsch, *Afterimage: Film, Trauma and the Holocaust* (Philadelphia: Temple University Press, 2004). Peter Reichel's *Erfundene Erinnerung. Weltkrieg und Judenmord in Film und Theater* (Munich: Hanser, 2004) has a narrower, German focus, but comes at the subject from the field of political science rather than film studies and is a better source of information than it is of analysis.

Chapter 1

A subtitled VHS recording of *The Nasty Girl* is no longer available: the best source of a copy is probably a Goethe-Institut library. The DVD version currently available has no subtitles, but its extras include the documentary *Das Mädchen und die Stadt.* It is possible to research the phenomenon of the 'Schülerwettbewerb Deutsche Geschichte' through its own publications, including Lothar Dittmer (ed.), *Historische Projektarbeit im Schülerwettbewerb deutsche Geschichte. Eine Bestandaufnahme* (Hamburg: Edition Körber-Stiftung, 1999). Two recent competitions dealing with the Third Reich (the second more directly than the first) are documented in Körber-Stiftung (ed.), *Denkmal: Erinnerung—Mahnung—Ärgernis* (Hamburg: Edition Körber-Stiftung, 1996) and in Johannes Rau (ed.), *Hilfe für Verfolgte in der NS-Zeit* (Hamburg: Edition Körber-Stiftung, 2002).

Chapter 2

For Schneider's indignant but thoughtful defence of *Vati,* see Peter Schneider, 'Vom richtigen Umgang mit dem Bösen', in *Deutsche Ängste. Sieben Essays* (Darmstadt: Luchterhand, 1988). For a deconstruction of the concept of 'generation' in German public and academic discourse, including a plea for a better understanding of female and non-middle class generational experience, see Bernd Weisbrod,

'Generation und Generationalität in der Neueren Geschichte', *Aus Politik und Zeitgeschichte*, 8 (2005), 3–9. Silke Wenk questions the retrospective sexualization of national socialist crimes in 'Rhetoriken der Pornografisierung. Rahmungen des Blicks auf die NS-Verbrechen', in Insa Eschebach, Sigrid Jacobeit, and Silke Wenk (eds.), *Gedächtnis und Geschlecht. Deutungsmuster in Darstellungen des Nationalsozialistischen Genozids* (Frankfurt/main and New York: Campus, 2002), 269–94.

Roland Suso Richter's film *Nichts als die Wahrheit* (FRG and USA, 1999) is a frivolous appropriation of the Mengele story employing formulae from the crime thriller and gothic horror film. Though it has little intrinsic value, it does point up the integrity of Schneider's approach and attests to the gap between the era of *Vaterliteratur* and the late 1990s: notwithstanding his tense relationship with his young defence lawyer, Mengele is not presented as a father but as a free-floating revenant from the past.

Though I recommend it a little hesitantly, Ulla Hahn's novel *Unscharfe Bilder* (Munich: Deutsche Verlags-Anstalt, 2003) offers a point of comparison with *Der Vorleser* in its contrived reversals of power. A Wehrmacht soldier unexpectedly finds himself under orders from an SS officer whom, as a schoolboy, he had helped with his schoolwork. Naturally—'naturally' in the stylized world of popular fiction about the Third Reich—the SS officer takes revenge for his earlier subordination by sadistically forcing the soldier to execute a partisan. Only the war veteran's subsequent admission that he has not been entirely truthful saves the plotline from outright cliché, allowing the possibility that the construction of SS brutality as the revenge of the uneducated against the educated might be a myth by means of which educated liberals avoid confronting their own capacity for evil. Hahn's novel is also, more obviously, a questionable response to the exhibition *Verbrechen der Wehrmacht*, which I discuss in Chapter 3.

Chapter 3

The results of a project to create and interpret a corpus of oral testimonies about Austria during the Third Reich are presented in Meinrad Ziegler and Waltraud Kannonier-Finster, *Österreichisches Gedächtnis. Über Erinnern und Vergessen der NS-Vergangenheit* (Vienna: Böhlau, 1993). A similar project with a narrower focus is recorded in Hamburger Institut für Sozialforschung (ed.), *Besucher einer Ausstellung. Die Ausstellung 'Vernichtungskrieg. Verbrechen der Wehrmacht 1941 bis 1944' in Interview und Gespräch* (Hamburg: Hamburger Edition, 1998). Jan Philipp Reemtsma's text 'Drei Patrioten' (in Reemtsma, *Stimmen aus dem vorigen Jahrhundert* (Stuttgart: Klett-Cotta, 2000)) is a montage of extracts from this testimony. Like Beckermann's film, it could be used to analyse mechanisms of exculpation in oral testimony about Wehrmacht crimes, or, more neutrally, the normalities of soldierly conduct in the Wehrmacht. On the other hand, as head of the Hamburger Institut für Sozialforschung responsible for the 'Wehrmacht Exhibition', Reemtsma is implicated professionally in the exhibition in a way that Beckermann is not, and one might discuss his montage in this light.

For a fuller discussion of television documentary, see Michael E. Geisler, 'The Disposal of Memory: Fascism and the Holocaust on West German Television', in Bruce A. Murray and Christopher J. Wickham (eds.), *Framing the Past: The Historiography of German Cinema and Television* (Carbondale: Southern Illinois University Press, 1992), 220–59. One could usefully contrast the work of Jewish-German documentarist Erwin Leiser, which goes through most of the phases I outline in my potted history of documentary (*Große-Männer-Geschichte*, *Alltagsgeschichte*, use of an autobiographical frame, use of *Zeitzeugen*) with the more conservative work of ZDF historian-in-chief Guido Knopp, which is concerned exclusively with prominent people and events, narrative in form, uncritical in its use of archive film and photographs, and male-centred in both content and voice.

Discourses on German wartime suffering, to which Sander's *Befreier und Befreite* makes an important contribution, are the subject of a major AHRC-funded research project at the University of Leeds, which will lead to a series of publications over the next few years (http://www.leeds.ac.uk/german/AHRC.htm).

The photographic heritage of the Third Reich offers a particularly rich field of study. The bibliography of *Ikonen der Vernichtung* (Berlin: Akademie, 1998), Cornelia Brink's seminal work on photographs from the concentration camps, records the extensive body of critical theory concerned with photography and memory. My necessarily brief analysis of the 1970 exhibition at Mauthausen draws on Brink's critique of the use of dramatic photographic enlargements in historical exhibitions about the concentration camps (Cornelia Brink, *'Auschwitz in der Paulskirche'. Erinnerungspolitik in Fotoausstellungen der sechziger Jahre* (Marburg: Jonas, 2000)). The temporary exhibition *Das Sichtbare Unfassbare. Fotografien vom Konzentrationslager Mauthausen* (Gedenkstätte Mauthausen, 2005) can be seen as a product of the more critical academic approaches that Brink's work has helped to shape. The catalogue (Vienna: Mandelbaum, 2005) has the same title as the exhibition and a bilingual German/English text. Two other excellent critical exhibitions of photography from the Third Reich are catalogued in Peter Jahn and Ulrike Schmiegelt (eds.), *Fotofeldpost. Geknipste Kriegserlebnisse 1939–1945* (Berlin: Elefanten Press, 2000) and in Klaus Hesse and Philipp Springer (eds.), *Vor aller Augen. Fotodokumente des nationalsozialistischen Terrors in der Provinz* (Essen: Klartext, 2002).

While several documentaries (including Leiser's *Die versunkenen Welten des Roman Vishniac* (Germany, 1978), Llorenç Soler's *Francisco Boix, un fotógrafo en el infierno* (Spain, 2001), and Dariusz Jablonski's *Der Fotograf* (Poland, France, and FRG, 1998)) deal directly with the work of photographers during the Third Reich, I have found that documentaries in which photography plays a peripheral role often have more to say about it. Hans-Dieter Grabe's *Er nannte sich Hohenstein* (FRG, 1994), whose main focus is a wartime diary, supplements readings from the diary with amateur photographs and home-movie footage that show how an otherwise decent German mayor in occupied Poland betrayed colonialist attitudes in his photographic endeavours. Similarly, Melanie Spitta and Karin Seybold's *Das falsche Wort. 'Wiedergutmachung' an Zigeunern (Sinte) in Deutschland?* (FRG, 1987) is concerned primarily with the failure of the German state to acknowledge Sinti victims of Nazism, but its visuals implicitly contrast the dehumanizing effects of National Socialist photography with the family photographic heritage of the

Sinti which, however constrained it may have been by the conventions of studio photography, nevertheless represented an authentic form of self-expression.

Finally, any study of photography and memory will benefit from addressing W. G. Sebald's photo-strewn texts, particularly *Die Ausgewanderten* (Frankfurt/Main: Eichborn, 1992) and *Austerlitz* (Munich: Hanser, 2001).

Chapter 4

In weighing Tournier's presentation of Goering as an ogre against Beyer's humanizing perspective on Goebbels, one might consider the debate triggered by Oliver Hirschbiegel's humanizing portrayal of Hitler in the film *Der Untergang* (FRG, 2004) (for instance, Georg Seesslen, 'Das faschistische Subjekt', *Die Zeit*, 16 Sept. 2004).

Like Schlöndorff, Gordian Maugg, in *Der olympische Sommer* (FRG, 1993), screens the Third Reich using its own techniques, but films with a primitive 1931 Askania camera rather than imitating Riefenstahl's state-of-the art techniques, resulting in a more alienating visual experience. Maugg's montage of original film footage and radio recordings is a common enough device, but where other film-makers stick to 'classic' images of the Third Reich (in the case of *Der Unhold*, Hitler at the Eiffel Tower) and play only clear or cleaned-up sound recordings, Maugg has hunted out deliberately obscure images of everyday reality in 1930s Berlin and particularly scratchy sound recordings from the war years. Whether the film's flimsy plot (after a story by Günther Rücker) warrants these technical exertions is a matter for debate, but the central motif of missing out on history (the hero sleeps through—or rather makes love through—the 1936 Olympic Games) contrasts with the narrative compulsion to be 'where it's at' that is acted out in Beyer's and Tournier's novels (and in other novels analysed by Lorna Milne). One could investigate a similar dialectic in representations of the *Wende*, where one finds both the protagonist who contrives to be in the thick of the historical action (Thomas Brussig's *Helden wie wir*) and the protagonist who sleeps through it all (Wolfgang Becker's *Goodbye Lenin*).

Chapter 5

Scholarly studies contextualize memorials to the crimes and victims of the Third Reich in different ways. One that places the Third Reich squarely centre-stage is Klaus Neumann's study of local community debates, *Shifting Memories: The Nazi Past in the New Germany* (Ann Arbor: University of Michigan Press, 2000). Other authors place the Third Reich on a historical continuum between earlier and later periods of German history: Rudy Koshar, *From Monuments to Traces: Artifacts of German Memory 1870–1990* (Berkeley, CA: University of California Press, 2000) and Brian Ladd, *The Ghosts of Berlin: Confronting German History in the Urban Landscape* (Chicago: University of Chicago Press, 1997). Koshar's study is the more ambitious of these, contending that attitudes towards preserving or eradicating traces of the Third Reich must be understood in the light of older German memorial practices, but Ladd's readable monograph exemplifies a growing interest in the way in which traces of the past survive in the built environment. For a synchronic rather than a diachronic approach, addressing the Holocaust as one aspect of European memorial culture, see Akademie der Künste (ed.), *Denkmale und kulturelles Gedächtnis nach dem Ende der Ost-West-Konfrontation* (Berlin: Jovis, 2000).

Gazetteers of local memorials, produced by a wide range of institutions and interest groups, are the best starting point for primary research. The *Bundeszentrale* and the *Landeszentralen für politische Bildung* (in Germany) and memorial sites (in both Germany and Austria) are good sources.

Unlike the museums at former concentration camps, Jewish museums serve to document, and to preserve what little remains of, German-Jewish and Austrian-Jewish life before 1933/1938. Sabine Offe's *Ausstellungen, Einstellungen, Entstellungen. Jüdische Museen in Deutschland und Österreich* (Berlin: Philo, 2000) provides a model for their study. Offe sees the tendency of towns to preserve the former synagogue in preference to other traces of Jewish life as a problematic centralization of memory. Shimon Attie's much-copied projections of photographs of Jewish life onto the original sites offer a more positive model for the dispersal of German-Jewish memory throughout the urban landscape (*The Writing on the Wall: Projections in Berlin's Jewish Quarter* (Heidelberg: Braus, 1993)).

For more on Austria's construction of its past, see Günter Bischof and Anton Pelinka (eds.), *Austrian Historical Memory and National Identity* (New Brunswick, NJ, and London: Transaction, 1997). Ransmayr's place in the Austrian tradition of *Anti-Heimatliteratur* is worth exploring further. Ransmayr has cited Hans Lebert's novel *Die Wolfshaut* (1960) as a model; more recent texts in this vein include Norbert Gstrein, *Einer* (1988) and *Der Kommerzialrat* (1995), Elfriede Jelinek, *Die Kinder der Toten* (1995), and Alois Hotschnig, *Ludwigs Zimmer* (2000). For an analysis of the genre see Andrea Kunne, *Heimat im Roman. Last oder Lust? Transformationen in der österreichischen Nachkriegsliteratur* (Amsterdam and Atlanta, GA: Rodopi, 1991).

Conclusion

For a survey of recent 'pop literature' see Moritz Baßler, *Der deutsche Pop-Roman. Die neuen Archivisten* (Munich: Beck, 2002). In his study *Popliteratur* (Hamburg: Rotbuch, 2001), Thomas Ernst is less inclined than Baßler to celebrate the recent revival in 'pop' writing, tracing the now mainstream trend back to its subversive origins. Both attempt to define the relationship between pop literature and literature that confronts the Nazi past: Ernst argues that the preoccupation of post-war writers with the difficulties of writing after Auschwitz delayed the arrival in Germany of US and French 'pop' thinking; Baßler's thoughtful analysis of *Der Vorleser* as 'pop literature' adds an interesting new perspective.

Select Bibliography

Literary texts discussed

Beyer, Marcel, *Flughunde* (Frankfurt/Main: Suhrkamp, 1995).
Ransmayr, Christoph, *Morbus Kitahara* (Frankfurt/Main: Fischer, 1995).
Schlink, Bernhard, *Der Vorleser* (Zurich: Diogenes, 1995).
Schneider, Peter, *Vati* (Darmstadt and Neuwied: Luchterhand, 1987).
Schubert, Helga, *Judasfrauen* (Berlin and Weimar: Aufbau, 1990).
Tournier, Michel, *Le Roi des Aulnes* (Paris: Gallimard, 1970).

English translations

Beyer, Marcel, *The Karnau Tapes*, trans. John Brownjohn (London: Vintage, 1997).
Ransmayr, Christoph, *The Dog King*, trans. John E. Woods (London: Chatto and Windus, 1997).
Schlink, Bernhard, *The Reader*, trans. Carol Brown Janeway (London: Phoenix, 1997).
Tournier, Michel, *The Erl-King*, trans. Barbara Bray (London: Methuen, 1984).

Films discussed

Beckermann, Ruth, *Jenseits des Krieges* (Austria, 1997).
Sander, Helke, *BeFreier und Befreite. Krieg, Vergewaltigungen, Kinder* (FRG, 1992).
Schlöndorff, Volker, *Der Unhold* (FRG, France, and UK, 1996).
Verhoeven, Michael, *Das schreckliche Mädchen* (FRG, 1989).

Secondary texts

Alldred, Beth, 'Two Contrasting Perspectives on German Unification: Helga Schubert and Brigitte Burmeister', *German Life and Letters*, 50 (1997), 165–81.
Arani, Miriam Y., '"Und an den Fotos entzündete sich die Kritik". Die "Wehrmachtsausstellung", deren Kritik und die Neukonzeption. Ein Beitrag aus fotohistorisch-quellenkritischer Sicht', *Fotogeschichte*, 85–6 (2002), 97–124.
Assmann, Aleida, *Erinnerungsräume. Formen und Wandlungen des kulturellen Gedächtnisses* (Munich: Beck, 1999).
—— and Ute Frevert, *Geschichtsvergessenheit, Geschichtsversessenheit. Vom Umgang mit deutschen Vergangenheiten nach 1945* (Stuttgart: Deutsche Verlags-Anstalt, 1999).
Assmann, Jan, *Das kulturelle Gedächtnis. Schrift, Erinnerung und politische Identität in frühen Hochkulturen* (Munich: Beck, 1992).

Avisar, Ilan, *Screening the Holocaust: Cinema's Images of the Unimaginable* (Bloomington: Indiana University Press, 1988).

Bartsch, Kurt, '"Spielen mit den Möglichkeiten der Wirklichkeit". Zu Christoph Ransmayrs Roman *Morbus Kitahara*', *Jahrbuch der Österreich-Bibliothek in St. Petersburg*, 3 (1997/8), 95–108.

Beckermann, Ruth (ed.), *Jenseits des Krieges. Ehemalige Wehrmachtssoldaten erinnern sich* (Vienna: Döcker, 1998).

Boa, Elizabeth, and Rachel Palfreyman, *Heimat—A German Dream: Regional Loyalties and National Identity in German Culture 1890–1990* (Oxford: Oxford University Press, 2000).

Burgess, Gordon, ' "Was da ist, das ist [nicht] mein": The Case of Peter Schneider', in Arthur Williams, Stuart Parkes, and Roland Smith (eds.), *Literature on the Threshold: The German Novel in the 1980s* (New York, Oxford, and Munich: Berg, 1990), 107–22.

Donahue, William Collins, 'Illusions of Subtlety: Bernhard Schlink's *Der Vorleser* and the Moral Limits of Holocaust Fiction', *German Life and Letters*, 54 (2001), 60–81.

——'Revising '68: Bernhard Schlink's *Der Vorleser*, Peter Schneider's *Vati*, and the Question of History', *Seminar*, 40 (2004), 293–311.

Fingerhut, Karlheinz, 'Das Lebensziel: "Nicht so zu werden wie ihre Väter". Zu Peter Schneiders Erzählung *Vati*', *Diskussion Deutsch*, 21 (1990), 416–23.

Foster, Ian, 'Alternative History and Christoph Ransmayr's *Morbus Kitahara*', *Modern Austrian Literature*, 32 (1999), 111–25.

——'The Limits of Memory: Christoph Ransmayr's Journalistic Writings', in Ian Foster and Juliet Wigmore (eds.), *Neighbours and Strangers: Literary and Cultural Relations in Germany, Austria and Central Europe since 1989*, German Monitor, 59 (Amsterdam: Rodopi, 2004), 159–71.

Gättens, Marie-Luise, 'Helke Sander's *Liberators Take Liberties* and the Politics of History', in Ingeborg Majer O'Sickey and Ingeborg von Zadow (eds.), *Triangulated Visions: Women in Recent German Cinema* (Albany: State University of New York Press, 1998), 261–71.

Grossmann, Atina, 'A Question of Silence. The Rape of German Women by Soviet Occupation Soldiers', in Nicole Ann Dombrowski (ed.), *Women and War in the Twentieth Century: Enlisted with or without Consent* (New York and London: Garland, 1999), 162–83.

Helbig, Louis Ferdinand, *Der ungeheure Verlust. Flucht und Vertreibung in der deutschsprachigen Belletristik der Nachkriegszeit*, 3rd rev. edn (Wiesbaden: Harrassowitz, 1996).

Hirsch, Marianne, 'Projected Memory: Holocaust Photographs in Personal and Public Fantasy', in Mieke Bal, Jonathan Crewe, and Leo Spitzer (eds.), *Acts of Memory: Cultural Recall in the Present* (Hanover, NH: University Press of New England, 1999), 3–23.

Höfer, Adolf, 'Vater-Sohn-Konflikte in moderner Dichtung. Symptome einer Ver-harmlosung des Faschismus am Beispiel von Peter Schneiders Erzählung *Vati*', *Literatur für Leser* (1994), 11–22.

Johnson, Sally, and Frank Finlay, '(Il)literacy and (Im)morality in Bernhard Schlink's *The Reader*', *Written Language and Literacy*, 4/2 (2001), 195–214.

Kaes, Anton, *From Hitler to Heimat: The Return of History as Film* (Cambridge, MA, and London: Harvard University Press, 1989).

Kittler, Friedrich, *Grammophon. Film. Typewriter* (Berlin: Brinkmann & Bose, 1986).

Koshar, Rudy, *From Monuments to Traces: Artifacts of German Memory, 1870–1990* (Berkeley and Los Angeles: University of California Press, 2000).

Köster, Juliane, *Bernhard Schlink. 'Der Vorleser'* (Munich: Oldenbourg, 2000).

Levin, David, 'Are We Victims Yet? Resistance and Community in *The White Rose, Five Last Days*, and *The Nasty Girl*', *Germanic Review*, 73 (1998), 86–100.

Lorenz, Dagmar, 'Austrians and Austria in Ruth Beckermann's *Jenseits des Krieges*, the Film and the Book', *Modern Austrian Literature*, 32/4 (1999), special issue: *Austria in Film*, 323–33.

Martin, Elaine (ed.), *Gender, Patriarchy and Fascism in the Third Reich: The Response of Women Writers* (Detroit: Wayne State University Press, 1993).

Milne, Lorna, 'Olfaction, Authority, and the Interpretation of History in Salman Rushdie's *Midnight's Children*, Patrick Süskind's *Das Parfum*, and Michel Tournier's *Le Roi des Aulnes*', *Symposium*, 53/1 (1999), 22–36.

Mitscherlich, Alexander, and Margarete Mitscherlich, *Die Unfähigkeit zu trauern. Grundlagen kollektiven Verhaltens* (Munich: Piper, 1967).

Morgan, Peter, 'The Sins of the Fathers: A Reappraisal of the Controversy about Peter Schneider's *Vati*', *German Life and Letters*, 47 (1994), 104–33.

Niven, Bill, *Facing the Nazi Past. United Germany and the Legacy of the Third Reich* (London and New York: Routledge, 2002).

——'Bernhard Schlink's *Der Vorleser* and the Problem of Shame', *Modern Language Review*, 98 (2003), 381–96.

Nora, Pierre, *Les lieux de mémoire* (Paris: Gallimard, 1984); in English translation: *Realms of Memory: The Construction of the French Past*, trans. Arthur Goldhammer (New York: Columbia University Press, 1996).

Paver, Chloe, '"Ein Stück langweiliger als die Wehrmachtsausstellung, aber dafür repräsentativer": The Exhibition *Fotofeldpost* as Riposte to the Wehrmacht Exhibition', in Anne Fuchs, Mary Cosgrove, and Georg Grote (eds.), *German Memory Contests: The Quest for Identity in Literature, Film, and Discourse since 1990* (Rochester, NY: Camden House, 2006).

Peitsch, Helmut, 'Communication, Generations, and Nation: Ulrich Woelk's *Rückspiel*', in Arthur Williams, Stuart Parkes, and Julian Preece (eds.), *'Whose Story?' Continuities in Contemporary German-Language Literature* (Berne and Berlin: Peter Lang, 1998), 317–40.

Perz, Bertrand, *Die KZ-Gedenkstätte Mauthausen 1945 bis zur Gegenwart* (Innsbruck: Studienverlag, 2006).

Pinfold, Debbie, *The Child's View of the Third Reich in German Literature: The Eye among the Blind* (Oxford: Oxford University Press, 2001).

Pliske, Roman, 'Flughunde. Ein Roman über Wissenschaft und Wahnsinn ohne Genie im Dritten Reich', in Marc-Boris Rede (ed.), Auskünfte von und über Marcel Beyer (Bamberg: Universität Bamberg, 2000), 108–23.

Reed, Donna K., The Novel and the Nazi Past (New York, Berne, and Frankfurt/Main: Lang, 1985).

Reimer, Robert C., and Carol J. Reimer, Nazi-Retro Film: How German Narrative Cinema Remembers the Past (New York: Twayne, 1992).

Ryan, Judith, The Uncompleted Past: Postwar German Novels and the Third Reich (Detroit: Wayne State University Press, 1983).

Sander, Helke, and Barbara Johr (eds.), BeFreier und Befreite. Krieg, Vergewaltigungen, Kinder (Munich: Kunstmann, 1992).

Santner, Eric L., Stranded Objects: Mourning, Memory, and Film in Postwar Germany (Ithaca, NY and London: Cornell University Press, 1990).

Schlant, Ernestine, The Language of Silence: West German Literature and the Holocaust (New York and London: Routledge, 1999).

Schlipphacke, Heidi M., 'Enlightenment, Reading, and the Female Body: Bernhard Schlink's Der Vorleser', Gegenwartsliteratur, 1 (2002), 310–28.

Schmitz, Helmut, On Their Own Terms: The Legacy of National Socialism in Post-1990 German Fiction (Birmingham: Birmingham University Press, 2004).

Schönherr, Ulrich, 'Topophony of Fascism: On Marcel Beyer's The Karnau Tapes', Germanic Review, 73 (1998), 328–48.

Sebald, W. G., Unheimliche Heimat. Essays zur österreichischen Literatur (Salzburg and Vienna: Residenz, 1991).

Simon, Ulrich, 'Assoziation und Authentizität. Warum Marcel Beyers Flughunde auch ein Holocaust-Roman ist', in Marc-Boris Rede (ed.), Auskünfte von und über Marcel Beyer (Bamberg: Universität Bamberg, 2000), 124–42.

Smith, Sabine H., Sexual Violence in German Culture: Rereading and Rewriting the Tradition (Frankfurt/Main: Lang, 1998), 258–85.

Snyder Hook, Elizabeth, Family Secrets and the Contemporary German Novel: Literary Explorations in the Aftermath of the Third Reich (Rochester, NY: Camden House, 2001).

Young, James E., The Texture of Memory: Holocaust Memorials and Meaning (New Haven and London: Yale University Press, 1993).

——At Memory's Edge: After-Images of the Holocaust in Contemporary Art and Architecture (New Haven and London: Yale University Press, 2000).

Zipfel, Gaby, 'Vom weiblichen Blick auf den männlichen Krieg', in Hamburger Institut für Sozialforschung (ed.), Besucher einer Ausstellung. Die Ausstellung 'Vernichtungskrieg. Verbrechen der Wehrmacht 1941 bis 1944' in Interview und Gespräch (Hamburg: Hamburger Edition, 1998), 141–60.

Index

I have omitted from the Index topics such as National Socialism and *Vergangenheitsbewältigung* ('coming to terms with the past'), that are addressed, explicitly or implicitly, throughout the book. In particular, although the sub-headings under 'majority experience' may seem to focus on experiences of hardship, this is not intended to imply an exculpatory equation of majority experience with suffering: crimes and failings of the majority culture are addressed throughout my study. Besides, many of the references under that heading point the reader to passages which, in one way or another, problematize or contextualize discourses of suffering in the majority culture.